THE GERMAN-HUNGARIAN-SWABIAN
TRIANGLE 1936–1939:

The Road to Discord

Thomas Spira

EAST EUROPEAN QUARTERLY, BOULDER
DISTRIBUTED BY COLUMBIA UNIVERSITY PRESS
NEW YORK
1990

EAST EUROPEAN MONOGRAPHS, NO. CCLXXXV

Thomas Spira is Professor of History at the
University of Prince Edward Island

THE GERMAN-HUNGARIAN-SWABIAN TRIANGLE
1936-1939:
THE ROAD TO DISCORD

PREFACE

This work resumes where my *German-Hungarian Relations and the Swabian Problem from Károlyi to Gömbös 1919-1936* (Boulder: East European Monographs, 1977) terminated. It begins with the death of Hungarian Prime Minister Gyula Gömbös in October 1936, and ends with Germany's attack on Poland in the late summer of 1939. These were fateful years for Germany, Hungary and for Hungary's German minority, the Swabians. All the tensions and problems during this period had been gestating since the end of World War I. After the rise of Adolf Hitler in Germany, discords between Germans and Swabians on one hand, and the Magyars of Hungary on the other hand, became accentuated and reached crisis proportions by the outbreak of World War II. Reich Germans, the Magyars of Hungary and Hungary's Swabians formed the sides of a triangle, the proportions and dimensions of which constantly alternated, mostly in response to various internal stimuli, and to events on the world stage.

This book analyzes the triangle comprising German-Hungarian economic relations, German-Hungarian diplomatic affairs, and the Hungarian government's Swabian educational and linguistic policies and practices. These issues are discussed separately in each of the years 1936-1937, 1938 and 1939. The book documents the interaction of Hungary's minority practices with the country's economic and foreign policies. This connection involved not only Germany, but also Italy, Austria, the Little Entente states of Czechoslovakia, Romania and Yugoslavia, as well as Poland and the Western European powers France and Great Britain. To familiarize readers with the intricacies of international diplomacy during that period, each year commences with a chapter that surveys international events and situations which directly or indirectly influenced the German-Hungarian-Swabian triangle and Hungarian diplomacy. Subsequent chapters analyze Hungary's economic, diplomatic and minority policies for each of the three years.

In this work, the adjective "Hungarian" identifies the political state of Hungary, or the people of Hungary. All Hungarian citizens belonging to the country's various ethnic groups or nationalities, as well as members of the Magyar nation, qualify for this designation. The term "Magyar" refers to the Magyar language and nation or to ethnic Magyars or Magyarized (assimilated) individuals. This includes those who had voluntarily adopted the Magyar language and Hungary's cultural and political norms. Magyars resided principally in Hungary, where they still form the dominant majority. After World War I, large numbers of Magyars also became citizens of Czechoslovakia, Romania and Yugoslavia, the three Successor States.

The difference between "ethnic group" and "nationality" is subject to interpretation and depends on a people's self-perception. Generally, ethnic groups are less politicized than are nationalities. The latter have an awareness of possessing a separate cultural and political status, regard themselves entitled to self-determination and might possibly desire autonomy or sovereignty. For example, Swabians belonging to the government-sponsored cultural association, the *Ungarländischer Deutscher Volksbildungsverein (UDV)*, regarded themselves as members of Hungary's German ethnic group and were content with moderate cultural and linguistic concessions from the Hungarian government. The *Volksdeutsche Kameradschaft (VK)*, a *UDV* splinter group created by *völkisch* (nationalist) dissidents, styled itself the sole representative of Hungary's German (Swabian) *Volk* (nation) and demanded administrative autonomy and cultural self-rule on this basis. The government and the majority of the public regarded only Magyars as a legitimate nationality. In their view, non-Magyars lacked legal or constitutional rights to qualify as a collectivity, although many conceded that non-Magyars ought to be able to practice their customs and speak non-Magyar tongues as private citizens. In rural areas where the number and proportion of non-Magyars warranted such a concession, they were to enjoy the option of sending their children to ethnic elementary schools.

As in my previous book, I have become indebted to numerous individuals and institutions. Professor Stephen Fischer-Galati urged me to write the continuation of my previous book, which he published over one decade ago. Professors Reginald C. Stuart and Douglas Baldwin read the manuscript and offered valuable suggestions on style and idiom. Professor Thomas Sakmyster inspected the text and advised me on organization and various diplomatic and social aspects of the pre-World War II period. Professor Nándor Dreisziger surveyed parts of the manuscript for accuracy and coherence. I wish to thank the staffs of the West German Federal

Archives in Koblenz; the Political Archives of the Foreign Ministry in Bonn; the Austrian State Archives in Vienna; the National Széchenyi Library and the Hungarian National Archives, both in Budapest; and various other library staffs in Europe and North America. I am grateful to the University of Prince Edward Island Computer Centre for permission to use its excellent facilities. I owe a debt of gratitude to my typist, Mrs. Wanda Bourgeau, who helped me immeasureably with the layout and other technical problems. My university's Interlibrary Loan Staff, especially Virginia Kopachevsky, effectively traced a number of elusive books and articles. And the U. P. E. I. Senate Research Committee provided the funds that covered some of the research, typing and other expenses.

My wife and daughter loyally supported my efforts. Other people too numerous to cite by name contributed to the genesis and progress of this book. These friends, colleagues and students deserve my gratitude. All errors of fact and judgement, of course, are mine alone.

Charlottetown
Prince Edward Island, Canada
August 1989

TABLE OF CONTENTS

CHAPTER I

HUNGARY'S POLITICAL, ECONOMIC AND ETHNIC BACKGROUND PRIOR TO 1937

As recent Hungarian history illustrates, small countries in strategic locations risk being overwhelmed by strong states and their allies in times of crisis. World War I ended Hungary's brief experience of shared sovereignty with Austria and exposure to great-power status. The Versailles peace settlement balkanized the defunct Austro-Hungarian Empire and destroyed its economic and political unity. The victors apportioned most of the twin-monarchy's former territories and populations among hostile neighboring states. The Trianon Peace Treaty of June 1920 severed Hungary's constitutional links with Austria, and granted the dismembered country sovereignty. It failed, however, to ensure Trianon Hungary's political stability, military security or economic solvency. Hungary lost 72% of its territory and 64% of its population (including about 3.5-million ethnic Magyars to Czechoslovakia, Romania and Yugoslavia) and a good portion of its natural resources.[1]

Following World War I, intense national rivalries in eastern Europe compromised Hungary's security. Two of the vanquished countries—Germany and the Soviet Union—and the chief victorious powers and their regional allies—Great Britain, France, Poland and the Little Entente (Czechoslovakia, Romania and Yugoslavia), sought to wrest economic and political control of the area. Only one of France's client-states—Poland—remained friendly to Hungary. The losers schemed to recoup their losses, whereas the victors hoped to preserve or augment their gains. Italy sought compensation in the Balkans to defray severe wartime losses. It appeared that, before long, Hungary, which commanded the strategic Hungarian Plain, would be caught in revived international rivalries. The duration of the peace would be determined by how rapidly the major losers and Italy recuperated before daring to risk confrontations to attain their expansionist objectives.

Trianon Hungary was considerably disadvantaged by having a small population of only about eight million, of whom over 800,000 were non-Magyars. Among these, the 550,000-strong Germans, the Swabians, predominated numerically, were the best organized ethnic group, and inhabited many of Hungary's strategically sensitive border areas. They consequently wielded the most influence among Hungary's ethnic minorities,[2] and shortly became the foci of ethnic strife in Trianon Hungary.

Ethnic disharmony in Hungary had been planted in the early Middle Ages. In the mid-thirteenth century, Mongol raids nearly destroyed the ethnic Magyar population. To remedy these losses, Hungary's Angevin kings invited Saxon artisans and merchants from Germany to settle in Hungary's new urban centers. Many of them became prominent in Hungary's financial and commercial life. Not until the nineteenth century did their descendants begin to assimilate into the Magyar stream.

Disasters continually dogged Hungary's people. The country's independence ended in 1526, when Hungary's secular and ecclesiastic elite met the invading Turks and perished on the battlefield of Mohács. For nearly two centuries, the Kingdom of Hungary remained fragmented. In the east, the semi-independent principality of Transylvania struggled to survive amid Austro-Turkish intrigues. Turkey appropriated the Great Plain in the center, and Austria seized a narrow strip of territory in the north and the west. During this period, various Balkan peoples moved northward and colonized vast stretches of the formerly Magyar-inhabited, but now depopulated and desolate, Hungarian countryside.

Liberation by Austria at the end of the seventeenth century brought no reprieve to the decimated ethnic Magyars. Hungary, its reduced Magyar population split between Roman Catholicism and Protestantism, became a hereditary Habsburg kingdom and lost all but titular sovereignty. The Crown declared most of the recovered Hungarian lands new acquisitions, and rarely restored abandoned property to Magyar owners or their heirs. The Habsburgs imported a new nobility, and installed Serbian soldier-settlers on Hungary's southern frontier to guard against further Turkish incursions. In order to counterbalance the Orthodox Serbian and largely Protestant Magyar population, the Habsburgs invited Roman Catholic peasants, mainly from southern Germany, including Swabians (*Schwaben*), to establish rural settlements throughout Hungary. Austria subsidized nearly one-thousand villages, enjoying tax and other privileges, in the eighteenth century alone. Austria hoped that the "Swabians," as these colonists came to be known, would excel other ethnic groups and remain devoted to the Habsburgs, their German ideals, and Roman Catholicism. These Austrian expectations proved realistic. Hungary's Swabians became Habsburg loyalists. Simultaneously, however, this Imperial policy ensured future strained relations between Swabians and ethnic Magyars.

In the late eighteenth century, these and other Magyar discontents with Habsburg policies erupted in a nationalistic reaction. Certain elements of the ethnic Magyar nobility and intelligentsia wanted to restore the neglected Magyar tongue and raise the culture to literary prominence. The movement, which began largely as a protest against Joseph II's Germanizing measures in the 1780s, flowered into a fully-fledged cultural and political renaissance in the early nineteenth century. By the 1840s, Magyar had replaced Latin as Hungary's official language, and it had begun to compete with German as the country's commercial *lingua franca*. Simultaneously, magnificent public works in Pest, Hungary's new capital city, imbued ethnic Magyars with intense national pride. The intellectual ferment of this Reform Age culminated in efforts by Hungary's Magyar leaders to restore the country's political independence.

This promising era terminated in disaster. After the abortive Revolution of 1848–1849, Hungary lost its freedom. In the revolutionary struggle, Hungary's non-Magyars, especially the Croatians, Germans, Romanians and Serbs, overwhelmingly supported Imperial Austria. Whereas the Habsburgs appeared to champion the national aspirations of each minority against the ethnic Magyars, by contrast, most of Hungary's revolutionary leaders, notably Lajos Kossuth, rejected a multiethnic society as a matter of principle.

For nearly two decades following Hungary's defeat, Austria governed the country as a conquered province and tried to Germanize it. But Prussian victory in the 1866 Six-Weeks' War forced defeated Austria to the bargaining table with Hungary's representatives. The Habsburgs had no choice but to make peace in the east, having lost all their influence in the German states in the west.

The 1867 Compromise (*Ausgleich*) settled most Austro-Hungarian differences. The Compromise established the Kingdom of Hungary as Austria's equal constitutional partner. Hungary gained the right to promulgate all manner of domestic legislation. By then, Hungary's population exceeded twenty-million, but only slightly over 50% professed themselves ethnic Magyars. German-Hungarians (mainly Swabians in Hungary and Saxons in Transylvania) may not have been Hungary's most numerous minority, but in the long-run, they proved to be the most formidable adversaries of exclusive ethnic Magyar domination.

When Hungary became a semi-independent state in 1867, many Magyars became determined to eliminate all alien influences. Nationalists insisted that all non-Magyar languages and cultures be removed from public life. Ferenc Deák and József Eötvös, the authors of the Nationality Law of 1868 (Law 54), were humanitarians and liberals and they wished to protect minority rights. Certain ambiguities of the Act nullified their good intentions, and eventually gave intolerance a free rein.

The Law enshrined the concept of a unified Hungarian state to be governed by Magyars or Magyarized members of the ethnic groups. It denied collective legal status to Hungary's non-Magyar nationalities, and proclaimed all citizens un-hyphenated "Hungarians," regardless of their mother tongue. But the law never clearly defined the precise meaning of the word "Hungarian," nor did it sufficiently elaborate or properly designate the provisions granting minorities a certain share in higher education. Subsequent legislation, especially after 1907, promoted Magyarization policies in the schools. Hungary's educational system became more efficiently centralized and almost completely Magyarized. Minority language instruction totally disappeared from kindergartens and all institutions of higher learning. The church-dominated rural elementary schools in the non-Magyar regions gradually reduced instruction in the minority pupils' mother tongue. Owing to the ambiguous phrasing of the 1868 Nationality Law, and thanks to subsequent restrictive government regulations, the authorities could declare minority cultures and benevolent associations "political," and subject them to harassment or outright closure.

Among all the non-Magyars, the Swabians suffered the most extensive relative decline in ethnic educational facilities. After the Compromise, many rural Swabian children lost access to instruction in their ancestral tongue. To cite but one set of examples, in 1869, Hungary's Swabians possessed 1,232 pure German-language elementary schools. By 1890, nearly half of these had been abolished, and by 1905, Swabian attendance was limited to only 272 German primary schools throughout Hungary. By the last date, the vast majority of Swabian children frequented either mixed-language German-Magyar schools or attended purely Magyar institutions.

The assimilation process in Hungary's minority schools had an ambiguous effect on the development of an ethnic intelligentsia before World War I. The minorities had far fewer educated members proportionately than the Magyars. Statistically, the Germans enjoyed broader opportunities for Magyar-language higher education than any of Hungary's other ethnic groups, although they had far fewer graduates proportionately than the Magyars. Many of these students, however, were German-speaking Jews, not Swabians. Conversely, numerous individuals listed as Magyars were assimilants who reverted to being Swabians. The Magyars did not discriminate against Magyarized individuals. This tolerance attracted many ambitious and intelligent members of Hungary's Swabian and other ethnic communities.

Magyarization in Hungary often proved misleading and superficial. Some "Magyarized" youths championed their respective minorities later in life. This change of heart resulted from inept assimilative techniques practiced in some of the Magyar-language schools, which frequently hurt the personal feelings and wounded the ethnic pride of pupils and parents. Insensitivity by overzealous Magyar teachers and other functionaries embittered many Swabian and other minority people against the Hungarian state, and often turned minority children into Magyar-speaking individuals who lacked emotional attachment to the Hungarian state.[3] Most of the postwar minority leaders came from the ranks of this disgruntled pseudo-Magyarized intelligentsia. Its anti-Magyar sentiments remained submerged until the passions of war and intense postwar nationalist propaganda claimed their allegiance for the various postwar nationality causes.

Hungary's defeat in World War I aggravated Magyar-non-Magyar tensions. As the Austro-Hungarian Empire disintegrated, most of Hungary's minority peoples defected, and joined or were annexed to newly-formed or enlarged countries across Hungary's shrunken frontiers. These desertions first shocked, then embittered the Magyars. Some of them became convinced that, had all the nationalities been assimilated, Hungary's dismemberment could have been averted. After Trianon, Hungary came close to being a purely Magyar-dominated nation-state. The country's new leaders had no enthusiasm to spare for protecting the language and culture of the remaining non-Magyars from the dominant Magyar ethos.

In every way possible, therefore, the war-ravaged country faced unique challenges. Impoverished Trianon Hungary, divorced from its former Austrian imperial partner, required new strategies for survival. Postwar Hungary's leaders concentrated their energies on the resolution of three troublesome problems—Hungary's diplomatic isolation, a depressed economy, and the threat to Magyar homogeneity caused by a relatively large and incipiently disloyal German (Swabian) minority.

In March 1920, the former Austro-Hungarian naval chief Admiral Miklós Horthy became Hungary's regent and head of state. Under his guidance, Prime Ministers Count Pál Teleki (1920-1921), Count István Bethlen (1921-1931), Count Gyula Károlyi (1931-

1932), and Gyula Gömbös (1932–October 1936) attempted to resolve these difficulties with varying degrees of success. The entire period may be conveniently divided into four distinct phases: 1920–1925, a time of chaos, isolation and reconstruction; 1925–1929, a time of relative prosperity and the beginnings of Italian and German influence; 1930–1933, a time of severe depression; and 1934–1936, a return to limited prosperity and growing German influence.

The first period saw an insolvent and friendless Hungary attempting in vain to dispose of its agricultural production and securing the support of political allies. In the mid-1920s, only the League of Nations' intervention rescued Hungary's economy from collapse, but not before Bethlen had pledged to rescue the Swabians and other ethnic minorities from imminent assimilation. Starting around 1925, Germany and Italy began to take interest in Hungary's territorial aspirations and economic problems. Bethlen and Károlyi hoped that Hungary would succeed in the recovery of its lost territories and improve the economy through the combined efforts of Germany and Italy. But Germany demanded substantial improvements in Swabian education and culture as the price of its support. Bethlen, Károlyi, and their successors responded but sluggishly to this challenge.

The depression that began after 1929 spurred the rise of National Socialism in Germany. Hitler's Third Reich vastly complicated Hungary's geopolitical situation. Although Germany became a prodigious importer of Hungarian goods and at first paid excellent prices, the new German government expected Hungary to improve the quality of Swabian life without further delay. To Hungary's chagrin, many Swabians became Nazi supporters who threatened to turn into a Fifth Column.

Gradually, Nazi Germany's might grew, whereas Italy's influence rapidly diminished. By the end of 1936, Italy was no longer in a position to protect Hungary against a revitalized and increasingly more aggressive Germany. Gömbös met this peril by trying to capitalize on his long-time personal friendship with Hitler. While demanding increasing economic aid from Germany, Gömbös refused to reciprocate by promoting the Swabian cause. Gömbös erroneously assumed that Germany and Italy would maintain parity, and that Hungary would remain the perennial linchpin of these two allies. Gömbös's successors would be forced to seek more imaginative and realistic solutions to ensure Hungary's survival.

The danger posed by a potentially powerful Germany supported by an incipient Swabian pan-German reaction was noted by more than one Magyar public figure after the war. The determination to extirpate the alleged German threat to Hungary's internal security became a primary objective throughout the interwar period. Not only the Swabians, but also Hungary's other ethnic minorities suffered the consequences of this defensive Magyar nationalism.

To justify the resultant policy of Magyarization, eminent personages such as Count Albert Apponyi, cited Hungary's "Historic Mission." According to this conception, the Magyars, augmented and aided by their loyal polyglot subject nationalities, constituted a natural economic and geopolitical agglomeration in the Danubian region. Leadership would devolve not on the most numerous people, but on the "culturally superior Magyar race," whose task was to protect Western Europe against attacks from the "barbaric East." The Magyar-dominated central government would grant the subordinate nationalities total personal freedom and adequate encouragement to nurture their cultural and linguistic individualities. Such a cooperative venture would ensure the mission's success.[4] The mystical basis of this Magyar-centered Hungarian nationalism elevated the issue of Magyar predominance in Hungary from the level of mundane politics to the realm of an ideology, and engendered a highly popular national crusade.

These Magyarization policies encountered certain difficulties. The Minorities Clauses of the Trianon Peace Treaty presented legal obstacles, which the Hungarian government easily evaded. Far more serious was the dilemma of what to do with the Swabian minority. Although determined to eliminate this potential threat to Magyar homogenization and dominance, Hungary's leaders recognized that a pro-Swabian policy offered possible advantages. After defeat and temporary insolvency that lasted until 1925, Germany became the only power able to offer adequate economic aid and support for Hungary's efforts to regain the lost territories. Germany, however, became keenly interested in the Swabians, and monitored their treatment and welfare. To resolve the clashing demands of its internal security and external diplomacy, Hungary tried to convince the Germans that the Swabians' cultural interests would be protected if Germany provided economic aid, actively championed Hungarian revisionism, and dissuaded the Swabians from challenging Magyar hegemony in Hungary.

In fact, the public and the Hungarian government wished to derive benefits from their German affiliation, but lacked enthusiasm to honor their commitments any more than was absolutely necessary. They were chiefly interested in regaining Hungary's lost territories, populations, and prestige, preferably by peaceful means. Through the application of a shrewd and calculating foreign policy, Hungary attempted to persuade friends and foes alike to permit, at the very least, the restoration of the lost territories with ethnic Magyar populations.

The Swabian cultural establishment, especially the rural elementary school system, was the ideal instrument for piecemeal Magyarization. Throughout the interwar period, Hungary promulgated a number of minority elementary school laws, purportedly to improve German and other educational facilities. Inept legislation and lack of good will virtually destroyed the effectiveness of these institutions.

The Magyarization program consisted of two steps. First, the government built superior Magyar-language primary schools, especially in German-inhabited areas, hoping to entice the brighter Swabian pupils into abandoning their own inferior, underendowed facilities in favor of the more attractive Magyar institutions. The second stage in the government's Magyarization strategy utilized the maxim voiced by Jakob Bleyer, leader of postwar Hungary's Swabians, that a minority without an intelligentsia must perish. The government believed that the unsophisticated Swabian peasants would be unable to resist assaults against their ethnic identity if they were deprived of their intelligentsia. The peasant home environment, with its tradition of oral culture, did not stress an appreciation of literary German, even though rural Swabians generally respected education. The minority schools, most of which divided their curricula more or less evenly between German and Magyar, failed to inculcate an adequate mastery of either tongue. As a result, ambitious Swabian pupils had to leave their minority schools and enroll in Magyar-language institutions. This was the only means of matriculating into higher institutions of learning and attaining a better station in life.

The basic outlines of this educational policy emerged almost immediately after the Armistice, when the influence of Hungarian diplomacy on Swabian school affairs, and the impact of Swabian minority education and cultural life on foreign policy, became direct and obvious. After the deposition of the monarchy, Count Mihály Károlyi's socialist coalition government and its successor, Béla Kun's Soviet Republic, introduced legislation designed to persuade Hungary's nationalities not to defect. Both governments focused on Swabians as the chief potential beneficiaries of German cultural and political programs. Swabians would regulate their own school affairs and enjoy regional autonomy in Hungary's only sizable compact German-inhabited region, in the western counties, next to

Austria. Through these regulations the government hoped to persuade the German majority not to secede. Both leftist regimes claimed the allegiance of numerous Swabian urban industrial workers, but nationwide, the latter constituted a Swabian minority. The Károlyi and Kun schemes for Swabian educational reform failed. Most German-Hungarians were religious rural conservatives, who defied the two governments' efforts to nationalize and secularize Hungary's school and church systems. Hungarians realized that Károlyi and Kun lacked the authority to persuade hostile provincial and church administrators that minority languages and cultures had a vital function to perform in postwar Hungarian life.

After the war, most Swabians believed that a display of Hungarian patriotism would endear them to conservative Magyars. As a result, many pro-Hungarian Swabians refused to collaborate with Károlyi or Kun, and instead played a vigorous and significant role in helping to restore an ultranationalistic, conservative government in the fall of 1919. In recognition for his counterrevolutionary services, Jakob Bleyer became Minister of Nationalities. Bleyer and many other Swabians assumed that the grateful Magyar-dominated government would deal equitably with the country's minorities, especially the Swabians.

Prime Minister István Friedrich, and his immediate successors Károly Huszár and Sándor Simonyi-Semadam, only appeared to champion minorities' rights. In fact, they wished to convince the victorious powers of Hungary's good intentions toward non-Magyars preceding the peace conference. Futhermore, they still hoped that a pro-minority policy would persuade the seceded non-Magyars to rejoin Hungary. None of the departed nationalities heeded Hungary's pleas. In June 1920, the Treaty of Trianon ratified Hungary's territorial and population losses.

In 1920–1921, Prime Minister Pál Teleki sought to convince the German-speaking Swabian population of Hungary's western counties that the region's economic welfare and German culture would prosper better under conservative Hungarian rule than in an unstable socialist-dominated neighboring Austria imperiled by bolshevism. Numerous Swabians heeded the pro-Hungarian patriotic pleas of Bleyer and his associates. In a 1921 plebiscite arranged by the League of Nations some residents of the western counties voted to maintain their ties with Hungary, although most chose Austrian rule.

These results angered most Hungarians. Many jumped to the conclusion that nearly all Swabians were "unreliable." Now that

Hungary's population distribution and territorial boundaries were firmly established, the public saw no reason why the remaining Swabian and other minorities should be pampered any longer. They not only castigated the seceded non-Magyar nationalities for desertion, they looked upon the remaining minorities as potential future traitors. Not surprisingly, most of Hungary's public was sufficiently disillusioned with the behavior of non-Magyars to demand clamping the lid on any future encouragement of minority cultures and languages on Hungarian soil.

The war had released intense nationalistic passions throughout the world. Hungary was no exception. The Magyars of Hungary meant to dominate their own small country. Only Magyars would qualify as a nationality, and their domination must be unchallenged. The Swabians, who were swept by a German nationalistic tide, became victims of Magyar nationalism. Bleyer modified his wartime blueprint of what the ethnic compositon of the Hungarian power structure ought to be. Earlier, he had conceded that the Magyars were entitled to dominate the Hungarian state. Now, he proposed a joint Magyar-Swabian hegemony in Hungary. Bleyer had enjoyed considerable popularity with conservative Magyars during and shortly after the war, but only because his nationalistic views and activities harmonized with their own. When it became apparent that Bleyer considered himself more of a patriotic German-Hungarian than a nationalistic Magyar of German origin, the Magyar public discredited him.

Deteriorating conditions in the rural Swabian elementary schools dramatized displeasure with the Swabians in postwar Hungary. The neglect of these institutions in Swabian regions violated both Hungarian law and the League of Nations' provisions designed to protect minorities' rights in all the states created by the peace settlements, including Hungary. In the first two years of Count István Bethlen's prime ministry, which began in 1921, pure German schools almost disappeared. In the 1923–1924 academic season the number of such institutions declined from nine schools serving 825 pupils to only four schools accommodating an indeterminate number of students. German elementary school teachers, who numbered only one-hundred for several years after the war, declined annually to fewer than eighty by 1927–1928.[5] Swabian pupils derived very little benefit, even from them, because the government dispersed most German-speaking teachers in non-German institutions throughout Hungary. In the few pure German schools, instructors were likely to be ethnic Magyars with inferior German skills.

The government introduced limited improvements in Swabian

cultural and educational facilities somewhat later, but only because Hungary had to appease the League of Nations and, later on, Germany. The Weimar Republic slowly recovered after suffering a severe postwar economic crisis, but by 1925 appeared ready to become Hungary's principal trade partner. Consequently, the nationalistic Weimar Germans had to be persuaded that their Swabian brethren in Hungary were not being oppressed. Bethlen also sought to convince the League of Nations' factfinding commission investigating the feasibility of granting Hungary a large loan that the country could be relied upon to observe the terms of the peace treaty, and to conduct sensible economic and social policies.

In June 1923, Bethlen unveiled his long-promised and oft-postponed minority education legislation.[6] The new law established three minority elementary school types. Pure minority schools were designated as A-type, mixed-language (50%-50%) institutions as B-type, and Magyar schools where pupils learned only their mother tongue as a daily subject, as C-type. The government failed to provide German schooling above grade school level. The authorities established German teachers' courses only later, and never in sufficient numbers to secure an adequate supply of competent German teachers. Decisions regarding school types to be adopted were left to the discretion of school boards assisted by unsophisticated parents' groups. Local administrators frequently coerced parents' conferences to choose C-type institutions. The German instruction they offered was invariably poor. Bethlen resorted to promises, delays and statistical manipulations to persuade the world that significant improvements were being introduced in Hungary's minority school system. Swabians, however, had little cause for rejoicing.

In 1924, shortly after the introduction of the school law, Bethlen authorized the establishment of the *UDV* (*Ungarländischer Deutscher Volksbildungsverein*). This was a Swabian cultural association sponsored and subsidized by the government.[7] The government appointed the trustworthy Transylvanian-born Saxon Gustav Gratz, a former foreign minister, as president, and Bleyer became his second-in-command. The government never permitted the *UDV* to function freely, yet the association served Bethlen's political purposes well. The German-Hungarian trade agreement of 1931 came into being because political circles in the Weimar Republic accepted Bethlen's assurances that the basic premises for a Swabian cultural renaissance were in the process of being firmly established in Hungary.

Fortunately for Bethlen, the grateful Bleyer had once more conceded Magyar hegemony, and demanded only that the rural Swabians' cultural and educational requirements be satisfied. By the end of the Bethlen era in 1931, Bleyer realized once more that even these modest pleas would not be heeded. Perceived Magyar duplicity disappointed and embittered him. During the brief ministry of Gyula Károlyi (1931–1932), Bleyer's disillusion turned to rancor. The Swabian leader despaired of ever reaching a satisfactory accommodation with the Magyar-dominated government without exerting duress.

Bleyer prepared an alternative plan. Swabian grievances would be settled not in Budapest, but would be mediated through bilateral German-Hungarian negotiations. The government rejected this scheme because it violated Hungarian sovereignty. Bleyer also toyed with the idea of forming a Swabian political organization to oppose the government's Unity Party. Finally, he founded the *DA (Deutsche Arbeitsgemeinschaft)*, a clandestine circle of trusted Swabian collaborators, who were to recruit *völkisch* cadres throughout Hungary's Swabian regions. The ultimate objective of this cabal was to unify all Hungarian Germans under one umbrella organization. Thus began the radicalization of Hungary's Swabians.

During the early postwar years, Bethlen initiated the painstaking diplomatic process that eventually destroyed the Versailles peace treaty system. Bethlen aimed at the restoration of Hungary's lost territories, populations and international prestige. The Prime Minister recognized the difficulties involved in executing this ambitious program. Some of the great powers, such as Great Britain and France, wished to maintain the *status quo*, whereas others, such as Italy, the Soviet Union and Germany, wanted to carve out spheres of influence in southeastern and east-central Europe at the expense of France, its regional allies, and each other. Bethlen's task was to decide which of the great powers would be most sympathetic to Hungary's territorial aspirations and commercial requirements and be willing and able to render assistance.

The Soviet Union played only a minor role in these early postwar Hungarian affairs. At first, the USSR isolated itself from world events, and under Josef Stalin, attempted to perfect its domestic socialist society before instigating a world revolution. Undoubtedly, Stalin was disheartened by the failure to establish communist regimes throughout Europe, including Hungary, immediately after the war. Fears of a second bolshevik revolution, however, ensured the unswervingly conservative thrust of Hungary's interwar foreign policy. This strategy included the avoidance of any dealings with the Soviet Union. This eliminated the USSR as a possible revisionist partner. Indeed, conservative Hungary's defeat of domestic bolshevism in 1919 inspired an institutionalized anti-communist crusade, which melded smoothly into Mussolini's and later Hitler's efforts to prohibit Soviet expansion in any part of the region. Hungary's interests clashed with those of France and the Little Entente. The strong likelihood of an eventual Franco-Russian military alliance further alienated Hungarian policymakers from France. In view of Great Britain's apparent disinterest, Hungary had no other choice than to seek the assistance of Italy, and/or Germany. At first, Bethlen's policy appeared to thrive. Between 1927 and 1933, when Germany's influence in Hungarian affairs was still relatively modest, Italy vigorously and effectively supported Hungary. After 1933, under National Socialism, Germany's influence in Hungary increased gradually. By 1935, Germany and Italy had reached parity in east-central Europe. For Hungary, these were days filled with breathless expectations. The wrongs of Trianon might be redressed shortly by the combined efforts of two evenly-matched, benevolent and powerful friends.

Hopes for an early territorial settlement in Hungary's favor had a negative impact on Hungarian-Swabian relations. When Gyula Gömbös followed Gyula Károlyi as prime minister in 1932, any illusions of a mutually satisfactory Magyar-Swabian settlement vanished. Gömbös, a Magyarized Swabian, was the first Hungarian leader to be openly rude to the Swabians. He berated Bleyer for allegedly having encouraged Swabians to embrace "harmful" German culture, and refused to offer them any further cultural concessions. One year later, in December of 1933, Bleyer died, a discredited and broken man. His final months were envenomed by demonstrations, denunciations, and lawsuits impugning his Hungarian patriotism.

The entire Swabian community shared in Bleyer's adverse publicity, and lost the public's slender support. Moreover, after 1932, the rise of National Socialism in Germany stimulated Hungarian hostility to Swabian assertiveness. Many Hungarians feared that *völkisch* zealots in Nazi Germany and assertive Swabians in Hungary might soon conspire to replace the influence Hungary desired in the Danubian region with exclusive German hegemony. The National Socialists in Germany vowed to march eastward. This threat intensified the skepticism of Hungarians regarding their country's future regional leadership opportunities. Most of them were convinced that, given the choice, numerous Swabians would be only too willing to promote Germany's expansionist objectives in the area at Hungary's expense.

Consequently, the advent of National Socialism in Germany had conflicting repercussions for Hungarian-German and Hungarian-

Swabian relations. National Socialism bolstered the Third Reich's economy and stirred revisionist aspirations in Germany and Hungary. The Hungarian government wanted to strengthen the country's agricultural sector, sought preferential commercial treatment in the Third Reich, but refused to placate the Germans by accommodating Swabian cultural demands. In 1934, Gömbös persuaded Nazi Germany to renew the commercial agreement of 1931. This was a significant, though temporary, economic windfall for Hungary's ailing agriculture. For the time being, the Third Reich overlooked Swabian grievances for the sake of establishing a firm strategic bridgehead and securing an economic grip in Hungary.

The rise of National Socialism in Germany inspired many Swabians who became outraged by Hungary's perceived repression of their cultural and political aspirations. This discontent brought about a Swabian backlash. During his lifetime, Bleyer had firmly dominated the obedient rural Swabians. After his demise, the *UDV*'s monolithic structure gradually crumbled. The patriotic German-Hungarian association, now led by Gustav Gratz and Monsignor László Pintér, still attracted most of the loyal members of the older generation, and continued to enjoy government support. In 1935, under the leadership of the *UDV* executive secretary Franz Basch and Debrecen University professor Richard Huss, a *völkisch UDV* faction, the *Volksdeutsche Kameradschaft* (*VK*), resigned en masse. This schism polarized Swabian society. Emboldened by the financial aid and moral support of *völkisch* Nazi circles in the Third Reich, and with the tacit blessings of influential members of the German government, the *VK* embarked on a vigorous campaign to hector the Hungarian government into granting extensive concessions to the Swabian *Volk*.

In an effort to arrest the growing Swabian disaffection and halt the drift toward Nazi radicalism, Gömbös promulgated the "Christmas" School Law (No. 4800) of 1935, a variant of its 1923 predecessor.[8] The statute established one uniform school prototype resembling B-type institutions. The new system was not slated to commence officially until the beginning of the 1938–1939 school year. It also failed to provide qualified German teachers, and the government flatly rejected the *VK*'s suggestion that autonomous *völkisch* German teacher academies be established in Hungary. The new regulations briefly raised Swabian hopes, especially among the older people with loyalties rooted in prewar royal Hungary. In some localities, the minority schools functioned well. In many others, however, zealous functionaries, teachers and clergymen ignored the new law, and used the interim period to persuade numerous

Swabian villagers to accept pure Magyar-language schools on a permanent basis.

These internal Hungarian developments partially coincided with the major event that altered postwar Europe's balance of power—Germany's occupation of the Rhineland on 7 March 1936. This audacious and successful German military operation thwarted French plans to prevent Germany's expansion into eastern Europe.[9] The Little Entente's security had been effectively breached, because a France intimidated in the west could no longer hasten to the aid of its eastern allies. Hungary also realized, however, that if unchecked, Germany would make a clean sweep of eastern Europe. Exclusive German hegemony in the region would injure Hungary's chances of becoming an influential middle power in Danubian Europe serving two equally balanced allies, Italy and Germany.

In order to prevent the Danubian region from falling under exclusive German dominion, Gömbös launched an intensive diplomatic activity. First, he wanted to reconcile Hungary's two allies, Austria and Italy, with Germany. Next, he planned to forge an alliance composed of all of Europe's anti-Marxist revisionist states. Finally, he wished to prevent a rapprochement among members of the latter group with the Anglo-French alliance system, composed also of Poland, the Soviet Union and the Little Entente. Poland, however, would be treated differently. This traditional friend of Hungary was in an anomalous position. It needed France's support for its survival against Germany, but it lived in mortal peril of France's ally, the Soviet Union. Therefore, Poland was to be detached from the French orbit and "rescued" under the slogan of an anti-bolshevik crusade.

Gömbös's approach recalled former Prime Minister István Bethlen's plan to revise the Peace Treaty of Trianon through simultaneous intervention on Hungary's behalf by Germany and Italy. By early 1936, this grand design verged on failure. Italy's influence in eastern Europe was rapidly ebbing, whereas the Third Reich had now eliminated French preeminence in the Danubian region. Hungary under Gömbös and his successors aimed at curbing Germany's hegemony in the east. They also endeavored to destroy the effectiveness of the Little Entente by isolating Czechoslovakia, its most powerful member, from Romania and Yugoslavia, and diminishing British and French influence in the region in favor of Italy.

After Germany's occupation of the Rhineland, Gömbös attempted to rescue Austria from being annexed by Germany. He also tried to reconcile Italy and the Third Reich, and attempted to establish Hungary as the chief central European ally of both these countries. Eventually, he hoped, the region would be transformed into a Christian bastion to protect Europe against Bolshevism. During the 13-16 March 1936 Budapest visit by Austrian Chancellor Kurt von Schuschnigg and Foreign Minister Egon von Berger-Waldenegg, Hungarian Foreign Minister Kálmán Kánya urged his visitors to be cautious with Germany. It was essential for Austria not to annoy Germany and avoid even the appearance of a pro-Czechoslovak or pro-French policy. Austrians must also rebuff any attempts by the Soviet Union to enter central European affairs under the pretext of aiding Austria. In view of Italy's preoccupation in Ethiopia, France's indecisiveness, and Great Britain's lack of interest in continental affairs, the Austrians felt isolated and defenseless. Consequently, they agreed to pursue the cautious course Kánya suggested to them.

At the 20-21 March conference in Rome, the three Rome Protocols signatories, Austria, Hungary and Italy, met to discuss a number of sensitive issues. Realizing that his influence in Europe was waning, Mussolini wanted to raise Italy's prestige by defying Germany. Gömbös tactfully dissuaded Mussolini, and guided deliberations into channels that might prove more acceptable in Berlin. The Germans, however, were far from reassured. they resented the fact that Hungarian diplomats dared to seize even regional initiatives. The Italians, on the other hand, feared gradually losing their influence in Hungary to the more aggressive Germans.

Following the Rome meetings, the Germans left no doubt that they distrusted the motives of their Hungarian allies. They were convinced that Hungary was trying to help construct a barrier against German expansion in the Balkans. Hungarian Ambassador Döme Sztójay in Berlin tried to convince German State Secretary Bernhard Bülow that the three allies were not engaged in forming an anti-German cabal. He pleaded for a German-Hungarian consultative pact and an Austro-German nonaggression treaty to diminish tensions. He also urged Germany to join the Rome Protocols without further delay. When Bülow refused, Sztójay threatened to sabotage improving Hungarian-Yugoslav relations. This offended Göring, who regarded a reconciliation between Hungary and Yugoslavia an essential prerequisite for German domination in eastern Europe. Sztójay also insinuated that if thwarted by Germany, Hungary might desert the Third Reich and join France. Germany would simply have to become more accommodating to Hungary's needs.

Hungarian audacity in the face of German might was foolhardy, especially since Gömbös was simultaneously defying growing German clamorings for an improvement in Swabian cultural conditions. Gömbös, in fact, continually kept tempers at fever pitch among Hungary's Germans by insulting the *völkisch* Swabian leaders on a regular basis. He was convinced that Hungary's vital strategic importance, reinforced by his own intimate personal friendship with Hitler, would shield Hungary against German retaliations.

In the short-run, Gömbös succeeded in harmonizing his foreign policy imperatives with the requirements of Hungary's internal security. Minor Reich officials might berate and threaten Hungary because the country allegedly mistreated the Swabians. Gömbös knew, however, that Hitler wanted to pacify Hungary's leadership. The Swabians would have to suffer petty oppression in silence. Of course, Gömbös the realist knew that Hitler's apparent indifference to the plight of Hungary's Swabians was merely a temporary expedient. Soon, Germany might apply various pressures to ameliorate the condition of the Swabians. Therefore, Gömbös thought, Hungary had to relegate the Swabians to insignificance by creating a homogeneous Magyar nation-state while Hungary still enjoyed total freedom of action.

Hungary's chief diplomatic weapons—daring, persistence and tenacity—paid handsome short-term dividends, especially after the complex international situation of early 1936 became clarified. On 5 May, Italy's Ethiopian campaign ended victoriously. In order to prevent Italy's rapprochement with Great Britain and France, Germany wished to pacify Italy, Austria and Hungary. This explains why Germany pursued a relatively conciliatory policy in Austria. Hitler tried to soothe Mussolini's fears of a German sweep to the East (*Drang nach dem Osten*). Having lost confidence in the Western powers, Mussolini needed Germany's support. Thereafter, reconciliation between Austria and Germany and Germany and Italy proceeded smoothly. Early in June 1936, von Schuschnigg obtained Italian assurances that a German-Italian agreement would not imperil Austrian independence. On 11 July, Hitler concluded a gentlemen's agreement with Austria that postponed *Anschluss* for nearly two years. This pact resolved remaining German-Italian differences as well. On 25 October, a secret protocol inaugurated the Rome-Berlin Axis. Its chief architect Gömbös had died of cancer on 6 October. German-Italian control of eastern Europe seemed to be assured now. The two governments pledged to collaborate in all respects, and promised to settle all economic and political problems in the Danube Basin in a friendly spirit. At this point, Hungary, as the trusted ally of the two evenly matched great powers, seemed to have its future assured.[10]

CHAPTER II

THE DIPLOMATIC PICTURE - EUROPE IN 1937

Hungary's leaders had failed to achieve their country's ambitious revisionist aims by 1937. Recovery of the territories lost to the successor states seemed as remote as ever. In the meantime, Germany's political, economic and ideological influence penetrated ever deeper into eastern Europe and the Balkans. Hungary stood in grave danger of being diplomatically outmaneuvered and militarily outflanked by the dynamic leaders of the Third Reich. The year 1937 offered some promise, because the war clouds of 1936 had lifted. This augured well for the peaceful long-range resolution of Hungary's revisionist aspirations. Even so, Hungarian policymakers faced formidable trials, owing in part to the complexities of the country's varied diplomatic involvements, and because by 1937 Germany's expansionist plans in the Danube Basin had matured. The countries lying directly in Germany's imperialistic path were most involved. Those situated on the peripheries, and even regions farther removed from the Balkans, also had a considerable stake in the outcome of the unfolding power struggle in east-central Europe. One way or another, Hungary's destiny depended on the position each of these countries adopted in the immediate pre-World War II period.

As Hungary's closest ally, Austria constituted the buffer against Nazi Germany. Austria commenced the year 1937 optimistically. Chancellor Kurt von Schuschnigg tried to resist National Socialist encroachments by urging his people to adopt a strong Austrian national consciousness. Improved economic conditions, which further stabilized Austria, should also have muted domestic National Socialism. But von Schuschnigg blundered. First, he encouraged Habsburg legitimism as a would-be safeguard to preserve Austrian sovereignty. Second, he launched Austria on an unrealistic "German *völkisch* and cultural Mission," which placed Austria on an ideological collision course with Germany. Hitler regarded only the Third Reich as morally entitled to promote German nationalism. The Austrian Chancellor also violated the 11 July 1936 gentlemen's agreement with Germany by persecuting Austrian National Socialists as alleged traitors.

A further difficulty for Austria arose from the fact that its gentlemen's agreement with Germany had to harmonize with the provisions of the prior Rome Protocols with Italy and Hungary, and subsequently with the Rome-Berlin Axis. For the present, von Schuschnigg was fortunate. Italy wished to maintain Austrian sovereignty, and France also renewed an interest in preserving Austria. Indeed, von Schuschnigg had every reason to believe that the twin-umbrellas provided by Italy (and hence Hungary) and by France (and hence Great Britain and the Little Entente) would shield Austria from an overt German attack.

Whereas Austria ranked as one of the best neighbors Hungary had, Czechoslovakia was only second to Romania as its bitterest enemy. In 1937, Czechoslovakia's external problems became gradually aggravated by internal difficulties. The combined weight of these pressures began slowly to strangle that awkwardly situated country with its restive, heterogeneous population. Czechoslovakia enjoyed good relations with France, its chief supporter, and with the Soviet Union. Whether effective military help would arrive from these two states in time to blunt a German attack was questionable, especially if the Third Reich should also enjoy the support of Poland and Hungary. Blossoming Austro-Czechoslovak relations wilted rapidly early in the year when Austria violated the Treaty of St. Germain and introduced military conscription. This buried a French plan to recruit Austria and Czechoslovakia as partners in an anti-German central-European *cordon sanitaire*.

The Czechoslovaks also clashed diplomatically with Italy over that country's invasion of Ethiopia. Later efforts to foster improved relations with Mussolini foundered on Czechoslovakia's support of the Spanish Republicans. Italy supported the Falangists. Ever since the creation of their respective republics after World War I, the Czechoslovaks and Poles had been feuding over possession of Těšín (Teschen), with its mixed Czech-Polish ethnic population and rich coal deposits. Poland also accused Czechoslovakia of mistreating Polish minorities. This mutual enmity proved so intractable that French designs for a central European bloc willing and able to stem Germany's expected eastward expansion had to be abandoned.

In 1937, Czechoslovakia's relations with Germany grew precarious over the Sudeten question. On 28 February 1937, Konrad Henlein, the Sudeten German leader, demanded territorial autonomy for his people. The Hodža government rejected this plan because it violated the Czechoslovak constitution. For many years, Hungary had been urging Czechoslovakia's Poles and Germans to make common cause with the Magyar minority to combat alleged government persecutions. Hungary wished to coordinate these efforts in order to force Czechoslovakia to the negotiating table, but Germany would not collaborate with Hungary to bring about frontier revisions. By 1937, however, Czechoslovakia's Little Entente partners Romania and Yugoslavia had written off their ally as virtually lost to German aggression, and sought loopholes in the Little Entente agreements to avoid having to support Czechoslovakia unconditionally in the event of war. Great Britain appeared totally uninterested in the destiny of eastern Europe. France seemed paralyzed, and the Soviet Union would not move without the collaboration of France. Czechoslovakia's relations with Hungary remained frosty but superficially correct.

Yugoslavia, which had been trying to foster good relations with all European countries, would not sacrifice existing diplomatic commitments or surrender Yugoslav territory to Hungary in exchange for security promises. Yugoslavia's rapprochement with Bulgaria (24 January) and with Italy (25 March), and the Kingdom's *de facto* recognition of the Franco regime in Spain, were the major events in Prime Minister Stojadinović's successful efforts to cultivate the friendship of Germany and Italy. Yugoslavia's relations with Hungary improved only marginally in 1937, despite, and perhaps because of, the assiduous exertions of Göring, who desired to build a strategic bridge linking Germany with the eastern Balkans via Austria, Hungary, Yugoslavia and Bulgaria.

With Poland, Hungary enjoyed a special relationship spanning several centuries. Even more so than Yugoslavia, Poland tried to avert dangers of aggression by pacifying most of its potential enemies, including the Soviet Union, despite unbridgeable ideological differences and mutual distrust. Although a major beneficiary of French funds and armaments, Poland sabotaged certain aspects of France's eastern European anti-German diplomacy, partly to injure France's allies Russia and Czechoslovakia, and partly to reassure Germany and purchase its good will. Poland cultivated the friendship of Romania and Italy as a means of counteracting Germany's eastward penetration, but these efforts met with limited success.

Internal problems played havoc with Soviet Russia's image abroad, and prompted most experts to dismiss the USSR's offensive military capabilities as ineffectual. Whereas the Soviet Union's relations with Germany, Italy and Japan approached the breaking point, Soviet leaders could not persuade France and England to join forces against Germany and Italy, the two chief Fascist powers. Deteriorating Russo-Romanian and Russo-Polish relations made it unlikely that either Romania or Poland would grant the Red Army or the Red Air Force transit privileges to defend Czechoslovakia against a German attack. With Hungary, the Soviet Union maintained cool but correct relations.

France's European security system, constructed painstakingly in the early postwar years, had begun to crumble by 1937. This was partly due to Germany's and Italy's resurgence and partly to Great Britain's professed aloofness from continental affairs. Internally, France had become politically and ideologically polarized by rightist and leftist extremists. The Spanish Civil War intensified the French domestic crisis. France's difficulty was further compounded by the financial chaos that Léon Blum's Popular Front reform government generated. In the event of hostilities with Germany, the French favored defensive warfare. They relied on the British navy to help defend France's overseas territories, and trusted the Maginot Line to frustrate a German invasion. Of course, in case of war, France could not reach any of its eastern European client states in time to save them.

Italy's defection from the shortlived Stresa Front, a French plan to detach Italy from Germany, could be ascribed to France's strategic difficulties. Without Italy's help, France could neither supply nor reinforce its eastern European allies. The Spanish Civil War further aggravated France's military problems. Under Italian tutelage, Spain might serve as a base for air strikes against France, in conjunction with an Italian invasion through Savoy and a German assault across the Rhineland and through Belgium. Italy could also strangle British naval traffic in the Mediterranean by blocking the Straits of Gibraltar. Axis bases on the Spanish Balearic Islands could sever French communications with colonial North Africa.

In 1937, Franco-German relations ranged widely from possible all-out war to attempted compromise solutions designed to settle major points of friction. France's military capabilities against Germany deteriorated steadily, especially after the Third Reich occupied the Rhineland, and constructed the Siegfried Line, a string of fortifications designed to neutralize France's Maginot Line. Belgium would not permit France to extend the Maginot Line to the Atlantic seawall. This exposed a long and vulnerable stretch of the Franco-Belgian frontier to possible German flanking attacks. Although publicly France and Poland proclaimed the effectiveness of their mutual defense treaty, these declarations rang hollow. Polish actions spoke louder than words. French Foreign Minister Delbos failed to conciliate the Czechoslovak-Polish dispute over Těšín. Furthermore, Romania's and Yugoslavia's growing doubts concerning the viability of the Little Entente and France's abilities to offer effectual military assistance to the Alliance against the Germans further weakened Czechoslovakia's strategic situation.

Yugoslavia's March agreement with Italy caused consternation in Paris, even though in October France and Yugoslavia extended their friendship treaty by five years. The Moscow trials, which eliminated the Soviet Union's top military leaders via the firing squad, shook France's confidence in the effectiveness of the Soviet armed forces. Franco-Romanian relations grew temporarily uncertain after Octavian Goga, a pro-German, became prime minister briefly in December 1937. The French public sympathized with Austria and Czechoslovakia, but doubted whether France had the will and capabilities to defend either country against a German attack. For the first time since the war, the outlines of a new European balance of power emerged. Under the new arrangement, Germany and Italy would become the power brokers in east-central Europe and the Balkans. France would have to withdraw from the area, or risk an all-out war.

On 28 May 1937, Neville Chamberlain became British prime minister, and inaugurated a new era, later deprecatingly dubbed "appeasement." Now that economic conditions had considerably improved in Great Britain, the new government intensified the previous Baldwin cabinet's determination to seek continental security through limited rearmament, cultivating the French alliance, and negotiating bilateral settlements with potential adversaries. Anglo-Italian tensions temporarily eased thanks to this approach. On 2 January, the two countries signed a gentlemen's agreement that defused an explosive situation in the Mediterranean, especially the Balearic Islands, and in Ethiopia. On 1 August, Chamberlain and Mussolini once again rescued deteriorating Anglo-Italian relations.

Great Britain's involvement with Germany followed an erratic course in 1937: first tension, then relaxation. Collective security, the status of Spain, and colonial questions were the chief divisive issues. The British government pointedly ignored eastern Europe, but influential M.P.'s and publicists championed Hungary's claims against the Little Entente. They particularly condemned the treatment accorded to ethnic Magyar minorities in the Successor States. This apparent concern by Britons in public life misled Hungary into the erroneous belief that sooner or later the British government would bow to public demand and help rectify the Treaty of Trianon in Hungary's favor.

Germany spent 1937 preparing for the destruction of Austria and Czechoslovakia. This meant that the Third Reich's other potential enemies would have to be temporarily pacified, and consequently, that the ardor of revisionist friends, such as Hungary, must be curbed. In line with this plan, Hitler negotiated tolerable relations with Great Britain and France. On 30 January, he promised to respect the neutrality of Holland and Belgium. On 13 October he pledged that Germany regarded Belgium's frontiers inviolable. The Third Reich also emphasized the need for friendly relations with Poland. On 5 November, Hitler promised that he would not permit the free city of Danzig to become the cause of a German-Polish conflict. In Yugoslavia, Germany counterbalanced Anglo-French and Italian influence with considerable success.

Despite rivalry in the Balkans, German-Italian relations thrived. The Rome-Berlin Axis proved its viability in Spain. On 6 November, Italy joined the German-Japanese Anti-Comintern Pact. Germany worried about Hungary's attempts to befriend the Little Entente and buttress Austria. A German-Hungarian trade agreement appeared to favor Hungary. This economic windfall resulted partly from Hungarian promises to rectify the worst abuses in the Swabian's cultural and educational conditions.

German venom focused chiefly on Austria and Czechoslovakia, the Third Reich's next two intended victims. Germany continued uninterrupted negotiations with Austria to rescue the July 1936 agreement that had obviously not borne fruit. Rumors of an Austrian Habsburg restoration and reports of an Austro-Czechoslovakian reconciliation, in which Hungary might have had a hand, upset Germany. As a result, Czechoslovak-German relations suffered. The German press castigated the Czechoslovaks throughout 1937, focusing on Czechoslovakia's close links with the USSR, the alleged persecution of Sudeten Germans, and the expropriation of German-owned lands along the Czechslovak-German frontier. The 17 October Teplitz-Schönau incident, in which the Czech police insulted Sudeten German minority leaders, further inflamed passions on both sides of the border. Russo-German relations were also poor, with no improvement in sight. This was due not only to ideological differences, but because the Soviet Union was determined to obstruct Germany's eastward expansion.

Throughout 1937, Italy's policies were characterized by impetuousness, ideological bombast and abortive *Realpolitik*. The harmful economic consequences of the "victorious" Ethiopian campaign and the continuing financial drain of the Spanish Civil War curtailed Italy's capacity to pursue effective politics in the Balkans. In late April, Mussolini had to abrogate the commercial clauses of the Rome Protocols. Austria and Hungary had depended on large-scale Italian purchases of their commodities. Austria never recovered from this economic blow, and Hungary was forced to seek remedies in Germany. *Anschluss* now became a foregone conclusion, especially after Germany and Italy settled their dispute over the division of the territorial spoils in eastern Europe and the Balkans.

Italy was also hard-pressed elsewhere in Europe. Franco-Italian relations cooled steadily, as Italy and Germany usurped France's formerly dominant position in Yugoslavia. Italy found it humiliating that France refused to recognize King Victor Emmanuel as the Emperor of Ethiopia. Anglo-Italian relations were more stable, but the Soviet Union and Italy neared the diplomatic breaking point. Italy and Hungary maintained cordial relations, and Italy produced a new, though ineffectual, trade agreement in August to pacify its ally.

Romania was plagued by social, political and ethnic dissension. The country contained an uneasy blend of mutually hostile Magyars, Saxons (Germans) and Romanians. The country was also split along rural-conservative, urban-liberal, and petit-bourgeois-fascist lines. France tried to retain Romania as an ally, but after October 1936, pro-German elements dominated the government. The Romanians had obviously despaired of effective French aid. They also feared sharing Czechoslovakia's impending doom, envied Yugoslavia's pampering by Italy and Germany, and wished to share economic and political benefits with Yugoslavia and Hungary. Italian-German friendship would also offer the best possible defense against persistent Hungarian revisionism. Yet Romania refused to settle its ethnic and legal quarrels with Hungary, feuded with the Soviet Union, and to a lesser degree with Poland. Romania hoped to attract Germany's support, based on its vast agricultural resources and oil reserves. One of Hungary's major frustrations in 1937 stemmed from Germany's firm insistence that Hungary must not tamper with Romania's and Yugoslavia's territorial integrity, at least for the present, and that Hungary must concentrate exclusively on Czechoslovakia to satisfy its insistence on frontier rectification.

For Hungary, as for all the small countries of eastern Europe, the perils of unchecked aggression by the Third Reich became a likely prospect. France had ceased being a great power in east-central Europe and the Balkans, and Italy's might was also diminished. The military purges had deprived the Soviet Union of its offensive striking capabilities, whereas Great Britain lacked the financial and military resources, and particularly the national will, to assert its presence in the Balkans. Virtually by default, Germany emerged as the only state sufficiently powerful and ruthless to fill the power vacuum from the Sudetenland to the Black Sea, and from the Baltic shores to the Mediterranean Sea.

CHAPTER III

GERMAN-HUNGARIAN ECONOMIC RELATIONS - LATE
1936–1937

Precarious global economic conditions curtailed Hungary's freedom of action before 1937. Even prior to Italy's renunciation of the economic provisions of the Rome Protocols in April 1937, the vast German consumer market had become an indispensable cornerstone of the Hungarian economy. After Italy's rapid decline as a first-class political and economic power, Hungary gravitated into Germany's orbit. Hungarian dependence on German generosity gave the Third Reich the means with which to curb the impatience of Hungary's statesmen for immediate revisionism.[1] After 1936, Germany gradually maneuvered Hungary into harnessing the country's agricultural production to accommodate the Third Reich's requirements. Hungary's industrial needs would be supplied mainly by German manufacturers.

Nazi Germany's aggressive and unscrupulous export-import program swept the small agricultural countries of eastern Europe and the Balkans into the Third Reich's economic orbit.[2] In September 1934, the German government introduced the "New Plan." This scheme integrated the exchange-control system and commercial policy with Germany's totalitarian armed economy.[3] The New Plan also revolutionized Germany's export-import pattern. It reduced trade with the industrial countries of the West, and intensified relations with eastern Europe's states such as Hungary, where the agriculturally-based rural structure complemented the Reich's technologically superior economy. The eastern European states had ample raw materials and excess agricultural products for export, and gladly purchased Germany's industrial manufactures in return. Germany therefore launched its New Plan in the vast region situated between the Czechoslovak-German frontier and the Black Sea. These areas enjoyed the advantage of being accessible to Germany by land and/or water, and of being situated beyond bombing range by France. These were essential considerations for Germany in case war erupted in western Europe.

Germany imposed efficient economic strangleholds on its eastern trading partners through clearing arrangements that benefited its industrial output. By paying these suppliers initially higher than prevailing world prices for their agricultural products, Germany effectively detached them from their former western European trading partners, and encouraged these fiscally vulnerable states to expand their agricultural production to suit Germany's requirements. Thereafter, the Third Reich held these countries effectively within its economic grasp. German industrial exports to these states never matched the cash value of agricultural imports which the Reich received. Germany accumulated huge trade deficits with the eastern European countries which forced these client states into placing nearly all their industrial purchases with Germany. By December 1934, the German-Balkan import-export deficit amounted to about 450 million Marks, of which Hungary's share was 44 million Marks.[4]

Germany had good reasons for pursuing this deficit financing policy. The accumulation of large payment balances in favor of agricultural states meant that their acquisitions of industrial products from western European countries had to steadily diminish. They constantly strove to close the export-import gap by purchasing German industrial products. Moreover, these countries lacked hard Western currencies with which to purchase industrial goods outside of Germany. Indeed, the Germans shrewdly cornered this sizable eastern European and Balkan market by forcing their trade partners to accept a new accommodation in the clearing agreements. Under the old system, Germany partially reimbursed its creditors in hard currency for agricultural shipments. This practice ceased in 1936. Thereafter, all trade agreements became straight barter arrangements.[5]

Germany's eastern European trade partners could not resist German pressures. They were individually weak and politically divided, and thus could not, as a unified bargaining unit, defy Germany. Neither could they prevail against Germany's superbly organized economic operations, which purposely pitted one small hostile country against another. Germany's buying power was so immense that in every one of these countries often the share sold to Germany decisively determined the price of the total available supply.[6] Germany benefited from its immense purchasing power and its partners' disunity. The Germans picked and chose only those commodities they desired, either to replace imports from distant or strategically vulnerable sources, or from countries that demanded cash payment on delivery in hard currencies. By forging firm economic links with the eastern European countries, Germany laid the foundations of a dynamic *Drang nach dem Osten* at a minimum risk and at small cost to itself.[7]

By 1936, most eastern European countries recognized that getting enmeshed in Germany's economic web was perilous.[8] Hungary was no exception. Although Prime Minister Kálmán Darányi realized that Hungary could not avoid being drawn into Germany's economic orbit, especially in view of Italy's lack of economic and political strength, he nonetheless decided to delay Hungary's rapid progress to economic satellite status. He wanted to soften the blow of German economic expansion, but do it discreetly, without antagonizing Hitler or imperiling Hungary's chances of sharing in anticipated German revisionist successes.

The six-year trade agreement concluded in July 1931, as amended in February 1934, regulated German-Hungarian commercial relations. Concluded during times of extreme agricultural stress for Hungary, these pacts virtually rescued the country from imminent economic ruin. Germany's share of Hungarian exports increased from 11.2% in 1933 to 23.9% in 1935, whereas German imports to Hungary grew from 19.7% in 1933 to 22.7% in 1935.[9] By the time of Gömbös's death in October 1936, Germany had become Hungary's principal trading partner.

By the end of that year, worldwide economic conditions had begun to improve. Poor harvests had created unprecedented global demands, and agricultural prices rose sharply. Between 1933 and 1937, wheat prices increased by 70% and corn by 150%.[10] For the first time since war's end, Hungary had the opportunity to become solvent by selling its agricultural surpluses freely in the world market. The clearing agreements, however, bound Hungary to accept payment in the artificially inflated German Mark. This destroyed the benefits of the high prices Germany had offered earlier. At the end of 1936, under Prime Minister Darányi, this situation led to a German-Hungarian trade controversy. The dispute centered on the volume of Hungarian grain deliveries and German recompense methods. Hungary had pledged to deliver various types of grains principally to its Italian and Austrian allies, but also to Greece, Great Britain, Switzerland, and Belgium. Hungary was to receive world prices payable in hard currencies. Darányi's efforts to remove Germany's economic yoke met the Third Reich's equally determined resolve to sabotage any economic liberation attempts, and return Hungary under German control.

German economic pressures on Hungary in the fall of 1936 roughly coincided with the inauguration of the National Socialist Four Year Plan under Göring's direction. In August of 1936, Hitler instructed Göring to make Germany economically battle-ready within four years.[11] Part of this scheme entailed the imposition of autarchy in Germany. This meant the securing and stockpiling of supplemental agricultural commodities from all countries eventually slated to become integrated into Germany's economic orbit. Hungary was one of these states. On 10 October 1936, while attending Gömbös's funeral, Göring forcefully intervened in routine German-Hungarian commercial discussions being conducted in Budapest. Hungary, he demanded, must provide a comprehensive listing of all those agricultural commodities that the country could deliver to Germany in addition to the items on existing clearing agreements. In return, Germany would provide Hungary with armaments.[12]

Other German officials immediately began pressuring various Hungarian colleagues to ensure the success of Göring's demands. On 14 October, Senior Counsellor Ulrich, who represented four German investment banks, arrived in Budapest to confer with Béla Darányi, the prime minister's cousin and director of *Futura*, the Hungarian wheat monopoly board. Ulrich demanded that Hungary release extra funding to subsidize additional German grain purchases, because supplementary grain acquisitions could no longer be financed through the clearing agreements. Ulrich urged Hungary to accept certain German industrial commodities to partially defray the existing German indebtedness.

Ulrich's demands stiffened Hungarian resolve to recapture the country's economic freedom. Hungary would accept only industrial products that were actually needed, and do so only at prevailing world prices, Darányi asserted. However, what Hungary required, Germany was unable to deliver in meaningful quantities. Ulrich next offered German-owned shares in Hungarian railway stocks as compensation. Darányi rejected this suggestion as well. In his view, Béla Imrédy, then president of the Hungarian National Bank, a known Anglophile and fiscal conservative, would reject such a transaction. Hungary insisted either that Germany offer payment in hard currencies, or deliver raw materials the country needed, and only at world prices. The meeting terminated inconclusively.

Ulrich thereupon urged Germany's diplomatic representative in Hungary, Hans Georg von Mackensen, to beg Imrédy to reconsider his negative decision on the railway stock offer. This proved unsuccessful. On 29 October, the German Foreign Ministry ordered von Mackensen to inform Darányi that Göring would discuss the supplementary grain delivery matter with him personally, and that Hungary's negotiating team "...should receive in advance the requisite instructions for giving effect to the Göring-Darányi conversation."[13] Darányi tried to dissuade Göring from insisting on such a course. Hungary could not deliver additional grain to Germany because of the recent poor fodder harvest. Nonetheless, Darányi stated, Hungary would make a symbolic goodwill gesture by offering Germany additional agricultural produce totaling 5.8 million Pengő (1.36P = 1.00RM). The shipment would include 3,100 tons of miscellaneous items, notably butter and meat products.[14] Throughout 1936, Darányi reminded Göring, Hungary had delivered approximately 220,000 tonnes of these commodities to Germany.[15]

As far as Hungary was concerned, Darányi's note should have temporarily satisfied German demands and salvaged Göring's ego. By then, however, the Germans had become very aggressive, and resolved not to let the Hungarians dictate terms. When, in mid-November, Alfred Nickl, director of the Hungarian Foreign Ministry's economic-political division, arrived in Berlin to negotiate the details of the compensation agreement (the occasion coincided with the 10-19 November annual meeting of the Hungarian-German Mixed Economic Commission), Göring emerged with a brand-new proposal. For years past, he explained, Germany had been maintaining a fund to be used specifically as a long-range emergency resource for Hungary's arms requirements. Now, owing to poor harvests, Germany needed more than merely a goodwill gesture from Hungary. In addition to Darányi's recent offer, Göring also demanded huge quantities of either wheat or flour.[16] Hungary would be reimbursed for all the additional shipments through armaments financed through the special defense fund. Moreover, Göring asserted, Germany expected Hungary to honor its commercial commitments even when harvests were poor.[17]

Nickl exclaimed that he knew nothing about German long-range armaments credits for Hungary. His distinct understanding, Nickl asserted, was that German food requirements rather than urgent Hungarian arms demands had prompted the latest Göring proposal. Still, Hungary would accept guns for butter, but only in exchange for the items and quantities the Darányi note had enumerated. Undeterred by this rebuff, Göring pressed his point: "Under these circumstances, Hungary will surely not forsake Germany."[18] On top of the Darányi offer, he persisted, Hungary must deliver an additional 75,000 tons of grain, and the total shipment must amount to between 20 and 25 million Pengő. On 31 December, Göring raised the quantity of grain desired in 1938 to 125,000 tons. He wanted even more later.[19]

Göring reinforced his tough negotiating tactic with a threat, delivered by Karl Ritter, head of the German trade delegation in Budapest. If Germany cannot depend on at least 150,000 tons of grain annually from Hungary, Ritter warned, then the Reich might have to seek other trade partners. If that ever happened, Hungary would suffer, because Argentina, for example, would insist on linkage, *i.e.*, selling frozen meats along with cereals. This, in turn, would force Germany to phase out Hungary as a source of pork and beef.[20] This ultimatum gave the Hungarians pause. Argentina almost always had large grain surpluses, and overseas transportation costs were generally cheaper than rail freight rates from eastern Europe to Germany. Moreover, Argentina did not insist on being paid in hard currency.[21] Under these circumstances, Hungary wisely forebore enraging Germany or humiliating Göring.

Even before this dialogue, Darányi consented to sell Germany additional grain, although he hedged on quantities. After several letters, Darányi pledged that Hungary would ship about 37,000 tons of grain and flour, and also raised the quantities of the other commodities to be delivered. The total cash value of all these export items amounted to 11-12 million Pengö. Actual delivery, however, lagged. Hungary shipped only 40,000 tons of corn and 5,000 tons of wheat flour during the first six months of 1937, and claimed to have sold the bulk of the harvest elsewhere.[22]

In itself, this disagreement was a relatively minor incident in German-Hungarian relations. But Göring had served notice that these German demands were only the first of many subsequent ones. Henceforth, Germany wanted to be a silent fourth partner in the Rome Protocols, and claimed Hungarian grain and flour shipments on the same basis as those enjoyed by Austria and Italy. Indeed, the message was loud and clear: Hungary must become an integral part of Germany's economic system.[23]

On 31 March 1937, the German-Hungarian Second Supplementary Agreement of 1934 (a renewal of the original 1931 agreement) expired. It took several months to get new negotiations started, because both sides realized how difficult these discussions would prove. In the interim, the earlier agreement remained in force by common consent. The German-Hungarian Mixed Commission met in Budapest between 16 June and 6 July. At issue were the clashing needs of the two countries' economies. Germany's poor wheat harvests for the past two years had precipitated a shortfall of over one-million tons each of bread and feed grain in 1937, whereas Hungary's bread grain surplus hovered only around 600,000 tons that year. Moreover, the global grain economy had now fully recovered. Consequently, by June 1937 Hungary had pledged its entire grain surplus to a number of European countries other than Germany for cash, at excellent prices, and at favorable exchange rates.[24]

Even before the negotiations began, the Germans announced

that the Reich expected Hungary to deliver at least 100,000 tons of wheat in 1937, and proportionate quantities of fodder grain.[25] German officials rebuked Hungary for having shipped only 40,000 tons of corn and 5,000 tons of wheat flour the first half year, whereas the 1934 agreement had allocated Germany 125,000 tons of Hungarian grain annually.[26] The Germans were more than annoyed. Over the past few months, Hungary had disposed of its surpluses lucratively elsewhere, and obviously meant to shirk its onerous nonprofitable contractual obligations with Germany.

In view of this unpleasant discovery, the German negotiators were in no mood for compromise or accepting excuses. Chief delegate Ritter demanded annual shipments of 200,000 tons of grain from Hungary. At least half would have to be wheat, thus nearly doubling the quantities specified in the 1931 and 1934 agreements. The Hungarians bargained. They offered only 50,000 tons of wheat to be delivered in 1938. The Germans rejected this offer as a piddling gesture, but promised to make the deal more attractive for Hungary by shipping chrome and manganese, two commodities Hungary had difficulties in obtaining in the world market.[27] Thereupon Nickl, head of the Hungarian delegation, complained to Foreign Minister Kálmán Kánya that the Germans were not negotiating, but dictating the terms of a new agreement.[28]

The Germans enjoyed both moral and legal advantage in this dispute, and they knew it. They now appealed to the farmers of Hungary, the main beneficiaries of any would-be German-Hungarian trade agreement, over the heads of their government. Dr. H. Reischle, Section Chief of the Third Reich's *Reichsnährstand*, Germany's central coordinating bureau for food products, released a strategically timed article in the July 1937 issue of the prestigious Hungarian agricultural periodical *Ungarischer Volkswirt*. He defended the commercial policies of Nazi Germany, the country that had rescued Hungary's economy in 1933 and 1934, when world prices for agricultural commodities had been dismal. At that time, when Hungary had no buyers for its produce, Germany purchased increasingly larger quantities of Hungarian grain at excellent prices. Currently, Germany was absorbing huge bulks of Hungarian food items, such as 83% of Hungary's fresh meat output, and 65% of the clover and lucerne harvest, that were not marketable globally. Thus far, Germany had generously helped an old friend and ally, and had tried to solidify German-Hungarian political friendship. Now that cereal prices had improved, Hungary was morally obligated to provide a fairer share of its harvest surpluses to Germany, which currently badly needed them. Reischle laced his benevolence with a threat. Hungarians must realize that they would suffer far greater economic hardship if Germany transferred its agricultural purchases elsewhere than if German manufacturers lost the Hungarian market. He assured readers, however, that Germany would continue absorbing prodigious quantities of Hungarian agricultural products in the future, regardless of market conditions. He hoped that Hungarians would magnanimously fulfill Germany's additional requirements.[29]

Hungarian negotiators knew the dangers that overwhelming German influence could pose for their country, but they feared even more that Germany might abandon Hungary in favor of agricultural competitors such as Romania or Yugoslavia, both of which enjoyed harmonious economic relations with Germany. They also recognized that Italy's days as a viable large-scale consumer for grain were numbered.[30] Austria, too, had begun to experiment with agricultural self-sufficiency. Moreover, Hungary had failed to introduce adequate land reforms after the war, and rural misery remained a running sore even in prosperous times.[31] The government feared social disorders, even revolution, should Hungary's agricultural price structure collapse. The loss of Germany as a steady, reliable client might be just the incident to precipitate such a catastrophe.

On this occasion, the Swabian problem decisively influenced the course of the Hungarian government's wheat diplomacy with the Third Reich. Most Swabians were farmers. Their prosperity depended on how well Hungary disposed of its agricultural surpluses not only in good times, but also during depressions. Many of Hungary's Swabians resided in sizable ethnic enclaves along the Austro-Hungarian border. They expected Hungary to collaborate economically with Germany. The government was literally forced to accede to Germany's harsh economic demands. Moreover, all Hungarians had good reason to believe that their country would decline agriculturally if it lost the German market. If such a disaster struck, most wavering Swabians, possibly even Hungary's hitherto faithful *UDV* supporters, might join the dissident pro-German *VK* led by Franz Basch—or so many Hungarians believed.

In view of these pessimistic auguries, Hungary could not afford to risk losing its best agricultural client. In the end, therefore, the Hungarian negotiators capitulated. Under the new agreement, Hungary pledged to ship 100,000 tons of bread cereals and 75,000 tons of fodder grains in 1937. To make the agreement more palatable for Hungary, the Germans promised to eliminate the clearing system from a certain portion of the cereal deliveries. But Imrédy, who subsequently negotiated the fiscal details of the agreement with

Ritter, found the German official uncooperative. He wanted to deny Hungary even this minor concession. At first, Imrédy demanded foreign exchange payments for nearly all grain deliveries, before gradually backing down. Finally, Ritter insisted on having the entire grain contract defrayed through the clearing system. Hungary thereupon sought assurances that deliveries of German raw materials would be maintained at current high levels. But the Germans rejected even this request, and in the Third Supplementary Agreement of 6 July 1937 (due to expire on 31 July 1940)[32] Germany would not commit itself to deliver any specific items Hungary desired.[33]

The agreement appeared to take some Hungarian sensibilities into consideration. Hungary was to provide Germany with only 10% of its annual wheat surplus, in addition to the regular quota, but the extra quantities to be delivered could never decline below 50,000 tons annually.[34] Consequently, in 1937, Hungarian exports to Germany grew by over 22% above the previous year, whereas German exports to Hungary rose by only 10%. This was so, because Germany substantially reduced the delivery rate of promised raw materials to Hungary.[35]

As a result of the expanding German-Hungarian export-import imbalances that mushroomed in a matter of months in 1937, German indebtedness to Hungary grew rapidly. By year's end, it reached the 12 million RM limit which the Hungarian National Bank and the Reichbank had agreed to maintain in the summer of 1937.[36] This occasioned further points of friction between the two countries. Just then, economic conditions favoring Germany intervened once more. A new recession, which began in the United States in the summer of 1937, soon spread, and caused steep decreases in raw material and food product price structures. This misfortune played into Germany's hands. The Western democracies had to reduce their agricultural purchases, especially in the more costly eastern European markets, and Germany immediately filled the void. Even before the *Anschluss* in March of 1938, Hungary was forced back into the German economic orbit, and theoretically was once again deprived of its freedom of action.[37]

TABLE 1

German Exports to Countries in the Danube Valley and the Balkans

Million RM					
Destination	1933	1934	1935	1936	1937
Austria	120.7	106.7	107.9	108.9	122.7
Czechoslovakia	160.1	184.4	130.0	139.0	151.0
Hungary	38.1	39.6	62.9	83.0	110.5
Yugoslavia	33.8	31.5	36.9	77.2	134.4
Romania	46.0	50.9	63.8	103.6	129.5

Sorurce: Lajos Jócsik, *German Economic Influences in the Danube Valley* (Budapest, 1946), pp. 6-7.

TABLE 2

German Imports from Danubian and Balkan Countries

Million RM					
Country of Origin	1933	1934	1935	1936	1937
Austria	57.6	66.2	71.1	76.6	93.5
Czechoslovakia ..	121.7	162.3	121.4	111.9	141.4
Hungary	34.2	63.9	77.9	93.4	114.1
Yugoslavia	33.5	36.3	61.4	75.2	132.2
Romania	46.1	59.0	79.9	92.3	149.5

Source: *Ibid.*

TABLE 3

Hungary's Commerce with Germany in the Most Important
Commodities 1936-1937
(In 1000 Pengö)

A) Exports

Category	In 1936 to		In 1937 to	
	Austria	Germany	Austria	Germany
Total Exports	86,956	115,198	99,379	141,586
Wheat	24,557	—	24,177	2,689
Rye	4,780	—	15,152	252
Corn	157	253	1,590	8,777
Clover and Lucerne	36	7,140	5	9,572
Flour	5,209	1,219	5,104	4,903
Fresh Fruit	4,189	4,030	3,200	4,057
Fresh Vegetables	1,203	2,027	1,221	1,324
Wine	355	3,115	485	3,002
Slaughtered and Live Animals	22,947	12,612	20,913	13,258
Cattle	3,130	6,116	3,116	6,718
Hogs	18,543	1,218	16,458	3,246
Horses	1,221	5,267	1,276	3,246
Poultry	5,867	8,516	7,576	7,029
Fats and Bacon	—	9,640	77	12,078
Fresh and Processed Meat	793	14,531	447	1,916
Fresh Butter	—	4,201	—	5,223
Eggs	2,352	2,216	4,142	3,701
Bauxite	1	4,166	7	6,238
Coal	2,233	—	2,695	—
Light Bulbs	141	2,833	192	3,160

Source: Mecsér, "Die Rückwirkungen," p. 26.

TABLE 4
Imports in 1936 and 1937
(in 1000 Pengö)

Category	In 1936 from		In 1937 from	
	Austria	Germany	Austria	Germany
Total Imports	72,435	113,353	85,368	124,762
Timber and Lumber	16,473	—	21,094	5
Coal	—	8,958	—	9,679
Metals	2,256	549	3,618	412
Iron Ore	1,058	7	574	1
Raw Hides	1,738	1,991	1,861	2,798
Iron and Scrap Iron	101	4,165	1,453	1,769
Cellulose	308	1,288	392	1,655
Dyes	3	8,380	5	8,678
Silk and Silk Yarn	82	5,596	97	7,109
Paper Products	15,992	5,702	17,623	5,997
Processed Iron Ore	2,015	1,023	2,313	1,312
Processed Furs	347	6,305	715	6,650
Cotton Yarn	567	353	1,213	188
Wool Yarn	1,478	1,997	1,248	2,200
Automobiles	780	4,302	755	5,731
Glass Ware	721	1,458	801	1,742
Instruments	172	2,087	263	2,899
Ironware	1,659	3,073	2,324	3,012
Machines and Apparatus	1,830	12,266	1,213	14,994
Electrical Machines and Apparatus	695	3,469	1,202	4,472
Cotton Material	1,267	697	1,401	549
Woollens	692	1,964	838	1,961

Source: Mecsér, "Die Rückwirkungen," p. 27.

CHAPTER IV

HUNGARY'S ABORTIVE 1937 RAPPROCHEMENT WITH THE LITTLE ENTENTE

In the latter part of 1936, changes in Europe's power distribution forced Hungary to reconsider the wisdom of using Bethlen's and Gömbös's formula for achieving revision by resorting exclusively to Italy and Germany, respectively. The new course called for a temporary settlement of Hungary's disputes with Romania and Yugoslavia, and the isolation of Czechoslovakia.[1] Regarding these Hungarian aspirations one observer noted: "With Germany's attitude [regarding Hungary's aspirations] unsure, and Italian support for Austria crumbling, it was clearly even more desirable than ever that Hungary follow a circumspect course." [2] Under Prime Minister Kálmán Darányi, Hungary's Foreign Minister Kálmán Kánya, a Bethlen protégé, adopted a "free hand" policy for Hungary, and he became more than ever determined to preserve Hungary's freedom for maneuver. In a strict sense, he was an opportunist who "wanted to wait and see which group emerged the strongest at the end of the period of rearmament, and then determine in which direction Hungary should be oriented."[3]

Together with Regent Miklós Horthy and numerous other Hungarian political figures, Kánya was also a pragmatist who respected Great Britain and believed in its alleged sense of fair play. He was convinced that the British would eventually champion "peaceful change" by scrapping the unjust Treaty of Trianon. Through patience Hungary would regain the lost territories. During his London visit in the spring of 1937 to attend George VI's coronation, Kánya felt encouraged in this belief when British statesmen urged him to "form a breakwater against German pressure along with Austria and Czechoslovakia."[4] Italy's Foreign Minister Count Galeazzo Ciano also feared the spread of Pan-Germanism in eastern Europe, and urged Kánya to consider an Italian-Yugoslav-Romanian-Hungarian alliance in the event of an Austrian *Anschluss*.[5] Other proponents suggested various degrees of amalgamation of the two regional alliance systems—the Little Entente (Czechoslovakia, Romania and Yugoslavia) and the Rome Protocols (Austria, Hungary and Italy).

On paper, these plans had much to recommend them. In practice, however, Hungary's strategic location athwart Germany's path to eastern Europe entailed considerable risk. In the event of a German attack, France and Great Britain would be unable to render military assistance, and Italy could not fulfill its ambitious military and economic commitments. Most Hungarians regarded the Soviet Union as a menace exceeding even the German threat. The Third Reich warned Hungarian politicians that if they wished to benefit from Germany's *Ostpolitik*, [6] they must obey, or face unpleasant consequences. Hungary must not negotiate with the Little Entente as a unit. Yugoslavia must be appeased, however. This meant abandoning hopes for Hungarian territorial claims there. Romania had to be pacified as well, at least temporarily. These two states, Hitler maintained, served as important outposts against bolshevism, and should not be weakened by war or intimidation.[8] Hungary must collaborate with Germany to dismember Czechoslovakia, a country which Hitler designated as nonviable. [9] This German scenario would have compelled Hungarians to bolster their country's two chief agricultural rivals for German favor. Czechoslovakia's disappearance would destroy French and British influence in eastern Europe, and reduce Italian power to the vanishing point.

Hungarians were deeply concerned as well because Germany apparently worked behind the scenes plotting with Hungary's enemies. In January 1937, according to C. A. Macartney, the "very real possibility [arose] that Hungary would find Germany installed as friend and patron of all three states of the Little Entente." [10] Kánya discovered that Hitler's emissaries were secretly negotiating with President Eduard Beneš in Prague, even though Hitler had assured visiting Hungarian dignitaries weeks earlier that rumors of a German-Czechoslovak rapprochement were false.[11] Kánya was convinced that the Germans had duped him and attempted to turn the tables on them. He was particularly alarmed because Hitler's foreign policy expert and personal confidant Joachim von Ribbentrop directed the German-Czechoslovak negotiations on Hitler's personal order, but without the awareness of Foreign Minister Constantin von Neurath. Apparently, Nazi functionaries were bypassing the traditional-minded career diplomats of the German Foreign Ministry. This might soon imperil Hungarian sovereignty.[12]

Counteracting these National Socialist moves entailed considerable risk for Hungary. Budapest was relieved when, on 2 January 1937, Great Britain and Italy concluded their universally acclaimed, though ephemeral, "Gentlemen's Agreement." The British sought to restore Italy's great power status in the Mediterranean and in eastern Europe. This would counterbalance growing German might, and hence contribute to the relaxation of tensions in these regions.[13]

An Italy buttressed and encouraged by Great Britain might offer Hungary some support to curtail monolithic German power in eastern Europe. Even so, Hungary would have been foolhardy to initiate a diplomatic offensive to contain Germany. When opportunity knocked, however, and Czechoslovakia, assisted by the rest of the Little Entente and Austria, began making pacific overtures at the beginning of 1937, Kánya decided to negotiate. He resolved to be discreet, drive a hard bargain, if possible detach Czechoslovakia from its allies, and scatter obstacles in the path of German imperialism in eastern Europe. These contradictory objectives made success questionable.

Austria's involvement with Hungary and Czechoslovakia in sponsoring anti-German intrigues arose from Austrian Chancellor Kurt von Schuschnigg's disillusionment with alleged German violations of the 11 July 1936 Austro-German Gentlemen's Agreement. Von Schuschnigg was also heartened by the apparent revival of Italy under British auspices.[14] Had the Chancellor's mediation efforts between Prague and Budapest succeeded, Germany's annexationist plans in Austria might have been prevented. Relieved from the perils of encirclement by the Third Reich, Czechoslovakia would have been able to assist Austria in case of a German attack. This, in turn, would have reprieved Hungary, and might have unified all of eastern Europe to resist any further German encroachments. These prospects dismayed the Germans. Hungary's ambassador in Berlin, Döme Sztójay, understated the case when he reported to Kánya: "Every time a scheme resembling the [Czechoslovak Prime Minister Miloš] Hodža plan [advocating east central European economic unity] surfaces, such as the sounding for a Prague-Vienna-Budapest triangle, the Germans become very nervous."[15]

Odo Neustädter-Stürmer, Austria's ambassador in Hungary, first broached suggestions for a Prague-Vienna-Budapest Axis on 21 January 1937. The ambassador queried Gábor Ápor, Hungary's permanent deputy foreign minister, on the feasibility of a Czechoslovak-Hungarian reconciliation. He noted that both Miloš Kobr, Czechoslovakia's ambassador in Budapest, and Kamil Krofta, the Czechoslovak foreign minister, had promised to reduce tensions with Hungary. Czechoslovakia would recognize Hungary's right to partially rearm, providing Hungary concluded a nonaggression treaty. Ápor replied that Kobr had already tentatively raised these issues, but Kánya had demurred. A nonaggression treaty would be worthless, because Czechoslovakia's agreement with Little Entente partners Romania and Yugoslavia would, under certain circumstances, force all three countries to attack Hungary jointly. Moreover, Kánya considered Hungary's right to rearm a nonnegotiable right, and hence not subject to reciprocal agreements.[16]

Two days prior to this meeting, Kobr had indeed revived the spirit of an informal pre-Christmas conversation held with Kánya on these same issues, but Kánya had rejected the suggestions. Unless Czechoslovakia improved the treatment of its Magyar minority considerably, and unless the little Entente modified its constitution to protect Hungary against a joint attack, Kánya saw no reason why Hungary should accommodate Czechoslovakia. This was particularly true at a time when the latter's diplomatic position was deteriorating, whereas Hungary's was improving.[17] Kánya wanted to intensify Sudeten-German pressures on Prague, supported morally, financially, and politically by the Third Reich.

Within days, the Yugoslav and Romanian ambassadors repeated Kobr's offer in Budapest.[18] Kánya regarded these efforts as a British-inspired plan to involve Hungary in a regional scheme, together with the Little Entente and Austria, to arrest the German steamroller.[19] Kánya wanted to conduct negotiations at a pace sufficiently brisk not to discourage his adversaries, yet cautiously, lest he arouse German suspicions. He replied evasively to the Yugoslavs. The Romanians received much the same answer as the Czechoslovaks. Sztójay was to acquaint von Neurath with the general tenor of Kánya's recent conversations with the Austrian and Little Entente ambassadors. He was to assure the Germans that the Kobr request had been treated "in a dilatory fashion," and that Kánya hoped Germany, too, would pursue "unshakeably" its current public policy of refusing to negotiate with Czechoslovakia. Kánya instructed Hungary's ambassador in Rome to advise Ciano about the Kobr interview, and to inquire discreetly whether Italy would support a Czechoslovak-Hungarian rapprochement.[20]

At this time, Mussolini lacked a definitive eastern European policy. Hitherto, Italian views on the inclusion of Czechoslovakia in any regional scheme had been largely negative.[21] Kánya believed that the latest diplomatic developments in western Europe would encourage Italy tacitly to tolerate bolstering Czechoslovakia against the Germans. The 2 January Anglo-Italian Gentlemen's Agreement had not only enhanced Italy's position in the Mediterranean and the Balkans, it also signaled a possible comprehensive great power settlement, from which Italy and Hungary wished to benefit. Apprehensive about Italy's sudden renaissance, Germany also began courting Great Britain.[22] For Italy, obstructing Germany's aggressive designs in Czechoslovakia at this point became not only feasible but profitable. Kánya wished to promote Hungary's interests while the Germans, "uneasy over Italy's flirtation with Britain,"[23] were on the defensive.

Kánya exploited Germany's temporary vulnerability by camouflaging Hungary's contacts with the Little Entente. On 23 January, he subjected Hans von Mackensen, Germany's minister in Budapest, to a long litany of Hungarian grievances against Germany. He focused on Alfred Rosenberg's 15 November 1936 article in the *Völkischer Beobachter*, in which the Nazi ideologue had intimated that Germany had no interest in the recovery of Hungary's lost territories. Kánya also scored German underhandedness in dealing secretly with Czechoslovakia behind Hungary's back. He cited various other anti-Hungarian German provocations. Von Mackensen defended his government's policies, and assured Kánya that not the slightest possibility existed that the Third Reich would conclude a Czechoslovak-German nonaggression treaty.[24]

A similar diplomatic exchange occurred in Berlin, except that Sztójay's dialogue with von Neurath on 6 February was more pointed than the Budapest interview. Sztójay warned von Neurath of the awesome consequences should Germany refuse to assist Hungary's revisionist efforts. The Little Entente countries had become convinced that Rosenberg's article irreparably damaged German-Hungarian relations. Hence they saw this as an auspicious occasion to draw Hungary into a Danubian confederation to combat the German menace. Sztójay maintained, however, that Kánya had rejected these overtures. Hungary's foreign policy rested on Germany and Italy alone. At the same time, however, the country's pro-German orientation would not survive another such severe blow as the Rosenberg article. Should Germany persist in being obstructive, Hungary would be forced to abandon the Third Reich and conclude nonaggression pacts with the Little Entente countries, even if this course entailed certain territorial sacrifices. Sztójay taunted von Neurath that the status of the Magyar ethnic minorities in the Successor States would improve once a settlement had been reached with the Little Entente and France, and economic conditions would revive in the region.[25]

According to Sztójay's report, this vigorous rhetoric left von Neurath "visibly surprised and unprepared." The presentation made a "deep impression" on the German diplomat, who assured the ambassador of Germany's fidelity to Hungary. In Sztójay's view, this interchange no doubt awoke von Neurath to the necessities of harmonious German-Hungarian relations. However, on 2 February 1937, Italy's negative reply discouraged the Hungarians for the time being from any further efforts to deal with Czechoslovakia. Italy advised Hungary to pacify Yugoslavia and Romania, in that order, and leave the Czechoslovaks dangling.[26] But by now, Kánya had achieved his limited objectives: he had driven the Germans on the defensive, and he had justified Hungary's need for further negotiations with the Little Entente.

Czechoslovakia's diplomatic offensive, which tried to exploit what appeared to be a widening German-Hungarian rift, misfired. In a 9 February dialogue, Kobr hoped to goad Kánya into action by taunting him of taking orders from Germany. The Third Reich, he charged, encouraged Hungary to befriend Romania and Yugoslavia, while Germany prepared an assault against Czechoslovakia. He accused Hungary of hoping to profit from this aggression. Kánya refused to be provoked, however, and merely reiterated his earlier reservations.[27] On the same day, the Czechoslovaks intensified the pressure on Hungary by releasing information to János Wettstein, Hungary's ambassador in Prague, that the Czechoslovak government seriously considered renouncing its mutual aid agreement with the Soviet Union, but only if Germany would grant Czechoslovakia an ironclad nonaggression agreement. Italy's ambassador in Prague Domenico de Facendis confirmed the accuracy of this report to Kánya, and Krofta did not deny it.[28]

The Czechoslovaks had thrown the Hungarians off balance, but not for long. Kánya wanted to counter the possibility of German punitive measures against Hungary in the form of a Czechoslovak-German accord. On 17 February Kánya instructed Sztójay to disparage at the German Foreign Ministry the 27 January Yugoslav-Bulgarian agreement of "eternal friendship." Acting State Secretary Hans Heinrich Dieckhoff boasted proudly how long and hard Germany had labored to reconcile the Yugoslavs with Bulgaria. By then, Bulgaria was one of Germany's client states. Presumably, Yugoslavia would soon follow Bulgaria's lead. In that event, Hungary would be strategically outflanked, and its importance to Germany at an end. Sztójay pointed out that by pursuing current policies, Germany might eventually suffer disastrous reverses in the east. The Third Reich was unwittingly encouraging the rebirth of a pan-Slav bloc in the Balkans. This would automatically strengthen Czechoslovakia. If the Soviet Union should ever become nationalistic, as tsarist Russia had before the War, then the entire Slavic world might combine to thwart German expansionism. Only Hungary could be depended on to serve Germany's interests by acting as a bulwark against the Soviet menace.[29] Sztójay's doomsday scenario made litte impact at the *Wilhelmstrasse.* Hitherto,

Kánya's skillful diplomacy had enabled Hungary to hold the Little Entente in check without rejecting its members' advances outright. Germany was being kept vaguely uneasy about Hungarian intentions, and guilty because Rosenberg had renounced past German commitments to Hungary.

At the same time, Czechoslovakia's efforts to tempt Hungary into a reconciliation scheme with the Little Entente had failed. Hungarian statesmen had derived considerable short-run diplomatic advantages by merely remaining on the negotiating scene. Von Schuschnigg appeared in Budapest on 18 March to break this impasse. He urged continued Czechoslovak-Hungarian conversations, in view of Austria's growing strategic and political peril. His timing was opportune. On 5 March, the Hungarian state police had uncovered an anti-government conspiracy hatched by MOVE, a Nazi-supported and German-financed clandestine racist organization. This revelation turned Hungary's government and public against Nazi Germany, and also roused fears that Hungary might soon share Austria's impending doom.[30]

Shortly after, the diplomatic waters were muddied, when, on 25 March, Italy and Yugoslavia signed a five-year nonaggression and neutrality pact.[31] The agreement improved relations between the two countries. Whether the pact would benefit or harm German or Hungarian interests remained unclear for some time. Apparently, though, it did relax Yugoslav Prime Minister Stojadinović's fears of an imminent German drive to the Adriatic Sea. On the other hand, Italy's protection made it far less desirable for Yugoslavia to seek closer German ties than before.[32]

For Hungary, the pact offered certain dubious advantages. Ciano pledged that the agreement would profit Hungary. Italy would not sacrifice Hungary for the sake of Yugoslav friendship. Amicable Italian-Yugoslav relations would loosen the bonds of the Little Entente, weaken Soviet, British and French influence in the Balkans, and bring a Hungarian-Yugoslav rapprochement one step closer to fruition.[33] On the debit side, if Hungary attacked Czechoslovakia or Romania, Yugoslavia would still be obligated to succor its Little Entente allies, whereas Italy would have to remain neutral. The Hungarians also believed that the economic clauses of the Italian-Yugoslav agreement injured their own and Austria's interests. Italy had agreed to grant Yugoslavia the same trade preferences formerly enjoyed exclusively by Hungary and Austria under the Rome Protocols. Indeed, Italy's economic absorption capacity was limited, and, despite disclaimers, the Italians had to reduce imports from these two states in order to accommodate Yugoslavia. This action partially accounts for the sudden chill in Austria's and Hungary's excellent relations with Italy, and also explains why Hungary soon heeded Czechoslovakia's overtures for an agreement once more. Hungarian-Yugoslav reconciliation became still another temporary casualty of the Yugoslav-Italian agreement. Contrary to Ciano's expectations, Yugoslavia, now having secure frontiers with Italy and Bulgaria, lost interest in a speedy accommodation with Hungary.[34] To complicate matters even further, Beneš publicly berated Stojadinović as perfidious, and termed the agreement a shoddy Italian attempt, abetted by Hungary, to entice Yugoslavia into the Rome-Berlin Axis.[35] In sum, the Italian-Yugoslav treaty created more problems than it solved, and sowed confusion and mutual suspicions in both political camps. Further progress in Czechoslovak-Hungarian reconciliation attempts nearly foundered on these and other obstacles.

Different events sustained Czechoslovak-Hungarian pacification efforts. A German diplomatic offensive to shatter the Little Entente by pretending to befriend its three members separately failed.[36] So did Polish attempts later that spring to detach Romania from its two allies.[37] Italy's growing preoccupation in Spain, and deteriorating relations with Great Britain for the second time that year, again diminished Mussolini's influence in eastern Europe. This left Hungary dangling. In order not to appear to compound the difficulties encountered by Germany and Italy, Kánya exercised extreme caution in dealing with the Little Entente. On 26 March, Hodža told von Schuschnigg that Czechoslovakia sincerely wished to normalize relations with Hungary, but he claimed to have become discouraged by Hungarian hesitancy.[38] Thus matters stood for one month, while the various European diplomatic relationships fermented.

The second stage in Hungarian-Little Entente contacts began on 27 April. At a private dinner, Yugoslav Ambassador Alexander Vukčević tried to convince Kánya to launch Hungary on the road to normalization with the Little Entente. Thus far, he asserted, Kánya had been dawdling. The Little Entente, he asserted, must find ways and means to permit Hungary to enjoy equality in armaments. He offered Hungary the choice of either dealing with the Little Entente jointly, or with each member separately. An agreement, he believed, would safeguard Hungary against individual or combined attacks by the Little Entente.

Kánya disagreed. In his view, reconciliation was unthinkable, because the Litte Entente's military provisions would clash with similar stipulations protecting Hungary. Vukčević accused Hungary of not being interested in a peaceful settlement with the Little Entente. Kánya countered that his country had tendered concrete proposals, but that the Little Entente had either rejected the overtures or had accepted, then repudiated them. Vukčević was offended. He warned Kánya that a unilateral Hungarian rearmament declaration would cause "great consternation," undermine slowly improving Yugoslav-Hungarian relations, and cause his transfer from Budapest.[39]

Kánya had extricated himself from a tight situation, although nearly at the cost of offending Yugoslavia. For the time being, he preferred quarreling with Little Entente ambassadors rather than with Germany and Italy, both of which objected, in varying degrees, to Hungarian attempts to negotiate with Czechoslovakia, Romania, and Yugoslavia simultaneously. Kánya was in no hurry to effect a reconciliation with Yugoslavia. Germany and Italy would sooner or later clear the path for any further Yugoslav-Hungarian negotiations, he believed, if and when Hungary truly desired such an agreement.

This phase of the Little Entente's diplomatic offensive was short-lived, at least partly due to internal dissension among the three allies. The Czechoslovak and Romanian ministers attending the 1—2 April Belgrade meeting of the Permanent Council of the Little Entente condemned Yugoslavia for not having notified its partners about the impending Yugoslav-Italian and Yugoslav-Bulgarian agreements. This was sheer hypocrisy, because in 1935, Czechoslovakia had also failed to publicize its nonaggression pact with the Soviet Union. Romania and Czechoslovakia insisted that, henceforth, member states must conclude agreements only jointly, or do so only after prior consultation and with unanimous agreement.[40]

The Belgrade conference made it impossible for Hungary to conduct negotiations with each Little Entente state separately, and complicated the efforts of Hungarian statesmen to isolate Czechoslovakia. The conference temporarily forced the suspension of even desultory and hitherto fruitless Romanian-Hungarian negotiations. Under pressures from Romania's Foreign Minister Victor Antonescu and Czechoslovakia's Kamil Krofta, Stojadinović temporarily also shunned further contact with Hungary. Sztójay notified von Neurath that, under the circumstances, Hungary would have to negotiate with the Little Entente *en bloc*, if it ever wished to get results. Von Neurath disagreed. Stojadinović had not bowed to Czechoslovak and Romanian pressures, but had to heed the views of domestic opponents of Hungary. Later, he would reopen talks, whether his allies liked it or not. [41] Von Neurath tried to intimidate the Hungarians, but they had once more forced Germany on the defensive. Sztójay asserted that the Third Reich would have to offer tangible evidences of support, in order to deter Hungary from launching negotiations with the Little Entente as a unit.

The third stage in Hungarian-Little Entente contacts was prompted indirectly by von Schuschnigg, who sought to bolster Austria's crumbling diplomatic defenses. First, he tried to obtain Mussolini's reassurances that Italy would parry the German menace, as it had in 1934. At the 22–23 April Venice conference, von Schuschnigg sensed Ciano's and Mussolini's vanishing desire to preserve Austria. The Italian leaders questioned the Chancellor on Habsburg restoration, which Schuschnigg favored in principle. They disapproved of Austria's emergence as "the point of friction in Italo-German relations." They cited Germany's displeasure over "how badly Austria was behaving...by applying the agreement of 11th July inadequately and with so many mental reservations." And finally, they criticized contacts between Austria and Czechoslovakia, both of which countries, von Schuschnigg asserted, shared "a common interest—that is, not to be attacked by Germany."

Mussolini lectured von Schuschnigg: Restoration was "impracticable." It would precipitate "a grave danger of disorders." Mussolini pledged to maintain Austrian independence, but only by "synchronizing it and bringing it into harmony with the Rome-Berlin Axis"—a euphemism for *Gleichschaltung*. On Czechoslovakia, von Schuschnigg required no prodding. He reluctantly pledged that "there is no possibility of authoritarian Austria's aligning herself with the ultra-democratic Paris-Prague axis." Despite the short-run advantages, therefore, to Austrian security, "no agreement of a political character exists or is foreseen between the two countries."[42] Having secured only vague pledges of further Italian economic support, von Schuschnigg returned home feeling uneasy. He sensed that, henceforth, Austria's chances for survival would depend more on the Western democracies than on uncertain Italian promises.[43]

In view of his failure to obtain reliable guarantees from Mussolini, von Schuschnigg redoubled his efforts to forge a Vienna-Budapest-Prague axis as a deterrent to Nazi aggression. When Austrian President Wilhelm Miklas arrived in Budapest on 4 May 1937 on an Austrian state visit, he was greeted with all the pomp normally reserved for crowned heads. This was a symbolic Hungarian anti-German gesture, and a rebuke to Mussolini as well for his abandonment of Austria. Von Schuschnigg and Foreign Minister Guido Schmidt accompanied Miklas. This demonstrated that the ceremonial visit would be accompanied by a conference, the object of which, Austria and Hungary announced defiantly, was "political rather than economic."[44] In view of the common Nazi threat, von Schuschnigg wanted to be reconciled with Czechoslovakia. He wanted to devise a scheme for Danubian collaboration, and invite Hungary to join Austria in some striking economic good-will gesture to Prague. The joint communiqué stressed deepening Austro-Hungarian friendship and promised vigorous cooperation. But the real intention of the conference was to create an Austro-Hungarian front to prevent "too much" Italo-German friendship. If German and Italian predominance in the Danube Basin was to be diminished, however, then, sooner or later, Czechoslovakia would have to be invited to augment such an accord. Hungary still balked at the suggestion.[45]

Krofta hoped that von Schuschnigg's pleas would sway Hungarian statesmen. On 15 May, he attempted to undo the damage caused by Vukčević's stormy 27 April interview with Kánya. He told Wettstein that the Little Entente would "regret" any unilateral Hungarian declaration of equality in armaments, but that, "of course, no great harm would come of it," even if Hungary should take this fateful step. Naturally, the three allies would treat Hungary with greater consideration in the event of a prior agreement. Sensing far greater flexibility by Czechoslovakia, as German and Sudeten pressures intensified, Kánya wrung the important concession from Krofta that Hungary indeed had the moral right to rearm.[46] This was a diplomatic windfall, indeed, that resulted from the negotiating perspicacity and patience of Hungarian diplomats over the previous months.

Krofta also relented on the question of a nonaggression treaty. Thanks to his missionary efforts, he said, Czechoslovakia's Little Entente partners now would ratify an agreement resembling the 1928 Kellogg-Briand Pact. The three allies only desired a friendly gesture from Hungary. Krofta hinted that the three countries would reconsider their minority policies, if Hungary cooperated diplomatically. Krofta stressed, however, that, for now this was merely a personal communication.[47] Presumably, the three partners wished to avoid being humiliated by still another official Hungarian rebuff. For Hungary, however, the new offers provided excellent diplomatic ammunition against Germany. As for the Little Entente countries, their increasing willingness to soften the concessions expected from Hungary while improving their own offers, had an excellent cause. Strategically, Czechoslovakia was in the front line blocking German imperialism. It was essential for all three of them to settle disputes with a hostile country that might find assisting a German attack against them profitable.

Italy was intimidated by the belligerent Germans, who currently plotted the destruction of Austria. On 21 May, King Victor Emmanuel of Italy arrived in Budapest on a three-day state visit, accompanied by Ciano. Agitated over developments in Austria, the Hungarians probed Italian intentions. Kánya chiefly worried about Austrian security. He no longer believed in Italy's "active interest in Austrian independence," and was convinced that "Italy was gradually withdrawing from her position on the Austrian question." But Ciano countered that only "Vienna's alignment with the Democratic-Bolshevik axis of Paris-Prague-Moscow" could possibly jeopardize Italy's support of Austria. Kánya also feared that Italy would abandon Hungary in the event of an agreement with Romania. Ciano pledged, however, that Italy would not negotiate with Bucharest unless Hungary approved. Concern over deteriorating British-Italian relations prompted Prime Minister Kálmán Darányi to inquire: "Does Mussolini want to make war on England?" Ciano replied that Italy would not flinch from any British threats. Finally, Darányi complained that Italy's commercial treaty with Yugoslavia would injure the Hungarian economy. Ciano promised that "Hungarian interests would be given special consideration by us."

The two Hungarian statesmen briefed Ciano on several current issues. Hungarian diplomacy was "based on friendship with Italy and collaboration with Germany," they explained. With the Little Entente, relations were confused. In view of the Little Entente's recent solidarity, "a separate agreement with Yugoslavia must be considered out of the question." Hungary's connections with Romania were even more difficult, they asserted. Momentarily, Czechoslovakia was "the only State with which [Hungary] could draw up a pact at any moment," but, for the present, this was not among the intentions of the Hungarian government. Economic improvements with Czechoslovakia, however, were possible. Finally, they explained, Hungary had the option "of carrying on negotiations with the three States simultaneously so as to arrive at bilateral pacts with each of them," and then permitting "the one which is not wanted in Hungary to perish—that is to say, the pact with Czechoslovakia."

A joint communiqué emphasized Mussolini's support of the idea of Danubian cooperation—a code phrase for resistance against German expansionism. Italy and Hungary reaffirmed their "full concordance of views on important political questions." This meant that, for the present, Hungary would not renounce the military clauses of the Trianon Peace Treaty unilaterally, but that—significantly—an attempt would first be made to reach an accommodation with the Little Entente countries.[48]

The fourth stage in Little Entente-Hungarian contacts began in Geneva on 27 May. The Little Entente's Permanent Council stood unified on a number of issues. This included a common front with Hungary, and a common procedure to be followed on Hungarian rearmament, whether it materialized through negotiations, or unilaterally.[49] Germany, and to some extent Italy, pressured Romania and Yugoslavia to break ranks with Czechoslovakia, but they failed. This show of strength made it ever more difficult for Hungary to refuse negotiating with the Little Entente as a unit.

In Geneva, Romania and Yugoslavia hovered in the background, while Krofta reiterated the gist of his 15 May conversation with Wettstein in the presence of László Velics, Hungary's League of Nations representative. Nothing had changed substantively since, except that the Little Entente's offer now represented official policy. Krofta thought an agreement with Hungary was long overdue, particularly in view of Yugoslavia's rapprochement with Italy, and Italy's growing influence in Romania. The inclusion of Czechoslovakia in an agreement might well follow this thawing process. Obviously, Krofta believed that the shortest route to Berlin led through Rome. Moreover, he declared, France and Great Britain favored universal rapprochement, and consequently he had requested their intercession. Unfortunately, he said, the French and the British did not wish to make it appear as if they tried to intervene in east-central European affairs and hence had declined. This gesture was meant to pamper German and Italian egos. Krofta implied the dawning of a new era in the region. The Little Entente had reduced its demands on Hungarian reciprocity to the point where treaty revision would no longer be taboo, but left in abeyance, and be settled at some later date. All Hungary had to do was to sign separate, identical nonaggression treaties with its three Little Entente neighbors. The next day, Krofta offered to replace the harsh word "non-aggression" with a more pleasing cognate, and as a further inducement hinted that, eventually, Czechoslovakia might emancipate itself from France.[50]

This time, Kánya did not disparage the Czechoslovak plan, but instructed Velics to thank Krofta for having made the offer. [51] Velics later told Kánya that, obviously, the Czechoslovaks felt isolated, and that was why they initiated the "Geneva campaign." Romania apparently enthusiastically supported the Czechoslovak effort, but Yugoslavia was a reluctant participant. For the time being, Little Entente unity versus Hungary was certain. Apparently, the Little Entente wished to place Hungary on the defensive by offering magnanimous settlement terms, thus leaving Hungary with the burden of guilt and international condemnation in case of refusal.[52]

Velics might have added that Little Entente solidarity resulted from the three countries' awareness that pacifying Hungary was a *sine qua non* for an understanding with all three members of the Rome Protocols, and that London and Paris greatly favored such a plan. Combining the two alliance systems would sabotage Germany's *Ostpolitik*, and restore the pride of Italy by letting that country become the West's chief guardian in the Danube Basin. It would also blunt the edge of Hungarian revisionism by removing it from aggressive German manipulations and intrigue. Hungary stood at the crossroads. Acceptance of the Krofta plan would either force Hitler to abandon his eastern European expansionist policy entirely, curb it, or he would be compelled to wage an aggressive war before his fighting machine was ready.

The Hungarians had to weigh certain other considerations as well. Kánya doubted, for example, whether Italy would go along with a settlement of which Czechoslovakia was a part, because Ciano held that country in low esteem, and preferred dealing with Poland. Berlin would certainly object, and without German acquiescence, any such agreement would be worthless.[53] Furthermore, Kánya believed that the Yugoslavs, and most particularly Stojadinović, were unreliable. While professing to support his allies, Stojadinović had promised von Neurath that in the event of a reconciliation with Hungary, Yugoslavia would immediately abandon Czechoslovakia.[54] Finally, Kánya pondered whether in the long run, Hungary would be better off to side with Germany, and thereby regain its former preeminence by sharing in the territorial spoils, possibly at the cost of a bloody and unpredictable armed conflict; or whether Hungary should support an Italian-monitored east-central European order blessed by Great Britain and France, in which Hungary's territorial aggrandizement would be meager and gradual.

The rapid flow of international events ought to have spurred Hungary to resolve its problems with the Little Entente speedily. Italy and Germany, which had disagreed on the Spanish Civil War and gradually drifted apart, were suddenly spurred into greater unity than ever before. The Spanish Republican Valencia government, France, Great Britain, and the Soviet Union had nearly driven a wedge between the two Axis partners. Hitler had counseled disengagement from Spain, whereas Mussolini had insisted on launching one more supreme military effort to end the conflict. Republican Spain's air attack on the German cruiser *Deutschland* on 29 May completely altered the international situation, and ruined whatever success the Spanish Republicans had had in fostering German-Italian disunity. [55] Reinvigorated German-Italian cooperation in Spain portended renewed Italian support of aggressive German initiatives in east-central Europe, and threatened to nullify Ciano's recently sanctioned cautious approval of Hungarian negotiations with the Little Entente.

Kánya continued playing for time. First, he informed Krofta that a Hungarian response to the Little Entente's offer would not be forthcoming, because the Prague and Geneva proposals were not identical, and neither of the two Czechoslovak drafts tallied with kindred Romanian and Yugoslav offers.[56] On 10 June, Wettstein submitted Hungary's reply, according to which any nonaggression treaties would have to be coupled with farreaching concessions to the Magyar minorities in the three Little Entente countries. This demand evoked such an angry outburst from Krofta that the friendly atmosphere instantly vanished. Krofta eventually calmed down, but he insisted that Czechoslovakia's minority policy was an internal affair that could not be linked to the terms of an international treaty. Czechoslovakia, he asserted, clung to a similar position in negotiations with Germany concerning the Sudeten Germans. He did pledge that his country would meticulously observe the minority provisions of the Versailles treaty system, provided that Hungary cooperated on Czechoslovak terms. Should Hungary declare equality in arms unilaterally, then the Little Entente would not only cancel its minority obligations, but repudiate all the other onerous duties arising from the peace treaties as well. Despite the airing of these, and other, contentious issues, the conference thereupon proceeded smoothly, and the negotiators parted "with the greatest friendliness." [57]

Hungary's recurring contacts with representatives of the Little Entente infuriated the Germans. The day after Wettstein's 10 June conversation with Krofta, von Neurath arrived in Budapest for consultations with Kánya and Prime Minister Darányi on a number of wide-ranging issues of common concern, especially Hungary's improving relations with the Little Entente. On this occasion, as before, von Neurath tried to promote the cause of Yugoslav-Hungarian rapprochement. But von Neurath blundered by presenting reconciliation not as a beneficial project to be sought for Hungary's own sake, but as a windfall for the good of German imperialism. Von Neurath wanted to secure Yugoslav neutrality in anticipation of the Austrian *Anschluss*, which he regarded as a foregone conclusion. Hungarian-Yugoslav amity would facilitate Germany's post-*Anschluss* annexationist ambitions in Czechoslovakia by destroying the Little Entente, and by removing the final vestiges of French influence in the region.

Kánya's negotiating skills exceeded von Neurath's. Germany's defensive shield in the Balkans was worthless, Kánya argued, because "just like Ciano, he [von Neurath] had too much confidence in the Yugoslavs." Kánya claimed to have had long and bitter experience with them. Consequently, he did not share Ciano's and von Neurath's optimism. Kánya regarded Stojadinović a crass opportunist who consistently lied to his allies, and who had misled Hungary on a number of occasions. Stojadinović thus had to be treated with extreme caution. Moreover, he complained, Italy and Germany had complicated Hungary's negotiations with the Yugoslavs by pampering the latter so ostentatiously as to diminish Hungary's relative importance. Kánya was convinced that the Yugoslavs would remain faithful to their present allies, while simultaneously they would promote friendly relations with Italy and Germany. In the end, they would choose sides on the basis of which country dominated the European power structure. In view of Yugoslavia's continuing fidelity to the Little Entente, Hungary had to engage in an exchange of views with all three Little Entente countries simultaneously. Kánya explained that he had rejected their nonaggression treaty offer, but that Hungary would accept a mutual declaration resembling the Kellogg-Briand Pact.

Kánya's mere mention of the phrase "non-aggression treaty" in connection with the Little Entente dismayed von Neurath, who interjected agitatedly: "I beg of you, please don't do it!" He apparently tolerated a more innocuous alternative wording, however. Von Neurath defended Yugoslavia's dependability, deplored Kánya's pessimism, and urged patience. In a few months, Kánya would see German confidence in Stojadinović vindicated. When Kánya inquired whether Germany had any agreement currently in force with Yugoslavia, von Neurath replied "no." Had the two countries concluded some sort of gentlemen's agreement whereby neither side would join a coalition inimical to the other? To this shrewd query, von Neurath refused to reply.[58]

If von Neurath wished to intimidate the Hungarians because their country was being surreptitiously outflanked by Germany and Yugoslavia, he failed dismally. Kánya knew that von Neurath's recent Belgrade visit had been a fiasco. Stojadinović had angrily bombarded von Neurath with a battery of accusations, centering mainly on what the Prime Minister considered intolerable German subversion in Yugoslavia. According to members of von Neurath's entourage, after a passage of sharp words, the German foreign minister left Belgrade "in a very ill humour."[59] Kánya, too, maintained the upper hand with the German diplomat, who returned home doubly empty-handed.

After this discussion, the diplomatic situation remained essentially static until the Little Entente's foreign ministers convened in Şinaia in August 1937 to reconsider their impasse with Hungary. On that occasion, the three allies satisfied Kánya's chief demands for combined Little Entente action. They tendered the draft of a jointly produced nonaggression treaty. Kánya's diplomacy stressing moderation thus bore fruit. Hungary gained an additional year's negotiating grace with the Little Entente, and could, if it wished, postpone decisions involving Germany, while awaiting further international developments.

In mid-June 1937, the Little Entente's negotiations with Hungary thus entered another dormant phase. But the new turn of events in Spain favored the Axis, and this revived German-Italian intimacy. This, in turn, prompted Hungary to observe caution. French weakness, compounded by Great Britain's deepening nonconcern with Europe's fate east of Germany, provided only that changes came peacefully, threatened to deliver the entire Danubian region into Germany's hands by default. Since Italy still lacked, and apparently never would possess, the might to "balance Germany in the Danubian area,"[60] the future seemed bleak for Hungary, if it should overtly defy the impending Nazi avalanche. Moreover, Hungary and Czechoslovakia were still too far apart on vital issues to reach an accommodation. The Czechoslovaks wanted to erect an ironclad shield against German economic encroachments, whereas Hungary would have still preferred to become the dominant small power in the region under joint friendly German and Italian auspices.

In this political environment Germany enjoyed far superior maneuverability than von Neurath's recent dismal eastern European tour would have suggested. Whereas Italy encouraged Hungary to seek commercial (but not political) accommodations with Czechoslovakia, and Austria favored political ones as well, von Neurath counseled Kánya and Darányi to avoid either course.[61] Hungary might have enjoyed a temporary tactical advantage versus Germany, but von Neurath's thinly veiled threats struck home at last. Besides, Hungarian pacification of the Little Entente would mean having to curtail revisionism, and the Germans knew that no Budapest government could possibly survive the resultant outburst of public outrage.[62] Consequently, prospects for even a limited Czechoslovak-Hungarian cooperation dimmed in Budapest, at least temporarily.

The Germans sought a permanent deadlock, and used both economic enticements and threats to get their way. The Third Reich was not above whipping recalcitrant agricultural countries such as Hungary into compliance.[63]

Many diplomats still believed, however, that an agreement joining Hungary, Austria, and Czechoslovakia might block the Third Reich's aggressive intentions. Gone was the extreme acrimony that had poisoned Hungary's postwar relations with the Little Entente. As one observer noted, Kánya and the diplomatic representatives of France and the Little Entente could parley on a much more practical and friendlier basis than before, even though concrete proposals, let alone solutions, seemed as far away as ever.[64] Hungary, too, exercised extreme caution in choosing the correct method of declaring military equality, and preferred to rearm gradually, avoiding fanfare. The Little Entente, on the other hand, sought not to humiliate Hungary again by extorting impossible concessions in return for meaningless gestures.

The other favorable development that might have promoted regional reconciliation was the Little Entente's apparent strength, confidence and unity. The alliance's 17 June Bucharest meeting revealed the birth of new hopes and demonstrated the three allies' vitality. The final communiqué showed that the Czechoslovaks had succeeded thus far in preserving and strengthening the alliance, even in the teeth of prodigious German efforts to isolate its members. The three countries also stressed their determination to bolster mutual security by coordinating their economies and through intensive cooperation in all other matters.[65]

For Hungary's Western-oriented statesmen, such as Tibor Eckhardt, Bethlen, Teleki, and Horthy, this flash of Little Entente spirit and viability was a welcome reprieve. It promoted Hungary's bargaining position "for Germany and Italy to feel that Hungary had a second string to her bow,"[66] and thus gave Kánya the breathing spell to consider other options besides abject submission to German economic, political and military demands. There might well have been a third solution in sight for Hungary, apart from total subservience to either England-France or Italy-Germany, as Henry L. Roberts pointed out:

> France was the one great power really committed to the status quo in Eastern Europe, and France, as it proved, was not enough, as Czechoslovakia was discovering to her sorrow. It could still be argued in mid-1937 that the same was also true of Germany, which,

unaided, could no more ensure Hungarian revisionism than France could guarantee the integrity of her Little Entente client states.[67]

Hopes for just such a settlement, one that was not entirely German-dominated, yet one that would restore some power to Hungary, dominated the thinking of Hungarian statesmen throughout 1937. Their expectations were not entirely unrealistic, considered in retrospect. As Franz von Papen noted shortly after the war, for a while it seemed that the year 1937 would bestow a new spirit of harmony on Europe,[68] and portend renewed Four-Power cooperation to settle grievances in the Danube Basin on the principles of equity and justice for all.[69]

These expectations came to naught. The Third Reich's potential for domination exceeded nearly everyone's expectations at the time. The geopolitical stakes in eastern Europe were sufficiently high to encourage Nazi intervention at great risk. The strategic importance of "Mid-Europe," an area comprising a group of small and weak states between the Soviet Union and Germany is so vital that, in the words of Henry L. Roberts, "if it is brought under the effective domination of the great powers on its flanks, Germany or the Soviet Union, these powers thereby gain such a preponderance of strength in Europe that the balance is to be redressed, if at all, only by calling in extra-European powers."[70] Hitler, who named this region "Inter-Europe," was determined, in view of current Soviet, British, Italian and French vacillation, to dominate it as a "German military protectorate."[71] If successful, these plans would have transformed Europe, including Hungary, into a vast Nazi-dominated political-economic vassalage system.[72]

Hungary's leaders justifiably dreaded exclusive German hegemony in the Danubian region.[73] It is not surprising that throughout the Nazi era and despite pro-German public rhetoric to the contrary, Hungarian statesmen, including the Germanophile Gyula Gömbös, sought to limit monolithic German control of the region.[74] The evidence suggests that during the first six months of 1937 Hungary refused to be recruited as Germany's accomplice to expedite German progress in eastern Europe. Rather, the negotiating tactic Hungary employed vis-à-vis the Little Entente in 1937 was an imaginative effort to preserve the country's national sovereignty and freedom of action. Hungary's Little Entente policy was part and parcel of a farreaching imperative. At best, Hungary had in mind to obstruct Germany's eastward progress until Italy and Great Britain might occupy the power vacuum created by the virtual abdication of France's regional responsibilities in 1936.[75] Then, perhaps, the Third Reich, which appeared to be the only power capable of dominating eastern Europe single-handed, would be unable to realize its extravagant ambitions in eastern Europe.

Even if negotiations with the Little Entente failed, Hungary hoped to gain time to defer the day when German troops in soon to be occupied Austria would be intimidating their country. Hungary's western counties contained the largest single concentration of Swabians; these would become the targets of intense National Socialist propaganda. Swabians, many of whom were seasonally employed in Austria, would be especially vulnerable to such appeals. Hungarians worried that if Germany ever menaced Hungary, these indoctrinated Swabians would welcome the National Socialist invaders with open arms. The mere presence of Germany on the Austro-Hungarian frontier would offer the Third Reich an immense psychological and logistical advantage in its dealings with Hungary. The Hungarian government wanted to avoid such a menace at all cost. The authorities felt justified, therefore, to attempt blunting the edge of Nazi propaganda by launching countermeasures in the form of Magyarization drives in all communities whose inhabitants professed to be Swabians, and by trying to weaken the heart and soul of the Swabian ethnic spirit, the German-language elementary school systems in the Swabian countrysides.

CHAPTER V

GERMAN-HUNGARIAN-SWABIAN RELATIONS -
LATE 1936–1937

Despite Darányi's promises and pleas to the Swabian public for understanding, conditions in the minority school system deteriorated, while the government tried to stem the growing tide of National Socialist influence and agitation among the Swabians. Even Gustav Gratz complained that only about half of the Roman Catholic Swabian schools provided religious instruction, including hymns and prayers, in the German language.[1] Lutz Korodi, a German writer, was far more critical than Gratz. He observed that it would be exceedingly difficult to find even twenty elementary schools in Hungary where the language of instruction was truly German.[2] *Grenzland,* a publication devoted to German minority affairs, criticized Hungarian government policy for tacitly permitting local officials to treat Swabians in a high-handed fashion. *Grenzland* cited several examples of various means of oppression. Violations allegedly were no longer regrettable exceptions. By 1937, infractions were pervasive and constituted "a part of an open plan [by the government] designed to prevent the introduction of bilingual schools." In Barsad, charged *Grenzland,* one of the parents engaged in collecting signatures on behalf of B-type schools was hauled before the notary, and then questioned and cautioned by the gendarmerie. In Soroksár and Nagymaros, parents had voted for the B-type school, but on registration day the school authorities arbitrarily classified many of their children as Magyars. In Szalatnak, the local school allegedly kept a so-called *szégyenkönyv* (literally, a book of shame), which contained the names of pupils caught speaking German on the way home from school.[3]

Violations of the school law committed by the civil authorities were equally numerous. Generally, their methods resembled those employed by the clerical leaders. They included deception and overriding the decisions of parents' conferences, delays, transfers of qualified German teachers to Magyar communities, and so on. Everywhere the picture was the same: communities demanded B-type schools in the spirit of the law of December 1935, but they were thwarted by uncooperative school officials.[4] *Nation und Staat* reported one of the methods officials used to influence parents and to repeal their decisions. In Nagykozsár, the school authorities summoned parents on 29 August 1937, to decide on the school type the community desired. After voting for the B-type school, parents were confronted by the local priest and the schoolmaster, both of whom tried in vain to persuade the villagers to opt for the pure Magyar school. After most parents had departed in the conviction that a B-type school had been decided on, a secretly assembled rump session, composed of Magyar and Magyarized Swabian parents, vetoed the decision by the majority.[5]

Confessional schools remained, as before, the worst offenders in the Swabian minority school complex. *Nation und Staat* hoped that Prime Minister Darányi would finally order the enforcement of the December 1935 school laws, and that the hostile church officials, under whose jurisdiction over 80% of the German schools functioned, would heed the orders of the prime minister.[6] Subsequently, *Nation und Staat* investigated school conditions in Gyönk, an Evangelical community. In the first grade of the former C-type school the pupils received no German instruction at all, claimed the journal. In the fifth and sixth grades German textbooks were not available. Four months before the inquiry, the parents had decided to adopt the new B-type institution over the strenuous objections of their minister. To date, the local school authorities had not honored the parental request.[7] A few months later, the citizens of Hárta, another Evangelical community, also decided to establish a B-type school, but the local minister refused the request on orders from Bishop Raffay.[8]

In 1937, the incidence of school law violations became so prevalent that the Swabians began to clamor for government action. To assuage the minority, Minister of the Interior József Széll pledged "to do something tangible about the German schools," but throughout that year nothing was done; on the contrary, conditions deteriorated.[9] The Ministry of Education issued its own set of directives to state school inspectors and church authorities concerning the multiple violations of the law in Swabian minority schools. The Ministry deplored obstructionism in these institutions. It bade local officials to investigate the methods used to circumvent the enforcement of the law in each community and to report their findings no later than 31 January 1938. The directive also ordered the transformation of all A- and C-type schools into B-type institutions in time for the 1938–1939 school year, wherever parents desired this change.[10]

The directive merely intensified pressures exerted by school and church officials on parents' conferences. According to G. C. Paikert, a Ministry of Education official assigned to the minority section, despite all promises of reform, it was basic government policy to remain opposed to real improvements in the minority schools. Paikert charged that "the government rejected the concept of developing a nationality-conscious intelligentsia, it being against the interests of the State."[11]

The failure of the German minority teacher training program best demonstrated the decline of the Swabian minority school system. The number of German elementary school instructors had diminished annually since 1933–1934.[12] By 1936, only 95 such teachers were left in Hungary whose mother tongue was German. Of these, only four taught in German schools that year.[13] In 1937, in response to complaints by Swabians, their number increased to between 40 and 50.[14] Early in his ministry, Darányi issued an order for the extension of teachers' vacation courses, but this was inadequate. An observer noted: "it is a well-known fact that most of the candidates are incompetent to teach the German language."[15] To be sure, in the 1936–1937 school year, eight academies offered special German courses for 330 teachers. As well, to meet the demands of the new B-type schools, the government provided a one-year continuation course for thirty teachers in 1937–1938.[16] But the Swabian school complex required at least 1,400 teachers. At the extremely high failure rates in the German courses it would have taken at least nine years to satisfy all the needs in the state schools alone, while leaving unsolved the needs of the numerically preponderant confessional schools.[17]

In 1937, the *VK* vigorously joined the chorus of those who demanded urgent government action in the minority schools. This publicity emerged on the pages of the *Deutscher Volksbote (DV)*, the *VK*'s official publication. Richard Huss explained that the German minority's spiritual harmony with the dominant non-German majority must not lead to assimilation, but engender spiritual devotion to the Germans' own *Volkstum*. In his view, two alien peoples could live side by side, share a fatherland, and both be equally concerned for its welfare and prosperity. Furthermore, a state had no right to interfere with *Volkstum*, because it was not a secular matter, but a divine right.[18] The Hungarian government was deliberately flouting these principles, Huss asserted, by eradicating pure German institutions in Swabian villages, and by substituting schools proclaiming the principle of "twin mother tongue" for Swabian children. He deemed this approach philosophically and pedagogically unsound. Even if the government created teacher academies to train instructors to serve in the new B-type institutions, the gesture would prove profitless. The only viable solution was for the

Swabians to establish their own German-language schools staffed with teachers rooted in the German community.[19] *DV* editor Georg Goldschmidt concurred with Huss' views. Swabian minority schools had two duties, he asserted. They had to serve sound pedagogical functions, and they had to educate children in the spirit of their *Volkstum*.[20]

On 14 May 1937, Prime Minister Darányi reported in the Hungarian Parliament on the status of the minorities. Regarding the question of Hungary's non-Magyar elementary schools, the Prime Minister promised to promote "equal opportunity" for minority education by allocating proportionate funds in secular, confessional, Magyar and non-Magyar institutions. He hoped that this even-handed policy would prove conclusively the government's good intentions. He expected the new B-type schools to solve all the remaining problems in minority education. He also announced that the government had extended minority teachers' training courses by one month, and would soon establish special classes of several months' duration for instructors who desired to earn certificates that would entitle them to teach in minority schools.[21]

The *Deutscher Volksbote* responded negatively to Darányi's speech. *Völkisch* Swabians opposed the government's bilingualism policy. They particularly scorned the government's avowed primary goal that Swabian and other minority pupils must be able to master the Magyar language by the end of their sixth school year. They, on the other hand, advocated German as the exclusive language of instruction, with the sole exception that the Magyar language be taught on a daily basis by qualified Magyar teachers. They swept aside Darányi's claim that the government was fair and concerned for the welfare of Swabians by funding the minority school system equitably. That entire issue was irrelevant. Only genuine German instruction held the key to the solution of the Swabian minority problem in Hungary. In the meantime, however, the *völkisch* Swabians argued, Swabian children were being denied even the limited benefits the B-type schools had to offer, because the government left decision-making concerning school types in the hands of impressionable parents' groups. These were being coerced into choosing Magyar schools and subjected to indignities by the local authorities.[22]

The *VK*'s followers found themselves in a conundrum regarding the school system. They opposed the government's B-type elementary school, but at the same time, they were forced to urge its preservation in support of numerous readers of the *Deutscher Volksbote*, whose complaints concerning interference by hostile functionaries poured into the editorial offices at a steady rate. The *VK*'s rural sympathizers were more concerned with the pragmatic aspects of their children's education than were the *völkisch* Swabian leaders, who saw education almost entirely from a doctrinal viewpoint. The *völkisch* Swabians either had to support the B-type schools they abhorred, or be stuck with no German schools at all.

The *DV* met this challenge in two ways. Its legal staff discovered a loophole in the school law. The pressure parents' groups encountered to abandon bilingual schools in favor of pure Magyar-language institutions could be averted by addressing written requests to the school authorities demanding B-type instruction in qualified communities. The *DV* published facsimile Magyar-language application forms in its pages for the use of interested readers with children attending non-confessional schools. In the clerical schools the situation was different, *DV* researchers discovered. Article 18 of the 1923 school law had not been repealed. This meant that parents with at least forty children attending confessional institutions could still demand the establishment of A-type schools in their communities.[23] Over the next few months, parents in a number of localities heeded Goldschmidt's impassioned pleas for action by utilizing the application forms and demanding A- or B-type instruction in their villages. One way or another, the rural functionaries sidestepped these requests, and by year's end, the *DV* reported numerous complaints from disappointed parents throughout Hungary.[24]

In August 1937, the *DV* engaged in still another dispute with a high government official. József Széll, the recently installed minister of the interior, declared that Hungary did not need new minority laws, it merely had to live up to the existing ones.[25] The *DV* disputed Széll's view that Hungary had no need of new minority statutes. The Swabians had to have laws that permitted the establishment of all types of organizations. Presently, only the *UDV* enjoyed a limited legal right to operate. Also needed were *völkisch* daily newspapers, a political party specifically geared to Swabian interests, and unilingual German schools of every type.[26]

In the October 1937 issue of the *DV*, the editor appealed to the Hungarian public's understanding and sympathy for the Swabian cause. He complained that even the most innocuous Swabian activity drew accusations of Pan-Germanism or Nazism from Magyars, who accused all *völkisch* Swabians of treason. Goldschmidt laced his plea with a veiled warning. The treatment Magyars experienced in the Successor States would never be better than what the Swabians endured in Hungary.[27] Shortly after the start of the 1937 school year, a member of the *VK* summarized the minority education situation in Hungary. According to the informant, the Swabians had been far better off before the introduction of the 1935 school law than since. The 1923 regulation had imposed no deadlines for the establishment of German minority institutions. The choices were never final, and parents could choose genuinely German A-type schools. Fourteen years later, Swabians still had no German teachers. Nearly all instructors were either ethnic Magyars or Magyarized Swabians. German textbooks were unavailable, and the government had not abolished parents' conferences as a means of determining the school types to be adopted in Swabian communities.[28]

Georg Goldschmidt's complaint that a significant segment of Hungarian society abhorred Swabians was accurate, but a number of individuals in authority conceded that the Swabians had a right to their own culture and language within reasonable limits. During the May 1937 budget debates in the Upper House of Parliament, several speakers expressed fear and dislike of Swabians. Dr. Sulyok charged, for example, that in the western counties of Hungary, Swabian landowners were accumulating land at the expense of the Magyar peasantry. Ultimately, they wanted to secede from Hungary. In the Lower House, representative Tildy rebutted Sulyok's charges. He saw no connection between increased Swabian landownership and secessionism. The Swabians were decent and patriotic folk. They were not to blame if Magyar peasants committed "national suicide" by producing too few children to maintain the numerical superiority of Magyars in the region, whereas the Swabians averaged two children per family.[29]

In the Lower House, Gustav Gratz asserted on 12 May that it was not National Socialist Germany that endangered Hungary, as was widely believed, but a handful of Swabian malcontents who wantonly disturbed the spiritual harmony between their people and the Magyars. Hungarian society must support the government's earnest efforts to promote the cultural welfare of Swabians. Opponents of such a policy harmed Hungary, because their negative attitude strengthened the influence of extremists who would alienate the Swabians from their fellow-citizens.[30] In his speech, Prime Minister Darányi urged the public not to thwart the fulfillment of Swabian cultural aspirations, especially in minority education. He pledged that his government would do all in its power to maintain both state and confessional minority schools and train suitable teachers, so that non-Magyar children would be able to learn their mother tongue as well as the Magyar language with equal ease.[31]

In July 1937, the Upper House again debated the minority issue. Dr. Konrad Heckenberger, an early opponent of Bleyer and champion of assimilation, now experienced a change of heart. He blamed the lack of progress in minority affairs on provocateurs on one side (presumably the *VK*) and the myopia of others (presumably local school officials). He believed that the new minority school system would enable Swabian children to become proficient in both German and Magyar. Only by pursuing this enlightened policy could the Hungarian government demand similar rights for Magyar children in the Successor States. Minister of Education Bálint Hóman and Reformed Church Bishop Dr. László Ravasz concurred with Heckenberger's views. Having examined conditions in the ethnic schools, the governing Unity Party's Minority Committee concluded that local authorities must change their negative attitudes, and stop blocking efforts by Swabian parents to educate their children as they wished. Apart from the justice of pursuing such a course, these local authorities had the golden opportunity to create trust and good relations between the Swabians and the Hungarian state.[32]

The Magyar-language press also expressed a variety of opinions regarding the Swabian presence in Hungary and the "German menace." Mihály Szabados, writing in the Roman Catholic publication *Korunk Szava*, exclaimed that neither before the war nor after was Hungary ever imperiled by ethnic mass movements. He was perturbed, however, because a few hundred well-educated opportunistic Swabian leaders were undermining the security of the Hungarian state and endangering Swabian-Magyar unity through a subversive whispering campaign. They wanted to lead an ethnic dissident movement, but they failed to realize that they were conducting both Hungary and their own people down the path to possible destruction. Szabados urged the government to take severe measures to nullify the efforts of these Swabian dissidents.[33]

The same writer also criticized the impending law that would introduce the secret ballot throughout Hungary.[34] The new statute would encourage many Swabians to adopt German ideological standards that would estrange them from other citizens. Most Swabians claimed only German cultural rights, but Szabados regarded cultural and political issues as inseparable. Moreover, the Third Reich was encouraging German ethnic groups abroad to adopt German culture as merely the first step in enlisting their support on behalf of Nazi Germany's political objectives. In Szabados's view, the government must prevent the formation of a German political party on Hungarian soil. The preservation of Hungary's security depended on it.[35]

Apart from the Swabian minority education dispute, the Hungarian government's name-Magyarization program emerged as the most bitterly disputed and volatile issue to disturb Magyar-Swabian and German-Hungarian relations. Name-Magyarization had begun in the mid-1920s, when Prime Minister István Bethlen's minister of war, Gyula Gömbös, initiated a name-Magyarization campaign in the armed forces, aimed mainly at Swabian recruits. As prime minister, Gömbös later extended the drive to all walks of public life. Gömbös agreed with Alajos Kovács, chief of Hungary's Statistical Bureau, that only 70% of Hungary's population possessed Magyar-sounding names, and hence the rate of conversions, as of 1930, was insufficient. Kovács regarded foreign-sounding names an "ugly blot on the face of Hungary." He was convinced that Hungary's honor would be besmirched if Hungarian citizens with Slavic or German-sounding names were to earn honors abroad. He therefore urged a thoroughgoing name-conversion campaign that would produce between 60,000 and 70,000 Hungarian citizens with Magyar-sounding names annually.[36]

Under Gömbös, schools, private industry, and all government offices relentlessly practiced name-Magyarization. The official Statistical Yearbook published annual progress reports based on the place of residence and nationality of the converts. People with foreign-sounding names were encouraged to Magyarize them by means of cash emoluments, special honors, and psychological pressures. A canvas of all Budapest ministries resulted in the publication of a carefully-prepared statistical table, indicating the percentage of employees in each bureau possessing Magyar and foreign-sounding names.[37]

In many instances the Swabians reacted truculently to the name-Magyarization drive. They had to concede that it was an eminently successful campaign. In 1935 alone, some 100,000 Swabians changed their names. This included two gold medal winning members of Hungary's Olympic team, who would otherwise have been left behind. On the other hand, some Swabians refused honors and material advantage and preferred to keep their German name. A Swabian peasant in Tolna County was a case in point. He refused to accept the honorific title "Vitéz," along with the gift of 24 cadastral yokes of land, which were his lawful dues as a decorated war veteran, because non-Magyars had to give up their names in order to be eligible for the honors.[38]

Under these circumstances it is not surprising that the name-Magyarization issue became a source of an irreversible rift in the *UDV* which shattered the unity of Hungary's Swabian community. In the course of the Hungarian parliamentary elections of 1935, Dr.

Franz Basch, then general secretary of the *UDV*, caused a furor in the legislature and in the press for declaring at a Swabian rally that "no Swabian ought to Magyarize his honorable German name." The remark cost Basch his freedom and his *UDV* post. He was arrested for slander against the Hungarian nation, tried, convicted and sentenced to a six-month jail term. He also lost his civic rights for three years, and received a peremptory command from Gratz to resign his *UDV* position.[39] It was this name-Magyarization issue that occasioned the schism in the centuries'-old Swabian unity in Hungary. It enabled the government to split the Swabians, and deal with the two hostile factions more effectively.

Unlike the *völkisch* Swabians, who minimized the importance of individual rights and stressed the collective aspects of nationality policy, the *UDV* leadership favored individual choice in all ethnic matters, including name-Magyarization. Gratz accepted name-Magyarization as a fact of life. It was neither a meritorious deed nor a criminal act. Some Swabians with German-sounding names might be better Hungarian patriots than those bearing a Magyar name, he explained. Hungary's national interests did not demand that all citizens had to have Magyar family names. The state should only be concerned with the loyalty of its citizens, not with their national origins. The government owed two duties to its citizens, Gratz asserted. It had to ensure that in the name-Magyarization process individuals suffered no official pressures, and that Swabians could, if they wished, maintain their language, German name, and customs without being accused of disgraceful conduct.[40]

In the closing months of the Gömbös ministry, the government's name-Magyarization techniques far exceeded the reasonable limits which Gustav Gratz envisioned as being fair. Some of these practices, on the contrary, bordered on hucksterism. Dr. Karl von Schandl, a parliamentary deputy, representing Bakonypölöske, "persuaded" 139 Swabian families to permit him to submit their names to the authorities for name-Magyarization.[41] *Nation und Staat* further reported that the Hungarian Ministry of the Interior had issued a confidential order to private and public organizations. They were to promote name-Magyarization among their employees, and provide two reports annually on the status of the conversion process. Budapest's chief of police, Dr. Ferenczy, issued a similar directive to all personnel under his command, and let it be known that those who cooperated would receive preferential treatment. In two of Budapest's institutes of higher learning, the rectors announced that only those bearing Magyar names, or those submitting name-Magyarization applications, would be considered for stipends. The institutions even offered to defray the expense of the application fee for candidates.[42]

Numerous complaints concerning the compulsory nature of name-Magyarization prompted Prime Minister Darányi to issue a statement on this problem during the May 1937 parliamentary debate. Darányi declared that, following the tradition of previous Hungarian governments, he had no objections which ethnic group any Hungarian citizen adopted as his own. Nobody in Hungary would be made to feel like a second- or third-rate citizen on the basis of ethnic affiliation. Hence it followed that in Hungary nobody could be either advantaged or disadvantaged for having a foreign-sounding name. His government deplored all attempts to deprive citizens of their personal freedom and rights in the process of persuading them either to keep or to change their foreign-sounding names. Thus, the law protected both those who wished to Magyarize their names and those who wished to keep their foreign-sounding ones. It must be understood, he asserted, that the name-Magyarizers must neither expect nor be offered any advantages by the authorities.[43]

The Swabian minority problem had been troubling German-Hungarian relations nearly since the end of the war. Under National Socialism the Third Reich became obsessed with the treatment of *Volksgenossen* residing abroad, whether they lived in hostile countries such as Czechoslovakia, or in nominally friendly ones, such as Hungary. While Gömbös lived, Germany was willing to condone the none-too-gentle treatment of the Swabians in Hungary. The prime minister had sympathized with National Socialist objectives. After Gömbös's death, however, the situation changed. Darányi, and other would-be prime ministers, clung to the parliamentary system, and rejected Nazi or Fascist-style authoritarianism. The end of 1936 constituted a watershed, therefore, in German-Hungarian-Swabian relations. As the *völkisch* Swabians became more belligerent and petitioned the Hungarian government for more and more concessions, the German government became steadily tougher in its dealings with Hungary. It is not surprising, therefore, that the Swabian problem grew in importance and became the source of discord in German-Hungarian relations.

On the eve of Minister of the Interior Miklós Kozma's impending Berlin visit to discuss the Swabian problem with German officials, Hans von Mackensen, Germany's minister in Budapest, briefed Friedrich Stieve, head of the German Foreign Ministry's cultural division, on the policies the Hungarian delegation was likely to promote in Germany. He pointed out that, in his view, the Hungarians employed erroneous psychological principles in connection with the Swabians. They apparently believed that anything connected with Germany must be suspect. They also felt endangered from all sides, surrounded as they were by traditional enemies. In fact, Mackensen thought, Hungarians were suffering from the effects of a persecution psychosis.

Mackensen regarded the Swabian problem as the only point of friction in German-Hungarian relations. Unless this situation became resolved to everyone's satisfaction, Mackensen asserted, Germany might as well kiss its political friendship with Hungary goodbye. Fortunately, however, he discerned a tiny glimmer of hope. A few leaders in government, particularly Darányi and Hóman, were adopting more sensible views regarding the Swabians. He considered Darányi's recent condemnation of forcible name-Magyarization a favorable sign.[44]

Mackensen listed a number of problems that plagued German-Hungarian relations. These were to be discussed and resolved during Kozma's visit. He emphasized the humiliating experiences in Hungary of a group of visiting female university students in the summer of 1936. These students apparently arrived nearly penniless in various Swabian localities, where, according to the Hungarian government, they exploited the hospitality of the villagers, and stirred up the peaceful Swabian peasants with National Socialist propaganda. They were under constant surveillance by the Hungarian gendarmerie. After being harassed, they were arrested. Mackensen blamed Hungarian feelings of insecurity, fear of the Pan-German menace, and the ineptness of Third Reich agencies that arranged the excursion, for the fiasco. Mackensen noted the Hungarians' fear of the *VK* and the Hungarian government's refusal to send athletes with German-sounding names to the Berlin Olympics as additional proof of excessive Magyar suspiciousness and lack of self-confidence.

Mackensen devoted a great deal of attention to the plight of the Swabian minority schools. This intolerable situation was rooted in the 1907 school law that severely curtailed the use of minority languages in education. Subsequently, the 1923 school law allowed parents to make decisions on minority education. The new B-type school he deemed superior to the old one, although it was still a far cry from the now defunct A-type institutions. Mackensen cited several dismal school statistics, and urged the creation of German kindergarten, nursery, trade and continuation schools, as well as the establishment of exclusively German religious instruction for all Swabians. Mackensen criticized the deplorable situation of German teaching personnel that required a German teachers' institute as a remedy. Finally, and most importantly, he thought, the Hungarian government must be persuaded to include confessional schools in the school regulations.[45]

Mackensen also reported a conversation he had had with Darányi, Kánya, Kozma, Hóman and Tibor Pataky. The latter was chief of the minority section in the Hungarian Ministry of Education. These talks centered on the Swabian problem and its repercussions. Kánya complained about the steady inundation of Swabian villages by German student propagandists, who masqueraded as scholarly investigators. He wanted the German government to issue a statement urging Swabians to remain loyal Hungarians. Kánya also complained about the unfriendly German press that irritated the Hungarian public with horror stories about the alleged mistreatment of Swabians. This hindered the government's efforts to improve Swabian cultural and educational conditions. He conceded that certain practical problems prevented instant success. Most minority schools were confessional institutions, they had not enough German teachers, and Hungary lacked sufficient facilities to train suitable instructors in appropriate numbers.

Kánya, Kozma and Darányi took turns enumerating certain limited achievements in minority education, and promised more improvements in the near future. A six-months' teachers' training facility would be established soon, and in the meantime, two female German instructors had begun teaching in two Swabian villages. In recent weeks, 8 state and 40 confessional C-type schools had been transformed into B-type institutions. A course designed to teach village notaries German had been created recently at Szombathely, near the Austrian border, the region with the largest Swabian population concentration in Hungary.

Darányi concluded the session by reiterating the complaint about student propagandists overrunning Hungary, and National Socialist agencies in Germany inundating the country with tons of Nazi propaganda. In Darányi's own electoral district alone, the authorities had confiscated 120 tons of such objectionable material.[46] The topics covered at this meeting would engage German-Hungarian conversations on the Swabian problem through 1937.

During Kozma's visit in Germany, these subjects dominated discussions. The talks on 12 November 1936 between Kozma and his German counterpart Wilhelm Frick, a few other Ministry officials, and finally with Hitler, revealed that the Germans expected a rapid improvement in the treatment of Hungary's Swabians. They were growing impatient with promises, excuses and lack of results. The Germans informed Kozma that, according to German minority leaders in Czechoslovakia, Romania and Yugoslavia, the Germans in those countries were so much better off in every way than the Swabians in Hungary that not one of them would consider returning under Hungarian rule. They urged Hungary to create "a minority Eldorado" to make the country a more attractive residence for non-Magyars in which to live. Kozma and his staff found themselves constantly on the defensive with their determined and well-briefed hosts, who refused to yield an inch on any issue. The Hungarian delegation appeared to flounder on most points. As a result, the Germans gained the erroneous impression that their visitors had no choice but to improve the condition of the Swabians.[47]

The Germans reacted optimistically to the Hungarian visit. On 23 December 1936, Friedrich Stieve informed director of the Ministry of Interior Vollert in this spirit. According to him, upon his arrival at home, Kozma had immediately issued releases to the Hungarian press regarding his promises made in Berlin. The German public appeared tremendously pleased and relieved, convinced that after all these pledges the Hungarian government would have all the minority laws carried out assiduously by the local authorities. Stieve foresaw the early introduction of *völkisch* elementary schools, the creation of a large body of qualified German teachers, and various associations, newspapers, and other facilities coming to life in Hungary. The establishment of total cultural and economic equality for Swabians would soon become a reality.[48]

German jubilation was premature. On 3 February 1937, Kozma resigned as minister of the interior. Until 10 April, when József Széll assumed the cabinet post, Prime Minister Darányi personally directed the affairs of the portfolio. Darányi did promise, however, for the benefit of Germans and Swabians alike, that Kozma's pledges would not be revoked.[49] Despite these promises, new difficulties with the Swabians and controversies with Germany kept cropping up throughout 1937, to exacerbate relations between the two countries.

German Foreign Minister von Neurath's 11 June 1937 talks with Kánya and Darányi in Budapest proved extremely contentious. Kánya complained that Pan-German propaganda continued among the Swabians. Neurath rejected this charge. He complained in turn that Kozma's promises had still not been institutionalized, whereupon Darányi interjected that the new school type and elimination of clerical influences in the minority schools would finally solve this problem.[50]

On 15 July, however, when Minister of the Interior Széll declared that Hungary did not require new minority laws, it merely had to carry out the provisions of existing regulations faithfully, the *VK* greeted the statement with indignation. Hitler's deputy, Rudolf Hess, on the other hand, welcomed the declaration with satisfaction. He stressed, however, that portion of the text in which Széll pledged to exert the full authority of the Hungarian state to activate the laws in a practical sense, regardless of obstacles. If, thanks to these new attitudes, the Swabians could gain political, economic and cultural equality in Hungary, Hess stated, then they would serve the Hungarian state faithfully, and act as mediators between Germany and Hungary.[51]

This uneasy German-Hungarian accommodation on the Swabian minority issue, announced with considerable fanfare by both sides, dismayed the *VK*. The truce, however, did not survive the summer. A new controversy clouded German-Hungarian relations with the appearance of an insulting article in Baldur von Schirach's youth magazine *Wille und Macht*.[52] The diatribe criticized Hungary for its ill-treatment of the Swabians, and pilloried the government for its unwillingness to remedy the violations against Swabians. This outburst drew an outraged reaction from Hungary. The controversy persisted throughout August. On 17 September 1937, the German government withdrew the offending publication from circulation. Of course, the damage was done, and German-Hungarian relations on the Swabian issue never fully recovered.

In November 1937, the German government's policy on the Swabian problem changed. Hitherto, the Third Reich had recognized the *VK* as the sole representative of the Swabians in Hungary, but had remained aloof of the organization, at least publicly. Third Reich officials preferred dealing with a congenial Hungarian government that had the authority to rectify some of the worst ills in Hungary's Swabian society. As illusions of voluntary government cooperation faded, Germany gradually intensified its support of the *VK*, and concentrated on having the *UDV* replaced by the *VK* as the official representative of Hungary's Swabians. This change in policy coincided with Hitler's decision, reached in mid-November 1937, to gear Germany for war, and to expand the country's eastern borders by military means. Under these changed circumstances, Germany could not afford to bolster an unreliable Hungarian government that failed to keep its word and persecuted *völkisch* Swabians, while it supported the collaborationist *UDV*. Sheer prudence demanded that Germany replace its laissez faire policy with a much tougher approach.

The idea of coopting the *VK* with the Hungarian government first arose in a conversation between Hans von Mackensen, recently named state secretary in the German Foreign Ministry, and Tibor Pataky. Mackensen tried to convince Pataky that Hungary ought to solve the Swabian minority problem by pacifying the *VK* and turning its opposition into support. As long as Hungary recognized the *UDV* and its president Gustav Gratz, whom Germany regarded as undesirable, the Swabian problem would fester, and the Hungarian government would be always condemned in Berlin. In fact, Mackensen told Pataky, the *UDV*, led by the Catholic, legitimist and freemason Gratz, was the Hungarian government's tool to subvert the Swabian minority. On a more positive note, however, Mackensen assured Pataky that the German government trusted Prime Minister Darányi's promises regarding improvements in Swabian minority life, but that the German authorities were uncertain whether Darányi could coerce the local functionaries, who were still sabotaging the minority regulations. Pataky assured Mackensen that Darányi was sufficiently powerful to deal with recalcitrant officials, although, he admitted, the government had much difficulty influencing confessional schools.[53]

Between 19-24 November 1937, Darányi held discussions with German officials on the Swabian minority question, and made the usual optimistic promises. German foreign minister von Neurath felt sufficiently encouraged by what he heard to dispatch a circular telegram to all German diplomats abroad to the effect that the Hungarians were finally determined to introduce meaningful changes in Swabian minority life, because they realized that friendly German-Hungarian relations depended on the execution of their promises.[54] Varying German reactions and attitudes regarding Hungarian pledges suggest that a definitive, strict policy toward Hungary was still in a process of evolution at that time. It would not remain tentative much longer. The Germans had become disillusioned with unfulfilled Hungarian promises. Dramatic changes in east-central Europe placed Germany in a commanding position by the end of 1938. The new situation substantially restricted Hungary's economic and diplomatic freedom of action and curtailed the extent to which the Hungarian government could repress the Swabians with impunity.

CHAPTER VI

THE DIPLOMATIC PICTURE - EUROPE IN 1938

Although developments in 1938 raised revisionist hopes and expectations in Hungary, the actual events that year impressed upon Hungarians the precariousness of their country's diplomatic and military situation. In the previous year they could still expect an Italian-led deterrent to unrestricted German expansion in the area situated between eastern Germany and the Black Sea, and between the Baltic and Mediterranean shores. By late 1938, undisputable German supremacy dispelled any such notion. In mid-March, Germany occupied Austria without firing a shot. This sealed Czechoslovakia's doom. In May, during the First Czechoslovak Crisis, Hitler failed to seize Czechoslovakia. The great powers averted war only narrowly. At the end of September, the Munich Pact truncated Czechoslovakia. Thereafter, the Third Reich extended its political, ideological and economic influence eastward unhindered by any other country or combination of states.

For Hungary, these difficult times demanded tact and wisdom. Former Prime Minister Count István Bethlen, commenting on Hungary's delicate position after the *Anschluss*, cautioned that a reinvigorated Germany might assist Hungary to defeat the Little Entente, only to emerge as an even greater threat than before. Germany would become an economic colossus, and through commercial and political pressures would incite eastern Europe's agrarian countries to compete against each other. Bethlen warned that Hungary might not be immune to the unreasonable demands of a Third Reich pursuing its own selfish national objectives.

In fact, the Munich Pact failed to bring Hungary the benefits its leaders expected through affiliation with Germany. Hungarian territorial demands were ignored. In early November 1938, the German- and Italian-sponsored Vienna Arbitral Award disappointed Hungary's revisionist aspirations. Hungary regained a small strip of Slovakia and Ruthenia inhabited almost exclusively by ethnic Magyars. The rest of prewar Hungary was still securely held by the Little Entente. Hungary desired to regain its lost lands and people from all three of these countries. Germany, however, had "befriended" Romania and Yugoslavia, and pledged to defend these two states against Hungarian aggression.

Under these circumstances, Hungarian leaders had to proceed with caution. If they offended Hitler, Hungary might become one of the Third Reich's victims instead of remaining an ally. On the other hand, Hungarians also had certain misgivings about having their country's prewar frontiers restored with German help. Should the Western powers declare war on the Third Reich and emerge victorious, they might partition Hungary among the three Successor States as punishment. Hungary had to choose between the Western Allies and the Axis—between potential advantages and possible future penalties. The country's leaders chose the middle road. They courted Germany by offering numerous seemingly friendly gestures, but in fact obstructed the Third Reich's eastward expansion.

In 1937, Austria had enjoyed relative stability and security. By 1938, it faced numerous difficulties. This was partly the fault of the von Schuschnigg regime's inept, vacillating domestic policy, partly due to Austria's geographic isolation, and partly because the Third Reich correctly judged the time ripe to destroy the Austrian state. In vain did von Schuschnigg seek support abroad. On 10 January, he attended the Rome Pact conference held in Budapest. By then, however, Mussolini had abandoned Austria and decided to support Germany. Hungary had neither the power nor the inclination to succor Austria beyond uttering expressions of concern. The Austrians appealed to Czechoslovakia, France and Great Britain for protection against Germany; but Czechoslovakia, too, was on Germany's "hit list," and President Beneš had no desire to antagonize Hitler. The two Western powers expressed deep sympathy, but refused to help Austria.

On 12 February, von Schuschnigg tried to reach a compromise settlement with the Führer, but he failed. On 9 March, von Schuschnigg announced that a plebiscite would be held four days hence. He predicted that his people would rally around "a free and Christian Austria." On election day, Hitler ordered his army to seize the country. The newly installed Arthur Seyss-Inquart government almost instantly joined Austria with the Third Reich. For the first time in history, Hungary shared a common frontier with Germany.

The new neighbor threatened Hungarian security in the west, as did Romania in the east and Yugoslavia in the south. Throughout 1938, however, Romania remained politically unstable. Right-radical Prime Minister Octavian Goga of the National-Christian Party conceded that the grievances of Transylvania's Magyar minority ought to be remedied. Goga pacified Romania's Hungarian Party through a few administrative reforms. He refused, however, to adjust Transylvania's borders in Hungary's favor. Moreover, Hungary feared that Hitler would befriend the ideologically congenial Goga. A German-Romanian alliance would outflank Hungary, and the latter's strategic advantages in the region would vanish. Hungary would be exposed to German penetration.

For two months, Hungarians lived in fear of a German-Romanian compact. But on 10 February, King Carol dismissed Goga, assumed dictatorial powers, dissolved all political parties, and appointed a royalist cabinet under Patriarch Miron Cristea. The new regime cancelled Goga's Magyar legislation, terminated administrative reforms, and dissolved the Hungarian Party. Cristea expressed concern for the welfare of Romania's minorities, but, in fact, Magyar minority life suffered during the remainder of 1938. King Carol also cancelled Goga's anti-Semitic legislation, which helped to restore Romania's close ties with the Western powers. These measures strengthened the Little Entente. Once again, Hungary faced encirclement, a peril that only a faithful pro-German policy might remedy.

King Carol intensified Hungary's predicament by concluding a major trade agreement with the Third Reich. This pact enabled Germany to establish firm control over Romania's economy. The Germans overlooked Romania's ties with the West for the sake of harvesting economic and strategic advantages. It was an ironical situation. Had Hungary behaved as did the Romanians, Germany would have retaliated against perceived Hungarian duplicity. Romania derived substantial economic benefits from Germany, whereas the Third Reich achieved more advantages through the exercise of economic control than if it had installed a puppet regime in that country.

Romania's advantageous diplomatic position enabled King Carol to appear generous to Hungary. The Cristea regime was friendly and polite, but refused to address Hungary's grievances. With other countries, however, Romania genuinely tried to mend fences. Polish-Romanian relations improved at the end of May. The rapprochement failed to survive the tensions of the Munich Crisis and its sequel, the Polish-Czech-Slovak dispute in October. On 31 July, Romania became reconciled with Bulgaria by recognizing its right to rearm. Good relations with Yugoslavia, a major ally, continued throughout this period. In November, the two countries decided to pursue a common policy against other states. In the same month, King Carol journeyed to Paris and London, presumably to solidify Romania's position in the West. Next, the King visited Hitler, no doubt to confirm Romania's equilibrium between the two Euro-

pean power blocs. Carol's strategy might have succeeded, had it
not been for the execution of Iron Guard leader Corneliu Codreanu
and twelve of his associates on charges of high treason. This action alienated German National Socialists, particularly Hitler, who
greatly admired the Iron Guard and its fallen leader. At this point,
however, Hitler was still willing to sacrifice his ideological principles
for the sake of achieving economic and strategic advantages. Romania escaped German retaliation and grew even more confident
in the pursuit of its "foolproof" diplomacy.

By year's end, Romania had little to show for all its vigorous
diplomacy. The League of Nations security system, which Romania supported, and which in turn had buttressed Romania, was
moribund. Czechoslovakia was dying. The Little Entente had disintegrated. The timidity of France and Great Britain during the
Austrian and Czechoslovak crises had demonstrated to the people
of eastern Europe the futility of relying on these two great Western
powers. Romania's relations with the Soviet Union, Bulgaria, and
Hungary deteriorated after Munich. Approaching the new year,
Romania was virtually isolated diplomatically, with the exception
of Yugoslavia. Whether or not Romania's altered circumstances
would benefit Hungarian aspirations depended on the convergence
of numerous complex factors.

Czechoslovakia, on paper the strongest, but in reality the most
vulnerable member of the Little Entente, entered its twentieth an-
niversary year with misgivings about the future. Czechoslovakia's
leaders, who regarded Germany, Hungary and Poland as implaca-
ble enemies, had in fact every cause for being pessimistic about the
future. Austria was in danger of being occupied by Germany. Its
extinction would intensify Czechoslovakia's peril. Poland and Hungary remained uncompromisingly hostile. Both countries desired
Czechoslovak territory, and awaited support from similarly inclined
Germany. The Czechoslovaks realized that their executioners would
gather as soon as Austria had ceased to exist. Germany needed Polish and Hungarian fellow-conspirators to distribute the wrath of the
Western powers.

Surrounded by enemies on nearly all sides, Czechoslovakia could
not muster its defenses effectively, despite having excellent fortifi-
cations and a first-rate military force. Most of the military in-
stallations facing Germany were located in the German-inhabited
Sudetenland. Against Hungary the country was totally defenseless.
Military aid or reinforcements could not reach the Czechoslovaks.
Diplomatically, too, Czechoslovakia was isolated. France and Great
Britain lacked the logistics to render military aid, and hence paid

only lip service to its preservation. The Soviet Union's offer to defend Czechoslovakia foundered on the refusal of Poland and Romania to grant the Red Army and Air Force transit privileges. Besides, the Soviets refused to fight unless France engaged Germany in the west. The Little Entente proved a slender reed. Whereas Romania supported Czechoslovakia even under Goga, Yugoslav Prime Minister Milan Stojadinović ostentatiously eliminated Prague from his itinerary en route to his 15 January meeting with Hitler. Italy's traditional hostility to Czechoslovakia was tinged with contempt. Czechoslovakia appeared doomed.

When Austria fell on 13 March, Czechoslovakia's fate was also sealed. Even so, Czechoslovak leaders responded to escalating demands by Germany, Hungary and Poland for frontier rectification "along nationality lines" so truculently that only French and British intervention prevented war on two separate occasions—in May and in September. Czechoslovakia surrendered only when Germany threatened to level the country, and when its own allies abandoned the Czechoslovaks. They capitulated to German demands on 30 September, granted autonomy to the Slovaks, and subsequently yielded to Polish and Hungarian territorial demands.

Prior to the Munich Conference, Hungary had expected to gain considerable territory at Czechoslovakia's expense. Disappointment reigned when the restituted lands and populations proved relatively modest. Ever since Trianon, Hungarian leaders had hoped that, with Germany's help and without risking a war, they would recapture all of the territories lost to the three Successor States. Hitler had ordered Hungarians to forfeit their possessions held by Romania and Yugoslavia, and to confine their revisionist demands exclusively to Czechoslovakia. Germany and Hungary would then jointly destroy and partition that country. At Munich, Hungary expected to retrieve all of Czechoslovakia east of Moravia. Instead, Hungary received small patches of land when the German and Italian foreign ministers announced their arbitral award decision in Vienna on 2 November.

Most Hungarians were indignant. Hungary had received only the southern, exclusively Magyar-inhabited portion, of Slovakia and Ruthenia. With the notable exception of Kassa (Košice), most major population centers, industrial and mining facilities, and large numbers of ethnic Magyars, remained with the autonomous province of Slovakia, soon to become an "independent" German protectorate. Like Slovakia, the remainder of Ruthenia also became an autonomous part of the Second Czecho-Slovak Republic. Large numbers of ethnic Magyars, most of them residing astride the Hungarian frontier, remained within this province as well.

This meager territorial settlement left Hungarian leaders with a dilemma that demanded early resolution. Hungary had gained some 12,000 km² (5,000 sq. miles) with a population of about one-million. These accretions were insufficient to ensure the creation of a strong and regionally influential Greater Hungary. On the contrary. By accepting the award from which the Western powers kept aloof, Hungary had become a German accomplice, and might have to pay dearly for its gains should Germany be defeated in a war against the Western powers. Hereafter, the fear of future negative consequences served as a major deterrent in Hungarian foreign policy. Hungary wanted to preserve European peace, restrain the pace of the Third Reich's eastward expansion, and maintain freedom of Hungary's diplomatic and economic maneuver.

Poland, an important friend of Hungary, resisted efforts by France and Germany to let itself be drawn into power-bloc politics. Polish policymakers cultivated bilateral agreements with countries of both competing alliance systems. This independentmindedness did not prevent Poland from supporting the formation of a north-south barrier that would stretch from the Baltic shores to the Mediterranean Sea, include (besides itself) Hungary, Romania, Yugoslavia and Italy, and act as a defensive shield against German eastward expansion. Poland also had an ulterior motive in advocating such a plan. The Poles hoped that reconciling Hungary with Romania and Yugoslavia would shatter the Little Entente, so that Poland and Hungary might dismember eastern Czechoslovakia without having to worry about Romanian and Yugoslav retaliation. None of these states, however, wished to risk arousing the displeasure of Germany. The scheme failed, despite lively interest by Hungary and Italy.

Hungarian-Polish relations remained excellent throughout this period. The respective governments, the press and the public enthusiastically supported each others' territorial aspirations, especially during the Sudeten Crisis. Earlier, the Poles had apparently acquiesced in the Austrian *Anschluss*, and calmly awaited Germany's diplomatic assault upon and destruction of Czechoslovakia, from which they hoped to benefit, as indeed they did. This action in turn injured Poland's close relations with France, a long-time ally, but one with its luster and power gone. Simultaneously, Poland appeared to be making headway in pacifying the Third Reich, an accommodation which the latter also seemed to favor at this time. But disagreement over the disposition of Ruthenia during the Munich Crisis soured German-Polish relations at a crucial point. Poland desired a three-way partition of Ruthenia with Romania and Hungary, and thereby gain common frontiers with these states. Germany, on the other hand, insisted that, for the time being, most of Ruthenia must remain an autonomous province of the Second Czecho-Slovak Republic. This would prevent the joining of three east European states in a possible anti-German confederation.

Poland concluded bilateral agreements with a number of other countries as well. The Soviet Union was a case in point. Although beset by mutual distrust and plagued by sporadic border incidents, the two countries nonetheless renewed their nonaggression treaty on 27 November, and in December they began trade negotiations in Moscow. Good relations with Romania suffered when the Romanians rejected Poland's partition plan for Ruthenia. The Romanians were not eager to share their border with Poland, and even less to antagonize Germany. With Yugoslavia, the Poles were sufficiently friendly to act—albeit unsuccessfully—as go-betweens to reconcile that country with Hungary. Poland invested a great deal of diplomatic effort in gaining the good graces of Italy, and—misjudging power realities—hoped to derive some protection from this fading great power against possible German hostile initiatives. On the whole, Poland pursued an opportunistic foreign policy that disregarded ideology as well as the mortal menace posed by Germany until it was too late to seek remedies.

The Soviet Union's position was still precarious after the purges of 1937, the consequences of which undermined the effectiveness of all branches of Soviet government. As a result, the USSR's credibility in the international community suffered, despite the fact that on paper, the Soviet Union wielded awesome manpower and weaponry. Nonetheless, all attempts by Soviet leaders to remedy the country's isolation failed. With the sole exception of Czechoslovakia, none of the European powers sought the Soviet Union's support or collaboration. The momentous events involving the demise of Austria and Czechoslovakia occurred without the benefit of Soviet participation or consultation. The USSR's prestige suffered considerable damage when Poland rejected a Soviet demarche in defense of Czechoslovakia on the eve of Poland's intervention in that country. Diminished British and French confidence in the Soviet Union's martial effectiveness was a natural consequence of this diplomatic fiasco. Soviet relations with Romania deteriorated over the dispute involving Bessarabia during Goga's term, improved afterward, but never became friendly. Soviet-Hungarian relations remained dismal throughout the first half of 1938, and then deteriorated during and after the Munich Crisis. The Soviet Union resented Hungary's seizure of Czechoslovak territory as much as it did Poland's, but was unable to aid Czechoslovakia. The Soviet Union suffered further difficulties due to the European consensus that, before long, the USSR would be fully engaged in the Far East against the hostile Japanese.

In 1938, France's continental policy suffered as the result of the Austrian *Anschluss* and the dismemberment of Czechoslovakia. These events rendered France's alliances with Poland, the Soviet Union, and the Little Entente strategically unviable and politically unrealistic. As the world saw it, France and Great Britain lacked both the will and the ability to honor their treaty obligations. This perception proved accurate. France's relations with Germany actually improved after the *Anschluss*, and amicable Franco-German contacts resumed after Munich.

France ceased condemning Italy's Ethiopian conquest after Munich. On 7 November, France recognized the Italian monarch's title of Emperor of Ethiopia. Thanks to this subservience, Italy treated France with contempt. In December, Italian Foreign Secretary Ciano rejected French complaints when the Italian Chamber of Deputies laid claim to Corsica, Nice, Tunisia and Djibouti. Italy also renounced the 7 January 1935 Laval-Mussolini agreement. By year's end, venomous press campaigns in both countries again poisoned Italian-French relations.

With Munich, French influence in Prague terminated, and relations with Poland, after the latter's seizure of Czechoslovakia's Těšín, so deteriorated that in December, Polish Foreign Minister Jósef Beck failed to make a courtesy call at the French Foreign Ministry during his sojourn in France. Apart from Great Britain, France maintained good relations only with Romania and Yugoslavia throughout 1938. The fact that the French public had become more sympathetic to Hungary and no longer condemned its territorial aspirations bore no practical results. Even after Munich, the French government stubbornly opposed any Hungarian acquisition of Czechoslovak territory, even in southern Slovakia, where the population was nearly 100% ethnic Magyar.

Perceived insensitive and unrealistic French behavior revived memories in Hungary of the abortive Franco-Hungarian negotiations in 1919 that had resulted in mutual recriminations. Excessive French demands at that time had alienated Hungary and shortly thereafter the French government sponsored a punitive peace treaty and orchestrated an encirclement strategy through the Little Entente. These policies eventually drove Hungary into the arms of a revived and vengeful Germany. Bitterness and anger over alleged past wrongs could not obliterate Hungarian policymakers' realization that if France did not exist, a substitute would have to be created to counter excessive German power. As a substitute, Italy had been found wanting. The cessation of French influence east of the Maginot Line therefore had dire consequences for Hungary. France, hitherto the only powerful continental deterrent to German imperialism, was impotent; Italy was too weak; and Hungary found the Soviet Union dangerous and ideologically objectionable. In view of these conditions, Hungary became progressively more dependent on the good graces of the Third Reich.

Great Britain managed to derive some dubious advantage from the *Anschluss* and Munich. These crises strengthened Anglo-French relations and intensified cooperation against further German and Italian aggression. In November, for example, Prime Minister Neville Chamberlain declared that Great Britain would defend France against an attack by Italy, even though his country had no legal obligation to do so. Despite this pugnacity, however, Chamberlain preferred to pacify Italy in order to safeguard Great Britain's vulnerable Mediterranean lifelines. Italophobe Foreign Secretary Anthony Eden's resignation on 21 February facilitated this reconciliation process. On 16 April, Great Britain recognized Italy's Ethiopian conquest, and approved the termination of Ethiopia's membership in the League of Nations. The agreement was ratified on 16 November, after Mussolini withdrew 10,000 Italian "volunteers" from the Spanish Civil War as a good will gesture.

Anglo-Russian diplomatic relations were strained in 1938. Even commercial contacts deteriorated. Guilty over the abandonment of Czechoslovakia after Munich, the British government made large sums of money available to that country, much of it as a gift. Little change occurred in British treatment of Romania and Yugoslavia after Munich. Great Britain's attitude toward Hungary was negative. By mid-1938, the British government concluded that Hungary had been irrevocably swept into the German orbit, and that all opportunities to help that country disentangle itself from the Nazi web would be in vain.

British influence in Czechoslovakia during the Munich Crisis led to that country's demise. During the early crisis Great Britain urged the Czechoslovaks to offer both the German and Magyar minorities generous concessions. As the crisis deepened, the British retained interest only in the destiny of the Sudeten Germans. Nonetheless, Great Britain agreed in principle to adjust Czechoslovakia's frontiers in favor of Hungary, but left the actual decision-making process to Germany and Italy. Hungary's leaders regarded the perceived abdication of Great Britain's duty as the upholder of fair play among all peoples, whether friend or foe, as a disillusioning experience, and despaired of attaining justice through conventional means. Henceforth, they believed, Hungary would have to seek the favor of Germany and possibly its junior partner Italy.

For Germany, 1938 proved the most successful year since Hitler's accession to power in 1933. The Reich gained 112,000 km^2 of territory with a population totaling about ten million. In that year, German influence replaced Anglo-French predominance in east-central Europe. These gains were made possible by the viability of the Rome-Berlin Axis, which served as the basic plank of German foreign policy. The Austrian crisis ultimately strengthened this connection. Italy rejected French suggestions for joint intervention against German aggression in Austria. In both Czechoslovak crises the two Axis partners cooperated smoothly and effectively.

After the settlement of the Sudeten Crisis, Germany made a temporarily successful effort to improve relations with France. On 6 December, the two governments decreed their respective frontiers as inviolable, and pledged to submit further misunderstandings to consultation. Germany made similar good-will gestures to Great Britain, also with favorable, if temporary, results. On 30 September, Chamberlain and Hitler pledged never again to let Germany and Great Britain wage war against each other and to submit future controversies to consultation. This era of good feelings failed to survive Germany's anti-Jewish pogroms of 10 November, which appalled and repelled the British public and government.

Germany's relations with Poland rested on the agreement of 1934, which both governments appeared to value. A few thorny issues and occasional incidents marred exemplary relations. Mutual complaints and recriminations involving the alleged mistreatment of Polish and German minorities, respectively, were endemic, and the expulsion of large numbers of Polish Jews from Germany in October caused consternation in Warsaw. But reciprocal diplomatic visits, and close consultations during the Sudeten Crisis by far outweighed the negative factors in German-Polish relations.

Germany's connections with Yugoslavia were amicable in 1938. Yugoslavia placed absolutely no diplomatic obstacles in Germany's path during the Austrian and the Czechslovak crises. In gratitude, Hitler proclaimed the German-Yugoslav frontiers inviolable, and showered economic benefits on Belgrade.

Goga's dismissal and Codreanu's execution caused consternation in Berlin, but Germany needed Romania's support, especially as a counterfoil against a possibly intransigent Hungary. Hitler received King Carol in Berlin on 24 November amid great pomp and circumstance. In contrast, the USSR bore the brunt of Germany's displeasure and invective during 1938. These sentiments were reflected in worsening commercial contacts, and in the exclusion of the Soviet Union from all aspects of the Austrian and Sudeten problems. The USSR had no voice in the decision-making process involving the two crises, and thus remained in diplomatic limbo throughout that year.

Seemingly normal, superficially friendly, German-Hungarian relations concealed hostile undercurrents. Three issues perturbed Hungarian statesmen: the spectacular and rapid rise of German power and prestige in the Danube Basin; Germany's proximity to Hungary following the Austrian *Anschluss*; and the relatively meager territorial gains achieved through the 2 November Vienna awards. Germany, on the other hand, feared that Hungarian opportunism would prevail over fidelity to the German cause. Hitler's suggestion in September that Hungary invade Czechoslovakia while the Chancellor negotiated had dismayed Hungarian statesmen. Upon the attack, Germany would terminate the talks, which Hitler had not desired in the first place, join the assault, and then the two allies would liquidate and partition Czechoslovakia. Hungarian leaders were struck with the coldbloodedness of the proposal. They noted Hitler's attempt to cast Hungary into the role of international villain, while at the same time the Führer reduced Germany's risks. Thereafter, Hungarian diplomats became extremely suspicious of German "suggestions."

On the surface, of course, German-Hungarian political and economic contacts proceeded amicably. There were frequent visits by statesmen and delegations. But throughout this year, Hungary tried to apply the brake to the Third Reich's inroads into eastern Europe. At the same time, however, the government saw the wisdom of harnessing German might not only to ensure restoration of Hungary's pre-World War I frontiers, but to help defend Hungary against the looming bolshevik menace and possible internal upheavals by the impoverished urban and rural lower classes.

On the other side of the coin, however, Hungarian statesmen knew only too well that Germany welcomed their country as a participant in the impending New Order—albeit as a junior member—only as long as they obeyed Germany's economic and political demands unquestioningly. Refusal would render Hungary expendable and transform it into a possible victim. Hitler had alternative plans. He could "leapfrog" over Hungary, and befriend Hungary's chief rivals, Romania and Yugoslavia. Hungarian statesmen recognized the perils of Nazi imperialism. Unlimited German hegemony in the area would interfere with Hungary's plans to become a regional power in the Danube Basin.

Italy, upon which Hungary depended to moderate German power in eastern Europe, proved unable to carry out this task, and became progressively more subservient to Germany. Mussolini entrusted Italy's destiny to the Rome-Berlin Axis, in view of his country's awkward strategic position. Control of the Suez Canal and Gibraltar enabled Great Britain to confine Italian forces in the Mediterranean theater. Only imports from Germany, Hungary, Romania, Bulgaria, and Yugoslavia would be secure in wartime. Since Italy lacked raw materials, none of these powers could satisfy all of Italy's requirements fully except coal. Faith in a German victory and ideological considerations overcame Mussolini's doubts in Italy's capability to cope strategically and economically.

Throughout 1938, Italy's decision to cleave to Germany bore ample fruit. Italy had resigned from the League of Nations on 11 December 1937, and thereafter treated the international body with contempt. Mussolini supported Hitler's aggressions against Austria and Czechoslovakia, and consequently gained considerable international prestige. By year's end, nearly every country had recognized Italy's Ethiopian conquest and accepted Victor Emmanuel's emperorship. But by 1938, Italy's impotence in eastern Europe had also become evident, and was noted particularly by Hungarian policymakers. Mussolini's soothing pro-Hungarian rhetoric and plans for an Italian and Polish-sponsored cordon sanitaire, the so-called "Horizontal Axis," to contain Germany, were empty talk. In this year, Hungary lost all its illusions about Italy, and recognized that only Germany's good will stood between Hungary and an unprecedented catastrophe.

Yugoslavia's position resembled Poland's in one important respect in 1938. Yugoslav statesmen wanted to preserve their country's maneuverability by forging tighter bonds with neighbors, but they did not wish to abandon existing commitments or alliances. Romania remained Yugoslavia's closest ally. Mutual visits and consultations, particularly at the Little Entente's Şinaia Conference in May, characterized their intimate relationship. The recently concluded Italian-Yugoslav agreement bred an excellent understanding that remained undisturbed by the dramatic events later that year. Italy's intermediary efforts made a rapprochement between Yugoslavia and Germany possible. Far from being upset by the *Anschluss*, Yugoslavs sighed with relief as the threat of a Habsburg restoration vanished. Yugoslavia seemed unworried about having the Third Reich as a neighbor on its western frontier. In contrast, however, during the Czechoslovak crises, when the government remained benevolently neutral, the Yugoslav public sided with the Czechoslovaks and condemned rapacious German behavior and its own government's inaction.

Germany assigned primary importance to maintaining Yugoslavia's friendship. In matters of exports and imports, the Germans offered the Yugoslavs preferential treatment. Nor did Germany object to Yugoslavia's energetic repression of Nazism among Yugoslavia's German minority. The reasons for this favoritism were obvious. By dominating Yugoslavia economically, the Third Reich hoped to establish a firm presence on the shores of the Adriatic Sea, impose its will on Italy and Romania, and intimidate Hungary into more cooperative behavior.

Relations with France progressed in inverse proportion to Yugoslavia's pro-German diplomatic and economic orientation, and in defiance of the Yugoslav public's pro-French sympathies. Friendly relations persisted throughout 1938 with Great Britain. Polish-Yugoslav relations suffered during the Munich Crisis, thanks to Poland's seizure of Czechoslovak territory. In general, however, the Yugoslav public did not condemn the Poles too severely for betraying fellow-Slavs.

After the accession of Prime Minister Milan Stojadinović, Yugoslavia's relations with Hungary improved steadily, due mostly to the exertions of Germany and Italy. The latter two countries wanted to forge an unbroken chain of eastern European states closely linked to the Rome-Berlin Axis. Hungary and Yugoslavia were not overly enthusiastic about an Axis-sponsored rapprochement. Both feared the loss of their freedom of action and sovereignty, and dreaded their eventual *Gleichschaltung* into the Nazi-Fascist political-economic imperium. They prudently moderated their formerly venomous press campaigns, however, and offered concessions to each others' minorities.

This spirit of reconciliation, which reached its zenith at the Little Entente's Bled Conference in August, brought about Hungary's partial reconciliation with the Little Entente, particularly with Yugoslavia. The Little Entente recognized Hungary's right to rearm, and renounced the use of force to achieve national objectives. Additionally, Romania, Yugoslavia and Hungary conceded that the condition of their respective minorities was unsatisfactory, and promised long-term solutions to eliminate all grievances. Although some of the conference protocols remained unsigned, Hungary and Yugoslavia regarded the provisions on the treatment of minorities as binding on both parties. Their press commented favorably on this bilateral decision.

From Hungary's point of view, the agreement with Yugoslavia formed an important part of broader Hungarian diplomacy. Hungary's attendance at the Bled Conference might have angered German statesmen, who suspected a Hungarian betrayal, but the accommodation ensured the virtual isolation of Czechoslovakia from its two allies, and hence paved the way for Hungary's participation in the dismemberment of that country without fear of attack by Romania and/or Yugoslavia. In Berlin, Budapest argued plausibly that, inasmuch as Germany had forbidden Hungary to recover Yugoslav-held Hungarian soil, Hungary had a duty to ensure the best possible treatment for Yugoslavia's ethnic Magyars, and to secure a risk-free intervention in Czechoslovakia.

Hungarian judgment proved accurate. Although in November the Yugoslav public condemned Hungarian acquisition of Czechoslovak territory, the Yugoslav government kept the peace and allowed the First Czechoslovak Republic to expire without a murmur. Within a few days of these events, on 11 November, Hungary and Yugoslavia transacted business as usual, and extended their 1936 commercial agreement by six months.

The events of 1938 demonstrated that, in view of the prevailing international amorality, national objectives could be best reached by abandoning orthodox and traditional diplomacy in favor of *Realpolitik* and irredentism. For all their short-term benefits, however, such chaotic and disruptive policies, especially when harnessed to National Socialist nihilism, carried the seeds of self-destruction, as Hungary's leaders discovered eventually, to their sorrow and dismay.

CHAPTER VII

HUNGARY'S ECONOMIC PROBLEMS IN 1938

The economic revival of 1937 enabled Hungary to block German pressures to force the country into the orbit of the Third Reich. The recession of 1938 placed Hungary at the mercy of Germany once again, although the German connection offered certain tangible benefits to Hungarian agricultural producers and government planners. Agricultural sales slumped to their lowest level since the Great Depression of 1929, yet Germany remained a dependable and stable consumer for nearly every product that Hungarian growers cultivated. Every food item raised in Hungary would fill less than 5% of Germany's total requirements. Germany's generous purchases benefited not only the producers of Hungary's bountiful and high quality 1938 harvest, but the country's entire economy enjoyed the ripple effects of full pockets and emptied granaries. For the first time since the 1929 Depression and its dreary aftermath, many Hungarian farmers were able to recoup their financial losses.[1]

Most Hungarians ignored the fact that their country would have to pay a steep political price for enjoying these economic benefits. By the beginning of 1938, German industrial imports dominated the Hungarian marketplace, and a larger proportion of Hungarian agricultural produce than ever before reached German consumers. The Hungarian National Bank accumulated a tremendous surplus of German Marks, because Hungarian exports exceeded German imports by a huge margin. (See Table 1) As a result, Germany began coercing Hungary to purchase unwanted consumer goods at artificially inflated prices. (See Table 2) A debtor country such as Germany could and did exploit weaker countries on current accounts to liquidate old, even prewar, debts.[2] This practice caused much bitterness in Hungary.

By 1938, therefore, Germany had thoroughly entwined Hungary in its economic tentacles. A contemporary observer noted: "It is easy to imagine the disastrous consequences which a sudden [German] decision to stop purchases would produce [in Hungary]."[3] For economic reasons, no less than political, Hungary dared not risk losing Germany as its chief agricultural client. As a price of support, the Third Reich demanded large-scale Hungarian arms purchases, whereas the Darányi government would have preferred to

proceed cautiously in view of the immense expenses of the armaments involved.[4] Germany, however, insisted on eliminating most
of its debts with Hungary by selling weaponry. Eventually, Darányi
had to accept this costly approach to appease the Germans. On 5
March 1938, he announced that Hungary would soon launch the
so-called Győr Program, an ambitious five-year one-billion Pengő
rearmament plan.[5]

Rearmament had unwholesome spinoff effects. Hungary's new-
found agricultural prosperity did not suffice to cover the vast sums
required to rearm the country. Darányi reluctantly increased tax-
ation on Hungary's large landowners and manufacturers. This was
risky policy, because Hungary's landed interests were the main pil-
lars of the country's social order, and alienating them ran the risk
of inviting political instability. (See Tables 3 and 3A) Worse still
for the large estates was Darányi's announcement that the government would soon attempt to help the hard-pressed landed and landless peasants through major land reform. These peasants were the
worst victims of the Depression, and the harsh economic climate of
1938 left them in desperate straights. Darányi hoped that the large
landowners would voluntarily surrender parts of their estates to help
the peasants. Leaving them in misery might lead to insurrection.
Hungary's native National Socialist parties agitated successfully for
support among the ethnic Magyar peasants by promising them fundamental land reform if elected. Unless the government helped the
peasants in time with the cooperation of the large landed interests, Hungary might suffer a native National Socialist revolution
that would overthrow the present conservative regime, and forfeit
Hungary's political sovereignty to the Third Reich.[6]

Bowing to intense German pressure, Darányi's Győr Program
also promised to introduce anti-Jewish legislation to curtail the alleged excessive economic influence of Hungary's Jews. This announcement had a disastrous effect on the peasantry. According
to a well-informed German Foreign Ministry observer, Darányi's
scheme caused a panic among Hungary's Jewish petty financiers.
They immediately revoked or curtailed numerous small loans, upon
which Hungary's small farmers depended for remaining solvent.[7]
German meddling in Hungary's internal affairs thus had created
a chain-reaction compounding social, economic, and political difficulties, from which the country never recovered during the Horthy
era.

Darányi had little choice in proclaiming these plans, even
though they had no rational justification in a globally depressed
economy. In the late 1930s' Hungary, however, common sense fre-

quently had to yield to political necessity, both domestic and foreign. The Hungarian government had to convince Hitler, who disliked and distrusted the country's leaders, that Hungary was determined to rearm, as much to actively assist the Führer's expansionist policies as to ensure a fair share of the spoils for Hungary, and to enable German arms to balance the Third Reich's trade deficit. The projected anti-Jewish legislation was also counter-productive. Hitler had been demanding a radical solution of Hungary's "Jewish problem" for some years. Hitherto, the government had ignored German entreaties. Recently, however, it had become apparent that the government party would lose the support of its small but influential ultraconservative wing unless it curtailed Jewish economic activity in Hungary. Darányi finally succumbed to the internal and external pressures clamoring for action against the Jews.

Intensive trade with Germany also caused difficulties of a different type in Hungary. About 80% of the country's export to Germany was regulated by clearing agreements. By 1938, Hungary could no longer fill Germany's export deficit with suitable imports. Germany would not part with certain strategic raw materials or machinery that Hungary needed. Other European industrial countries, on the other hand, refused to extend Hungary credit, and demanded payment in hard currency upon delivery. Hungary, however, lacked cash or gold reserves.[8] Throughout 1938, Germany required deliveries of mounting quantities of agricultural commodities from Hungary. Unable to dispose of its agricultural surpluses elsewhere, and lacking either cash or credit to purchase industrial goods on the open market, Hungary was being swept involuntarily into compliance with Germany's growing demands. The late 1930s witnessed the economic envelopment of Hungary and its *Gleichschaltung* into the Third Reich's political-economic orbit.

The best way to appreciate the extent of Hungary's economic dependency on Germany in 1938 is to survey the situation the year before, when wheat and wheat flour comprised Hungary's principal agricultural export commodities. In 1937, Hungarian wheat and flour surpluses flowed in immense quantities to Austria and Italy, Hungary's two Rome Protocols allies. Both countries had agreed to pay Hungary premium prices. Italy obligated itself to purchase one-million quintals of wheat annually at about twice the global price. Italy also exercised the option to buy an additional one-million quintal of wheat, and pledged to reimburse its ally for any losses if the latter quantity had to be sold elsewhere at a cheaper price. With Italian backing, Austria promised to purchase 2.2 million quintals of wheat or wheat flour at only a slightly lower price than Italy's.

These arrangements also included highly preferential secret credit and transport subsidies that enabled Hungary to reap handsome profits. In all, Hungary sold 3.5 million quintals of wheat and .5 million quintals of wheat flour to these two countries in 1937, or over 80% of Hungary's total output of these two commodities.[9] Italy and Austria were practicing economic bribery pure and simple in Hungary. Both countries wanted to keep Hungary out of Germany's orbit—Austria out of the necessity of sheer survival, whereas Italy wanted to create a satellite zone in the Balkans before Germany became strong enough to challenge Italian supremacy. This explains why Germany's share of Hungarian wheat and wheat flour was only about 8% that year. The Third Reich paid Hungary only 30% above world market prices for these two items in 1937.[10] The German-Hungarian trade agreement, struck in the midst of the Depression in 1931, and then renewed in 1934 and 1937, lacked the lucrative fringe benefits the Rome Protocols arrangement provided.

For Hungary, this opportunistic economic policy made eminent sense. Shunting valuable agricultural resources into the relatively unprofitable German market in 1937 would have destroyed Hungary's most profitable postwar moneymaking opportunity to date. To prevent any chance of this occurring, the Hungarian National Bank ordered the suspension of certain shipments to Germany through various bureaucratic expedients. These schemes worked well, but only as long as Hungary could gain access to other than German markets.[11]

The Third Reich resented Hungary for turning a quick profit and abandoning an old and trusted friend and ally. Germany had subsidized chronically depressed Hungarian agriculture and rescued the country's tottering economy for years. After November 1937, German leaders grew tired of Hungarian behavior. Hitler placed Germany on a war footing and proclaimed domestic autarchy, followed by the regimentation and incorporation into the Third Reich's orbit of all the small east European agricultural economies. Fortunately for Hitler, Hungary's economic bonanza faded later in 1937, as international agricultural prices began to sag in the summer, and virtually collapsed by year's end.

At this point, Hungary's excellent economic performance proved counterproductive. In December 1937, The League of Nations Financial Committee issued a progress report based on Hungary's spectacular economic achievements a few months earlier. It drew favorable attention to Hungary's balanced budget, and lauded the Hungarian government's generous offers for the retirement of the bulk of Hungary's debts. Foreign creditors gratefully lined up to enjoy these windfalls. On the basis of the faithful performance of Hungary's duties to the international community, in fact to the Western powers and their smaller allies, the League Council in January 1938 terminated the office of the Financial Committee's representative in Budapest as of 31 March. The League also discontinued the post of Adviser to the National Bank on 31 January. Hungary had regained control over its finances, but it lost the League's protection against the perils of bearish market forces, or against the quasi-legal exploitations of an unscrupulous country such as Germany.[12]

Hungary, which had clearly miscalculated the stability of the world market, realized too late to appreciate the negative repercussions of Italy's decline, and minimized the political consequences of that weakness for the survival of Austria. Italy's financial exhaustion, caused by the costly Ethiopian venture, the expensive Spanish Civil War, and large-scale rearmament expenditures, severely curtailed Italian power just as the depression of 1938 struck again. While Germany grew vigorous by swallowing Austria and later that year the most prosperous parts of Czechoslovakia, Italy had to abandon its extravagant dreams in the Balkans, and surrender economic and political leadership in the region to Germany. The Rome Protocols were dead, Italian power had evaporated, and Hungary found itself totally at the mercy of a vastly strengthened Third Reich considerably annoyed at Hungary's economic "betrayal" of 1937.[13]

With the disappearance of Austria in March 1938, Italy's strategic and commercial advantages in the Danube Basin crumbled. Italy had to yield the economic field to Germany throughout the region, particularly since Great Britain and France also gradually conceded control of east-central and southeastern Europe to the Third Reich.[14] After the Munich Conference in September of 1938, German appeasement dominated the thinking of Western statesmen. The British and French permitted Germany to stake out the entire area as its economic sphere of influence. Although French and British investments continued to flow into the Balkans at a relatively high rate throughout 1938, the two Western partners made it crystal clear that they sought no competition with Germany, and would make every effort to shun a confrontation.[15]

These fundamental geopolitical changes meant that Hungary had to swallow several bitter economic pills in 1938, apart from enduring the negative consequences of the agricultural downturn that year. By early 1938, Italy's economic support slipped away. In March, Hungary lost Austria as an important sovereign trade partner, the only friendly industrialized country able to offer Hungary the consumer products Germany withheld. Throughout 1938,

France and Great Britain ignored Hungary's economic difficulties, and concentrated on placing their investments in countries they hoped to rescue from total German domination. For a short while, Czechoslovakia, Romania, Yugoslavia, Turkey, and Greece derived some minor benefits from this policy. Even the most confirmed Anglophiles in Hungary had to concede that their country had been abandoned by the West. Following the *Anschluss* and Munich, Hungary lost the battle of free choice between the West or the Axis. After September 1938, Hungarian commercial sovereignty had become a fiction. Economic policy for Hungary was fashioned in Berlin. Hungary might procrastinate, but eventually had to obey the Third Reich.[16]

Hungary had no choice but to accept the Third Reich's economic tyranny in 1938. In that year, Germany changed tactics. Hitherto, the Third Reich had exercised political and economic coercion upon countries selected to be in its orbit. Now, it resorted to outright aggression and threats of war as a penalty for noncompliance. Such punitive measures, inflicted upon the region's two highly industrialized countries, Austria and Czechoslovakia, tremendously increased Germany's potential to wage large-scale war, force the remaining agricultural states of central and eastern Europe into cooperation, and deter the Western powers from further interference. All of these small eastern European countries competed with each other to be in the Third Reich's good graces. The Germans played Machiavellian politics with them all.

What made the situation difficult for these small states and easy for Germany was the fact that the former were agricultural competitors, and Germany was the only consumer able to absorb their entire production. After Munich, the Third Reich was also the only industrial producer in continental Europe that could supply these agricultural states. As a result, Germany demanded that their trade policies, delivery schedules, qualities, and volumes conformed strictly to the Third Reich's specifications. Hungary could not afford to be outmaneuvered by its competitors in eastern Europe, especially Romania and Yugoslavia. Germany's imports and exports with some of these countries grew tremendously after 1933. (See Tables 4 and 5) One contemporary observer noted that after the *Anschluss*, Germany enveloped the region east of Austria and brought all the countries under its economic and political tutelage.[17] Or, as *The Economist* explained the situation, with the acquisition of Austria and Czechoslovakia, the two leading industrial countries east of Germany, the Third Reich's economic position in the remainder of the region was so strong that the small countries there

found it impossible to escape the German orbit by normal, orthodox methods, so enmeshed had they become in Germany's clearing
system.[18]

The Austrian *Anschluss* and the acquisition of the Sudetenland
half a year later enabled Germany to derive other benefits that
weakened the independence of Hungary and the other countries of
eastern Europe. These annexations temporarily solved Germany's
clearing difficulties. Austria and Czechoslovakia were creditors to
their eastern neighbors, had large-scale investments in Hungarian,
Romanian, and Yugoslav banking houses, and held large shares in
a variety of food processing and small manufacturing enterprises.
Now that these assets were in German hands, the Third Reich expanded its ownership in selected strategic industries throughout the
region. In other words, instead of relieving their trading partners'
dependency by using the seized assets to retire their own indebtedness, the Germans utilized these funds to infiltrate their victims'
non-agricultural sectors.[19]

Great Britain and France had not realized the full implications
of the Third Reich's economic imperialism until after the *Anschluss*.
By then, they could not prevent the success of Germany's economic
imperialism. The two Western allies were confused and indecisive,
and were unable to present a unified front to German expansion.
They did not want the Germans to dominate the Balkans exclusively, but neither did they wish to give the Third Reich cause
to complain about Western interference. The feeble Anglo-French
trade offensive, launched in the wake of the April 1938 London Conference, could not overcome Germany's overwhelming advantages.
Such half-hearted efforts as Great Britain's purchase of 200,000 tons
of grain from Yugoslavia at world market price, proved an entirely
insufficient gesture to reverse the German economic tide.[20] After
Munich, France and Great Britain diminished commercial ties, not
only with Hungary, but with Romania and Yugoslavia as well, even
though all three countries wished to continue trading with them.
The two Western powers had surrendered the region to Germany
at Munich by default. Now they feared offending Hitler, and soon
reduced even their restricted commercial presence in the region to
a mere token.[21]

The Munich Conference had eliminated France and Great
Britain as power brokers in eastern Europe. Hungary rapidly adjusted its policies and tactics to reflect the new situation.[22] During
a 14 October 1938 conversation between Hitler and ex-prime minister Kálmán Darányi, the Imrédy government's plenipotentiary,
economic matters also emerged. Hungarian statesmen feared that

Germany's economic demands would prove unreasonable. The past few years had amply demonstrated that Germany desired as much cereals and other food products as could be extracted from the Hungarians, and that each trade negotiation session brought demands for bargains. Hungary was weighing the possible advantages of concluding a long-range trade pact with the Third Reich to stabilize their economic relationship. Such an idea had surfaced during Darányi's recent discussions with Reich Minister for Food and Agriculture Walter Darré. Darányi inquired what Hitler thought of Darré's suggestion that future German-Hungarian economic and trade agreements ought to cover a decade or more. Hitler agreed that such long-term arrangements would be helpful. He urged German and Hungarian negotiators to explore the scheme further.

A long-range economic accommodation favored Germany's plans to rearm Hungary. For the past few years, Germany had been insisting that its huge trade deficits with Hungary be reduced by armament sales. Hungary, on the other hand, had demanded consumer goods and essential raw materials. Darányi capitulated. He assured Hitler that Hungary was ready to purchase weaponry in large quantities from Germany and Italy, either by making barter arrangements or on credit. Hitler appeared pleased with this changed Hungarian attitude that implied a long-range commitment, and expected the details to be formulated during subsequent negotiations.[23]

Neither Germany nor Hungary believed that a trade agreement of ten years' duration was feasible. Darányi had to demonstrate Hungary's interest in a long-term relationship with Germany, and show confidence in German initiatives. Sagging German-Hungarian relations needed a boost. Hungary had defied Germany all too often in the past. During Munich, Hungarians had spoiled Hitler's plan for a German-Hungarian-Polish lightning strike against Czechoslovakia. Hitler had been forced to negotiate because in the last minute Hungarian leaders had taken fright. To his chagrin, Hitler had to conclude an unwanted agreement with France and Great Britain, lest he appear as a warmonger. Hitler had wanted to occupy all of western Czechoslovakia by the fall of 1938. Instead, that country was severely crippled but survived. Thanks to alleged Hungarian trickery or cowardice, the destruction of Czechoslovakia had to be postponed, which in turn interfered with Hitler's timetable for subduing eastern Europe. By committing Hungary to serve Germany's economic needs for ten years or more, Darányi hoped to persuade Hitler that Hungary was repentant and desired a long-term commitment to Germany. Acquiring armaments from the two Axis powers,

Darányi hoped, would signal Hungary's eagerness to participate in future military operations on Germany's side. Convincing Hitler of Hungary's benevolent intentions in trade and war had a special significance in the weeks following the Munich Pact. Only Hitler could ensure that Hungary received a "fair" share of present and future Czechoslovak spoils. Hitler would not let Hungary go empty-handed in any event, but his restored faith in Hungary might bring unexpected windfalls.[24]

Following this meeting, Hungary provided further proof of its determination to serve German interests, even to the point of transforming the structure of the country's industrial and agricultural infrastructure. On 21 November 1938, Sztójay notified the German Foreign Ministry of major impending changes in Hungarian economic and foreign policy. Hungary would soon cooperate more closely with the Rome-Berlin Axis, especially economically, would shortly join the anti-Comintern Pact, and hinted that Hungary might be persuaded to resign from the League of Nations.[25]

Emil K. J. Wiehl, director of the German Foreign Ministry's economic bureau, analyzed the content of Sztójay's 21 November statement. Sztójay had proposed a rationally coordinated plan that would permit Germany and Hungary to exploit each others' productive capacities for their mutual benefit. Hungary pledged to intensify the production of agricultural staples that Germany regarded as essential, and to introduce new crops, such as cotton, hemp, flax, wool, soybeans and lucerne. Hungary would also curtail its industrialization plans, and terminate the manufacture of such non-profitable items as automobile parts, in order to create a viable market in Hungary for German industrial products. Hungary expected no adjustments in Germany's industrial or agricultural output, because Hungary could use every possible item presently manufactured or grown in the Third Reich. Sztójay also suggested the conclusion of long-range economic agreements, that would specify firmly established quantities, delivery schedules, and prices. He pointed out, for example, the immense advantages Germany would derive if Hungary kept former Austria supplied with cereal products in exchange for timber.

Theoretically, Wiehl believed, Sztójay's plan would benefit both countries. In practice, however, success depended on whether Hungary indeed could, or would, transform its agricultural establishment efficiently and promptly, and whether the country was truly willing to curtail the production of superfluous industrial products. Off-the-record comments by various Hungarian cabinet members suggested that the government intended to execute these plans. Despite these hopeful auguries, however, Wiehl doubted the plan could succeed in the foreseeable future. For years, Hungarian imports had been enjoying secretly kept preferential tariffs in Germany. This traffic now averaged 45% of Hungary's annual capacity. If new agreements should reveal the existence of these preferential tariffs, then countries with which Germany had been trading on the basis of most favored nation principles would demand similar advantages for themselves. Germany and Hungary would require the forging of a customs union. Italy, however, would balk at such a plan. A thoroughly integrated German-Hungarian system dominated by Germany would be the only viable economic scheme. Germany would have to control the Hungarian economy, and eventually the German Mark would have to replace the Pengö as Hungary's legal tender. In Wiehl's view, this plan was unrealistic because it would cause the virtual disappearance of Hungarian sovereignty.[26]

Wiehl's views harmonized with those of most German statesmen. They were well-acquainted with Hungarian fears regarding sovereignty questions. On 26 July 1938, Baron Johann Plessl, a German official attached to the German Embassy in Rome, analyzed Imrédy's impressions after meeting with Italian leaders. Plessl thought that the Hungarian prime minister's publicly professed pro-German sentiments were misleading. Privately, Imrédy feared growing German influence in Hungary. Imrédy confided to Plessl that the *Anschluss* had exposed Hungary to the perils of exclusive German economic domination. He insisted that no sovereign Hungarian government would ever tolerate such an imposition.[27] At the time, Imrédy was still an Anglophile, and hence his opinions had to be judged accordingly. Germany's leaders realized that Hungary's dominant economic and political élite would not voluntarily permit the cessation of the country's hard-fought sovereignty. Events in the near future would prove the accuracy of this prediction. Within months, it would claim the by then excessively pro-German Imrédy as its first victim.

Hungary's economic negotiations with Germany in 1938 should not be viewed in isolation. Their outcome in Germany's favor had resulted from the profound geopolitical changes that had occurred in east-central Europe after the liquidation of Austria and Czechoslovakia. Hungarian leaders were deeply concerned about the disappearance of these two states, both of which had served as convenient buffers against German might. These developments altered how Hungarians viewed the Germans, the Italians, the Little Entente states, and their own country. The new reality was that the entire east-central European land mass was suddenly dominated by Germany.

Basic Hungarian strategy remained unchanged. It was to slow, but not totally arrest, German extension over Danubian Europe. Hungary supported some type of collective regional economic, political, and strategic accommodation to counteract exclusive German hegemony in the area. In 1938, Hungarian diplomats used delaying tactics and petty obstructionism to slow Germany's pace. Budapest defied the harsh economic terms the Germans had imposed on Hungary, bolstered the crumbling Little Entente, and continued trading with the Western powers.

TABLE 1

Germany's Indebtedness to Hungary 1934 - 1939
(in millions)

1934 - 1935	7.5 DM
1935 - 1936	10.6 DM
1936 - 1937	18.3 DM
1937 - 1938	23.3 DM
1938 - 1939	26.0 DM

Source: Berend & Ránki, *Magyarország a fasiszta Németország életterében*, pp. 173-174.

TABLE 2
Hungarian and German Imports and Exports 1933 - 1937

Year	Imports			Exports		
	1000P	Index	% of Total Imports	1000P	Index	% of Total Exports
1933	61,507	100	19.7	43,701	100	11.2
1934	63,025	103	18.3	89,866	205	22.2
1935	91,295	148	22.7	108,098	247	23.9
1936	113,353	184	26.0	115,198	263	22.8
1937	125,352	204	25.9	141,334	323	24.1

Source: *Ibid.*, p. 175.

TABLE 3

Distribution of Land by Size of Holdings in Trianon Hungary, 1935[1]

Size in holds[2]	Number of holdings	Percent of holdings	Total area (1,000 holds)	(1,000 hectares)	Percent of area
Less than 1 ...	628,431	38.5	236	136	1.5
1-5	556,352	34.1	1,395	803	8.7
5-10	204,471	12.5	1,477	850	9.2
10-20	144,186	8.8	2,026	1,166	12.6
20-50	73,663	4.5	2,172	1,250	13.5
50-100	15,240	.9	1,036	596	6.4
100-200	5,792	.4	805	463	5.0
200-500	3,840	.2	1,181	679	7.3
500-1,000	1,362	.1	944	543	5.9
1,000-2,000 ...	581	.0	798	460	5.0
2,000-3,000 ...	187	.0	452	260	2.8
3,000-5,000 ...	117	.0	451	260	2,8
5,000-10,000 ..	101	.0	680	391	4.2
10,000-20,000 .	48	.0	691	398	4.3
20,000-50,000 .	25	.0	855	492	5.3
50,000-100,000	10	.0	671	386	4.2
over 100,000 ..	1	.0	209	120	1.3
Total	1,634,407	100.0	16,081[3]	9,254	100.0

Source: S. D. Zagoroff, Jenő Végh, et al., The Agricultural Economy of the Danubian Countries 1935-1945 (Stanford, 1955), p.160.

---

[1]Data from Hungary, Magyar Központi Statisztikai Hivatal, Magyarország földbirtokviszonyai 1935-ben. II. Birtok-nagyságcsoportok szerint (New Ser., Vol. 102 [1938]). See also Hungary, Magyar Központi Statisztikai Hivatal, Magyar Statisztikai Zsebkönyv, 1948, p. 103.

[2]One cadastral hold equals .5755 hectare, or 1.422 acres.

[3]Sum of rounded figures

TABLE 3A

Ownership Distribution of Land in Trianon Hungary, 1935

Category	Persons
Owners of holdings of 1-5 holds	1,093,030
Tenants of holdings of 1-5 holds	552,700
Agricultural laborers[1]with holdings of under 1 hold	271,767
Landless agricultural laborers	455,621
"Farm hands[1]"	599,622
Total	2,972,740

Source: Zagoroff, Végh, *et al., The Agricultural Economy of the Danubian Countries,* p. 161.

TABLE 4

Development in the Trade of the Seven Countries
of Central and Southeastern Europe, 1933 and 1937

Country	Exports to Germany as a Percentage of Total Exports		Imports from Germany as a Percentage of Total Imports	
	1933	1937	1933	1937
Bulgaria	36	43.1	38.2	54.8
Greece	17.9	31.0	10.2	27.1
Hungary	11.2	24.1	19.6	26.2
Romania	16.6	19.2	18.6	28.9
Yugoslavia	13.9	21.7	13.2	32.4
Austria	15.7	14.9	19.7	16.3
Czechoslovakia	20.0	15.0	19.8	15.5

Source: Adapted from Antonín Basch, *The Danube Basin and the German Economic Sphere,* p. 191.

---

[1] "Agricultural laborers" are occasionally-employed workers; "farm hands" are employed under the respective law (Act XLV, ex 1907) at least for a one-year period and are obliged to do all kinds of work on the farm.

TABLE 5

Hungarian Exports by Geographic Distribution 1925-1938

	1925-30	1929	1930	1931	1932	1933	1934	1935	1936	1937	1938
	%	%	%	%	%	%	%	%	%	%	%
Hungary's Immediate Neighbors (excluding Poland)	61.9	57.2	53.8	43.3	46.4	43.2	37.4	31.3	28.3	26.7	28.4*
Germany & Italy	17.8	18.6	23.2	23.5	22.0	19.8	30.4	37.1	36.1	36.3	36.1
Other Countries	20.3	24.2	23.0	34.2	30.6	37.0	32.2	31.6	35.6	37.0	35.5
Total	100.0	100.0	100.0	100.0	100.0	100.0	100.0	100.0	100.0	100.0	100.0

Hungary's immediate neighbors are Austria, Czechoslovakia, Romania and Yugoslavia.

*These figures do not include Austria after the Anschluss.

Compiled from *Statisztikai Havi Közlemények*, Vols. 24-41.

CHAPTER VIII

HUGARIAN FOREIGN POLICY IN 1938 - GERMANY, ITALY AND THE LITTLE ENTENTE

PART I - The Anschluss and the First Czechoslovak Crisis

For Hungary, the most important external events in 1938 included the Austrian *Anschluss* on 12-13 March, the First Czechoslovak Crisis in May, the Second Czechoslovak Crisis which culminated in the Munich Conference in September, and the First Vienna Arbitral Award of 2-3 November. The disappearance of Austria weakened Czechoslovakia's position. Hungary planned to isolate Czechoslovakia from its Little Entente allies Romania and Yugoslavia, and then hoped to dismember it with the assistance of Germany and possibly Poland. Hungarian statesmen tried to persuade Hitler and Mussolini to support Hungary's ambitious expansionary policies against the Little Entente, and endeavored to block Germany and Italy from deserting Hungary in favor of Romania and Yugoslavia.[1] The Little Entente states, on the other hand, attempted to pacify Hungary in order to deprive Germany of an important ally. Hungary, however, was determined not to be outflanked by the Little Entente states, nor to offend the Third Reich by openly negotiating with Czechoslovakia. These complicated cross-currents created what Stephen Kertesz termed "a diplomatic whirlpool" in a different East European context.

Early in the new year, Hungary's leaders queried Italy's position on several issues vital to Hungarian interests. On 4 January 1938, Mussolini assured former Hungarian prime minister Count István Bethlen that Italy would never conclude an agreement with any other country, presumably Romania, without Hungary's acquiescence.[2] *Il Duce* promised to coordinate this and other related matters with German officials. Germany and Italy would examine Hungarian grievances, decide if these complaints were justified, and help remedy legitimate problems. He hinted at issuing a joint German-Italian guarantee to protect Hungary against a Czechoslovak or Yugoslav attack. But the Italian leader omitted any specific reference to Romania, Hungary's chief antagonist at that time.[3]

Mussolini's evasiveness alarmed Hungary. Ciano intensified the unease by denouncing the Rome Protocols as "more and more impotent," because its raison d'être was based on "purely economic content."[4] In his view, economic considerations alone were insufficient to ensure the viability of any treaty. Ciano believed that Hungarian clamor for a Magyar minority protection declaration by the Little Entente would prove counterproductive. Pressure of this sort would help to preserve the Little Entente alliance. Ciano also deplored Kánya's indiscriminate hatred of all three Little Entente countries. Contempt for their leaders, especially of Romanians, would injure Hungarian interests, he thought.

The Italian leaders' apparent loss of interest in Hungary caused difficulties at the 10-12 January 1938 Budapest meeting of the Rome Protocols signatories. According to Ciano, Austria, Hungary and Italy experienced "friction on many points."[5] Ciano and Mussolini were exasperated with Austria and Hungary. Both countries were "only too ready to beg," but when it came to discharging responsibilities on Italy's behalf, they knew how "to make themselves scarce."[6] Ciano urged the two allies to support the Axis with more enthusiasm, embrace Italy's anti-Comintern crusade, and resign from the League of Nations.[7]

The final three-power communiqué tried to conceal fundamental disagreements and publicly affirmed Austro-Hungarian-Italian solidarity. In fact, however, Italy was forcing Austria and Hungary to endorse the Rome-Berlin Axis, and refused to guarantee Austria's independence. Such a pledge would offend Germany, Ciano explained. He therefore urged Austria to settle its disputes with Germany. This implied that Italy had abandoned Austria to the Germans.[8] The Hungarians realized that an independent Italian Danubian foreign policy had ceased to exist. Italy had become Germany's junior partner, whereas Austria and Hungary had become insignificant.[9]

Nearly three weeks elapsed before the Hungarians received any indications regarding Germany's latest plans concerning eastern Europe. Ernst Wilhelm Bohle, State Secretary of the German Foreign Ministry and chief of the National Socialist Party's organization for expatriate Germans, conveyed these impressions indirectly during a visit in Budapest. While there, he soothed his hosts with platitudes. His reports to the German leaders, however, criticized Hungary's statesmen. They kept harping on common German-Hungarian grievances against Czechoslovakia, he asserted. They were urging that their countries move in unison to dismember that country. In Bohle's view, this was mere bluster. Faintheartedness paralyzed Hungarian resolve every time the opportunity beckoned to settle the score with the Czechoslovaks. One of the reasons for this timidity, Bohle believed, was the Hungarians' "obsession" with being attacked by Yugoslavia while Hungary launched military operations against Czechoslovakia.

According to Bohle, Count Csáky intimated that Hungary would be willing to renounce its claim to Yugoslavia's Magyar-inhabited territories in return for Yugoslav neutrality. He expected Germany to enforce the agreement. Bohle promised to submit Csáky's proposal to his superiors in Berlin. Csáky assured Bohle that Hungary preferred having a strong and friendly German neighbor to a weak Austria. This was why Hungary did not object to the impending *Anschluss*.[10] Moreover, Hungary was convinced that Germany would never attempt annex Hungary. Bohle agreed. Hitler opposed the subjugation of non-Germans. During his five-day sojourn in Hungary, Bohle heard numerous rumors that Germany would soon abolish its pro-Hungarian policy and befriend the more cooperative Yugoslavs and ideologically congenial Romanians.[11] Back home, Bohle described Hungary as a demanding, overcautious and undependable ally. The influential Bohle's unfavorable impressions had a negative effect on Hungary's expansionary plans that could not succeed without Germany's collaboration and sympathetic support.

Hungary's first contact in 1938 with a Little Entente country occurred due to a lack of confidence in Germany and Italy, fear of Yugoslavia, and the desire to neutralize the Octavian Goga regime that King Carol of Romania had commissioned on 28 December 1937. The possible disadvantages of this political change outweighed any benefits Hungary might derive by befriending the new regime. The Little Entente alliance might be weakened and possibly disband. Under a Fascist-type dictatorship, however, Germany's and Italy's influence would be strengthened in Bucharest. Hungary's privileged strategic and economic advantages as Germany's and Italy's ally would disappear. Supported by an ideologically congenial Rome-Berlin Axis, Romania would refuse to return parts of Magyar-inhabited Transylvania to Hungary, or improve the treatment of its Magyar minority.[12] The political change in Bucharest forced Hungarian statesmen to devise a new strategy to be applied not only against Romania, but against the Little Entente alliance as a unit.

During Goga's brief ministry, Romania and Hungary wanted to maintain the illusion that uninterrupted diplomatic contacts were being maintained. Neither side wished to be blamed for having broken off relations, yet both countries tried to avoid engaging in serious negotiations on one pretext or another. Goga needed time to forge a new foreign policy, Hungary had to weigh whether the

Little Entente could survive the strains of having a member state toying with Fascism. When Kánya discovered that Romanian Foreign Minister Istrate Mîcescu wished to confer with him in Geneva around 17 January, the Hungarian foreign minister postponed his trip until mid-February, even though Romania temptingly offered to negotiate "a purely Hungarian-Romanian settlement without the participation of alien [*i.e.*, Czechoslovak and Yugoslav] elements."[13] Shortly, however, Mîcescu also changed his mind, and no longer desired an early meeting with Kánya. Kánya's caution stemmed from Italian reports that the Goga regime was unstable and verged on collapse. The last of these communications reached Kánya on 10 February. On that day the Goga government fell. The Romanian crisis was over. Another international complication directly affecting Hungary, the Austrian *Anschluss*, was barely more than one month away.

Shortly after Goga's departure, Italy suggested a tempting, albeit impractical, diplomatic grand design to Hungary. Ciano explained to Hungarian Ambassador Baron Frigyes Villani that Austria and Czechoslovakia were doomed, but that Italy did not dread sharing a common frontier with Germany. Italy would remain loyal to the Axis no matter what. Nonetheless, Italy wanted to create a defensive "horizontal axis" composed of friendly states. This organization would stretch from the Baltic shores to the Mediterranean Sea, and besides Italy consist of Yugoslavia, Hungary and Poland. The latter two countries would share a common frontier, presumably when Czechoslovakia's partition yielded Ruthenia to Hungary. The projected alliance system would not compete with Germany, but rather complement the Axis. To be effective, however, the pact had to be at least as strong as the Third Reich, yet remain on friendly terms with it. In order to expedite the plan, Ciano urged Hungary to pacify Yugoslavia immediately.[14]

On paper, Ciano's scheme sounded plausible. From a practical viewpoint, however, it was worthless. Italy could not influence the disposition of Ruthenia. Hungary could not seize that Czechoslovak province without German permission, and that was unlikely until after Germany had annexed Austria and occupied the western portion of Czechoslovakia. By then, however, Germany would be so overwhelmingly strong that no combination of states would be able to match it. A Hungarian-Yugoslav rapprochement seemed unlikely. Thus far, all Italian and German mediation efforts had failed. Without such an agreement, the horizontal axis scheme appeared doomed, even if the Third Reich approved it, which was out of the question. The matter of Slovakia, a Czechoslovak province coveted by Hungary, did not figure in Ciano's blueprint. Despite its flaws, Kánya took Ciano's scheme seriously enough to explore it with Polish leaders.[15] The prudent Kánya's lack of circumspection is difficult to explain. The foreign minister should have known that Germany would resent Hungary and distrust its involvement in a thinly disguised attempt to forge a north-south barrier that would block the Third Reich's expansion in southeastern and eastern Europe.[16]

The Goga interlude and the Third Reich's growing might forced Czechoslovakia to adopt desperate defensive measures. By the end of January, Czechoslovakia's quarrel with the Sudeten Germans and the Third Reich had reached an impasse. Czechoslovak leaders feared that Romania's Goga regime might desert the Little Entente, join the Rome-Berlin Axis and leave Czechoslovakia and Yugoslavia defenseless. Without Romania, the alliance lacked spatial continuity and thus was militarily and politically unviable. A rightist Romania would resist Soviet attempts to reinforce Czechoslovakia via Romanian soil or airspace. Hungary and Poland were hostile to Czechoslovakia, and the Western powers lacked both military power and moral resolution to deter Germany. Seeking breathing space, Beneš offered Hitler a deal. Czechoslovakia would settle all outstanding issues with Germany, prohibit Czechoslovak territory from being used as a base by any foreign power (obviously the Soviet Union) for an attack on Germany, and his country would join the struggle against Communism.[17]

For strategic reasons, Hitler accepted Beneš's proposal. The Führer desired a non-controversial, uncomplicated and smooth Austrian *Anschluss*. A frightened Czechoslovakia would precipitate a major international crisis. Hitler therefore promised to improve Germany's relations with Czechoslovakia. To prove it, Hitler ordered the Sudeten German Party to cease subversive activities, terminate its cooperation with the Slovak separatists and Slovakia's Magyar minority, and he refused to set a date for negotiations with the Hungarian general army staff regarding the coordination of military operations against Czechoslovakia. Hitler promised never to claim any Czechoslovak soil or population for the Third Reich, and pledged to keep German troops in Austria at a distance of fifteen kilometers from the Czechoslovak border.[18] While this tactical accommodation lasted, the Czechoslovaks relaxed. Hungarian policymakers, on the other hand, feared the loss of Germany's support.

The second phase in Hungary's contacts with the Little Entente occurred when the Czechoslovaks realized that political uncertainties in Romania would persist even after Goga's departure. They therefore decided to normalize relations with Hungary with or without Romania.[19] The Czechoslovaks naïvely and erroneously believed that Hungary desired a settlement with them as eagerly as they did with Hungary. Beneš magnified the consequences that Romania's instability had on Hungary, and he misinterpreted German-Hungarian tensions as signs of an irrevocable breach. Disagreements did plague German-Hungarian relations, but these stemmed partly from Hungarian impatience with the secretiveness of the Third Reich's eastern European diplomacy. Both countries concurred that the Versailles treaty system, particularly its chief creation, Czechoslovakia, must be destroyed. [20] In fact, as German strength waxed, Hungary grew more rather than less interested in enlisting German assistance to help bury the Trianon peace treaty. Consequently, Hungarian statesmen planned to treat Czechoslovakia with outward friendliness, but would try to delay negotiations in order to avoid German suspicions. In the meantime, Hungary would attempt to persuade Romania and Yugoslavia to resume bargaining. Ultimately, however, Hungary wanted to isolate and destroy Czechoslovakia.[21]

The Czechoslovak thaw toward Hungary began during Goga's ministry, and continued unabated after the installation of a moderate regime in Romania under Miron Cristea. Czechoslovakia declared the time ripe to pacify Hungary, even if negotiations had to proceed without Romania and Yugoslavia.[22] Hungary took three weeks to agree to bilateral talks,[23] but then declared that it preferred negotiating with the Little Entente as a unit.[24] The Czechoslovaks had no choice but to let one of the other Little Entente states continue negotiating for them. Romania was in the best possible position to act as proxy for Czechoslovakia.

The Cristea regime also desired bilateral negotiations with Hungary, and relied on Romania's strong and secure strategic and economic position to drive a hard bargain. The Romanians pledged to remove all obstacles to a Hungarian-Romanian agreement, and promised to inaugurate a new era in good relations. Romania threatened to withdraw, however, if Hungary insisted that Romania rectify the Transylvanian Magyar community's ethnic and economic grievances. Romania wanted to remove the minority issue from the agenda entirely, renounce the Trianon Peace Treaty minority protection clauses, and settle the grievances of Romania's minorities unilaterally. The Romanians explained that minority management was strictly an internal matter, in which Hungary had no right to interfere. The two countries, however, would solve all the other political and administrative problems that plagued their relationship.

Ambassador Bárdossy would not accept these Romanian proposals. He insisted on utilizing the earlier Geneva and Şinaia agenda that included the minority issue. Negotiations with the three Little Entente countries—singly or jointly—had to be preceded by a settlement of Magyar minority grievances. Furthermore, Hungary regarded renunciation of the minority protection clauses of the peace treaty as a flagrant violation of a binding international compact. Bárdossy thought that the Romanian government's benevolent intentions were praiseworthy but irrelevant to the minority issue. The Romanians remained non-committal, but as a good will gesture they promised to initiate negotiations with Romania's Magyar minority leaders no later than 15 March.[25]

While encouraging talks with Romania, Hungary also wished to resume negotiations with Yugoslavia, which had lapsed since Hungary's 25 November 1937 proposal to that country had remained unanswered. At that time, Hungary wanted to have its postwar frontier with Yugoslavia recognized as final, but at a price. Yugoslavia would have to remain neutral if a war erupted between Hungary and other states.[26] In other words, Hungary expected Yugoslavia to abandon Czechoslovakia. Yugoslavia ignored this offer, even though in January Hitler personally appealed to Stojadinović to accept it. Also in January, Csáky had inquired in Berlin whether Germany would guarantee Hungary's frontier with Yugoslavia. Germany responded evasively.[27] On 5 March, Kánya instructed Sztójay to revive the issue with the German Foreign Ministry. Kánya wanted to put Hungary's house in order, because he expected "serious developments in the near future;" whether this meant a German attack on Austria or on Czechoslovakia, or both, he could only guess. Kánya thought, however, that Yugoslav neutrality would be an asset in any event.[28]

Clearly, for Hungary, the road to Belgrade led through Berlin, and possibly through Rome. It was unlikely, however, that Germany would honor Hungary's persistent request to guarantee the Hungarian-Yugoslav frontier. For Germany, such a pledge was more than one ally might expect of another. This particular Hungarian plan could embroil Germany in a Hungarian-Yugoslav conflict at a time when the Third Reich lacked a common frontier with either country. Perceived Hungarian duplicity also disturbed the Germans. As the *Anschluss* approached, and afterward, Hungarian diplomats publicly rejoiced that their country would share borders with an "old, reliable friend,"[29] rather than with weakling Austria.

In fact, Hungary feared the *Anschluss*. The German envoy in Budapest reported that most Hungarians, including even "sympathetic" supporters, dreaded the nearness of the mighty Third Reich. Hungarians expected to benefit economically from the Austrian *Anschluss*, yet they only cheered when Germany threatened Czechoslovakia.[30] Hungary was the first country to congratulate Hitler on the *Anschluss* and to recognize the seizure *de jure*.[31] On 13 March, when Austria formally joined the Third Reich, Hungary's Minister of the Interior József Széll demonstrated Hungary's fear of Germany by launching a vigorous campaign to curb domestic Nazis. The Hungarian High Court extended the sentences of more than seventy convicted Hungarian Nazis by several months each.[32] The Germans retaliated by branding Hungarians as materialists. Rather than promoting ideological purity, they cynically exploited their idealistic German friends to recover a few square miles of lost territory. As a result, the Germans either ignored or remained noncommittal about Hungarian statesmen's continual pleas to guarantee Hungary's frontier against Yugoslav retaliation.[33]

Hungary prudently forbore criticizing the *Anschluss* publicly before, during and after the event. Afterward, Hungary pursued two seemingly contradictory diplomatic objectives. On the one hand, Hungary wanted to collaborate with Germany against Czechoslovakia, provided the risks of war were minimal, and then only if the Western powers condemned the action merely as a formality. On the other hand, Hungary continued negotiations with the Little Entente in order to promote frontier rectification with Czechoslovakia, or at least to alleviate the alleged mistreatment of the Magyar minority. Hungary temporarily renounced revisionist aspirations against Romania and Yugoslavia, but only because Germany and Italy wanted to patronize these two countries. In view of these limitations Hungarian negotiators tried to separate Czechoslovakia from its two allies, conclude separate treaties with the latter, and secure their neutrality in the event of action against Czechoslovakia.

Attempts to isolate Czechoslovakia and regain Hungary's lost Magyar-inhabited territories contained various elements of risk. France and the Soviet Union might honor their treaty obligations and attempt to rescue Czechoslovakia. This would precipitate a world war, which, most Hungarian leaders were convinced, Germany would lose. Horthy believed that naval supremacy would turn the tide in a global conflict, and he had no doubts that the British navy ruled the seven seas. Since most Hungarians regarded the British as a fair-minded people who belatedly regretted the "follies of Trianon" and were eager to restore "justice" in the Danubian region, Hungarian statesmen tried to avoid any action that might offend the British. Fears of being attacked by Romania and Yugoslavia while their own backs were turned greatly worried Hungarian statesmen. They had hoped that the Axis would dissuade these two powers from trying to rescue Czechoslovakia, but Little Entente unity seemed unshakeable.[34] Throughout the coming months, Hungarians pondered the question of peace or war with Czechoslovakia on the basis of whether the possible gains justified the risks of starting a world war. Incurring the wrath of the Western powers, especially of Great Britain, seemed foolhardy.

The Little Entente, the two major Western powers, and the Soviet Union were aware of the Hungarians' uncertainties. They warned the revisionist countries that the Western alliance would firmly oppose any separate or joint hostile act against Czechoslovakia by either Germany, Hungary, or Poland. On 17 March, Hungarian Ambassador Szilárd Masirevich advised Kánya that the general staffs of the three Little Entente countries had decided to launch a joint military action in case of an attack by any country. Masirevich counseled Kánya to take this sign of solidarity seriously.[35]

France probably planted this information to frighten Hungary into inaction. Ambassador Gaston Maugras informed Kánya the next day that the French worried about the perils confronting Czechoslovakia. The Ambassador tried to wring information from Kánya regarding any hostile moves Germany planned against Czechoslovakia. Kánya's claim that a German attack against that country was unlikely in the near future failed to reassure Maugras. He retorted that Germany's intentions must surely be aggressive, because the Third Reich would not permit Czechoslovakia and Hungary to conclude an accord, even if Hungary desired an accommodation.[36]

The same day, Soviet Foreign Commissar Maksim Litvinov proclaimed the USSR's determination to help stamp out aggression anywhere, and promised to invoke the alliance with France and Czechoslovakia in the event of an unprovoked attack anywhere.[37] Great Britain belatedly joined the interventionists on 22 May. British Ambassador Nevile Henderson explained in Berlin the absolute need for a peaceful resolution of the Czechoslovak crisis, and warned Poland that its application of force in Czechoslovakia would have "incalculable consequences." The British ambassador stationed in Rome informed Ciano that any aggression launched against Czechoslovakia would compel France to honor its treaty obligations, and that Great Britain would support its continental ally.[38]

During the First Czechoslovak Crisis, Germany heeded these

warnings and avoided an armed conflict with France, Great Britain and the Soviet Union. In the early phase of the crisis the Germans had been confident that no country would defend Czechoslovakia. British and French resolve to fight left German leaders shocked and discouraged.[39] Once the initial dismay had worn off, however, Germany became more than ever resolved to destroy that country.[40] Hitler no doubt heeded a pro-German British politician's counsel on how to liquidate Czechoslovakia: "You mustn't shoot, but strangling is fine!"[41] This explains why Ernst von Weizsäcker, a German Foreign Ministry official, rejected Sztójay's 19 May suggestion to launch a simultaneous German-Hungarian attack on Czechoslovakia. Sztójay conceded that such a conflict would not remain localized, but he assured Weizsäcker that nonetheless, Hungary "would in that case have to act, and act promptly."[42] Sztójay, a noted "hawk," most likely acted without his government's knowledge or approval. The Germans assumed that he was following instructions. They came to regard the Hungarians as irresponsible and impetuous. As a result, they kept Hungarian statesmen in the dark regarding their own battle plans and timetables.[43]

In view of German taciturnity and secretiveness, Hungary's diplomatic position turned awkward. Until the end of May, when the First Czechoslovak Crisis terminated peacefully, Hungarian diplomats had pursued two objectives. First, they wanted to entice Romania and Yugoslavia to the bargaining table, settle the Magyar minority issue in both countries satisfactorily, persuade them to formally recognize Hungary's right to rearm, and obtain neutrality guarantees in case of a joint German-Hungarian campaign against Czechoslovakia. Second, they wished to avoid settling outstanding grievances with Czechoslovakia. The Hungarians would have preferred a surgical solution, possibly a limited war and dismemberment of Czechoslovakia. Hungarians saw no point in effecting a reconciliation with an intended victim.

György Ránki has pointed out, however, that Hungarians also entertained a third option. They realized that Hungary might have to settle for a far more modest territorial accommodation with the Little Entente than they had planned. In this scenario, Germany and Italy would have no role to play. By then, Pál Teleki and István Bethlen regarded Italian promises of support of Hungary as ambiguous,[44] involvement with Germany as dangerous, and confrontation with Great Britain as a perilous military gamble. After the Kiel Conference, Horthy and Kánya fully appreciated the wisdom of this viewpoint.[45] Others, such as Csáky and Sztójay, believed in an ultimate German victory, and sought to involve Hungary in a war on Germany's side, regardless of the cost.[46]

The third phase of Hungary's talks with the Little Entente resumed on 18 March. Apparently, Hungary's efforts to involve Yugoslavia in the talks had borne some fruit. The Romanian foreign ministry acquainted Ambassador Bárdossy with the Little Entente's counterproposal to Hungary's August 1937 four-point Şinaia Conference brief that formulated Hungary's preconditions for peace. This, then, superseded Hungary's subsequent November 1937 proposals to Yugoslavia. Point 1 accepted Hungary's offer of a mutual nonaggression treaty. Point 2 supported Hungary's quest for rearmament. Point 3 proposed abolition of the mixed arbitration commission, a body which the peace treaty had installed to protect the interests of Hungarian citizens with properties situated in the Successor States. This resolution violated Hungarian wishes. The Romanians pledged, however, to include a rider in any new agreement that would obligate the three allies to rectify the grievances of their Magyar-speaking citizens.

Bárdossy still refused to accept the proposal. The Romanians would first have to issue an unambiguous statement that Magyar minorities possessed certain rights. Bárdossy also objected to a few "tricky" legal terminologies that would enable Czechoslovakia to turn the rearmament provisions of the Little Entente against Hungary. The Ambassador accused Czechoslovak Foreign Minister Kamil Krofta of trying to entrap Hungary, and of using the Romanians as proxies. The Romanians conceded Krofta's authorship of the idea.

The Romanian negotiators were embarrassed. They begged Bárdossy to ignore the offer. The Little Entente would not insist on imposing objectionable clauses on Hungary, they assured Bárdossy.[47] Nevertheless, the talks seemed on the verge of collapse due to Hungarian indignation. Romanian Foreign Minister Petrescu-Comnen (hereafter Comnen) thereupon urged Bárdossy to submit the objectionable Romanian proposal in Budapest. A Hungarian counterproposal would be far more useful than negotiations that had been suspended in rancor. This would create an "extremely bad impression" abroad.[48] Despite this warning, negotiations languished at this point.

Romania, and to a lesser degree Yugoslavia, tried to persuade Hungary to be more flexible. Since Hungary seemed obdurate, they asked a few countries wielding influence in Hungary to intercede on their behalf. On 24 March, Polish Foreign Minister Jósef Beck related to Hungarian Ambassador András Hóry the gist of a conversation between the Polish ambassador in Bucharest and Romanian foreign minister Comnen. Since the *Anschluss*, Comnen had declared, Romania sincerely desired a rapprochement with Hungary. The Romanian ambassador in Moscow had expressed similar sentiments to his Polish colleague the day before.[49] Subsequently, Stojadinović allegedly assured Italy that under no circumstances would Yugoslavia attack Hungary.[50] In the meantime, German diplomats pressured their Hungarian colleagues repeatedly to make peace with Yugoslavia at any cost.

Kánya explained his concerns regarding Hungary's three troublesome neighbors to German officials. He assured the German foreign minister via Sztójay that Hungary had been striving to resume negotiations with the Little Entente ever since these talks terminated in the fall of 1937. Now again, Hungary desired good relations with Yugoslavia, and sought a *modus vivendi* with Romania. Thus far, these exertions had been futile, because both countries insisted on honoring their treaty obligations with Czechoslovakia. Obviously, Czechoslovakia would have to be drawn into the negotiating process as well. The current impasse prevented anything but a limited normalization of relations between Hungary and the Little Entente.[51] This was a clever explanation. German leaders disliked Hungarian diplomatic contacts with Czechoslovakia, because they always suspected a betrayal. Kánya's rationale enabled the Hungarians to clear the way for bargaining sessions with Czechoslovakia without incurring German suspicions, or so they hoped.

By mid-April, the Little Entente was as pessimistic as Kánya regarding the likelihood of resolving outstanding issues with Hungary soon. On 11 April, Hungarian Ambassador János Wettstein in Prague, quoting Krofta, informed his superiors why the talks had reached a dead end. Krofta considered the choice of Romania as negotiator for the Little Entente as unfortunate. Czechoslovakia and Yugoslavia had earlier accepted Hungarian criteria for a settlement, whereas Romania had not. Czechoslovak and Yugoslav negotiators saw no reason to participate in the Bucharest talks. An overall settlement now hinged on Romania alone. According to Krofta, Czechoslovakia and Yugoslavia would automatically ratify any agreement the Romanians approved. The mistreatment of Romania's Magyar minorities was a major impediment to a rapprochement. Romania refused to ratify any clause that recognized Magyar minority rights which the Romanians regarded as an internal affair. Romania also wanted to abolish the mixed arbitration commission, on which Romania and Hungary had reached an impasse not long ago. Krofta hoped, however, that an agreement might yet be achieved shortly despite these obstacles.[52] The Hungarians disagreed with Krofta. They saw Krofta's optimism as the wishful thinking of a desperate statesman conducting the affairs of a country in dire peril and clutching at straws.

The same day, the Hungarians approached the Third Reich to ascertain whether Germany had reached a solution on the Czechoslovak problem. The Hungarians were surprised to discover that German diplomats had not been as evasive as they had believed. They truly had no idea when or if Germany would invade Czechoslovakia. Apparently, only Hitler knew for certain. Gábor Ápor, a highly-ranked Hungarian foreign ministry official, instructed Sztójay to query Ribbentrop regarding Germany's intentions, and to remind Hitler of his November promise to Foreign Minister Kánya and Prime Minister Darányi that Germany had no territorial ambitions in Slovakia. This implied that Hungary had a free hand in that province. The Führer had also advocated a joint German-Hungarian frontier. The Hungarians chose to believe that Hitler had not meant Hungary's border with the Ostmark, but the frontier where Slovakia and Moravia met. In other words, in the course of a joint German-Hungarian campaign against Czechoslovakia, Hungary hoped to incorporate Slovakia and Ruthenia. Ápor explained that by presenting these suppositions as foregone conclusions, Hungary might trick Hitler into revealing his intentions.[53] This ploy failed. Instead, Hungarian inquisitiveness aroused resentment in Berlin. Numerous German officials regarded the Hungarians as insolent and pushy.

As the First Czechoslovak Crisis intensified, copious behind-the-scenes maneuverings unfolded between Hungary and the three Little Entente states.[54] The major sticking point was the Magyar minority problem in Romania. Hungary and Romania refused to budge on this issue. All four countries tried to keep negotiations from total and permanent collapse. Each country blamed the other side's blundering, stubbornness or insincerity for the languishing talks.

On 14 April, Comnen agreed with Krofta that the talks were temporarily suspended. The former accused Hungary of stalling tactics and of bad faith. Bárdossy, he exclaimed, had not produced Hungarian counterproposals, but created procedural difficulties. This demonstrated Hungary's determination to sabotage the proceedings. Bárdossy defended Hungary's actions. His government saw no sense in discussing any issues as long as Romania refused to relent on the main question, namely, the treatment of Romania's Magyar minority. Bárdossy promised, however, to seek instructions from his government.[55] At first, Kánya refused

to resume the talks. He saw no reason why Hungary should negotiate on the basis of two brand new issues, namely, abolition of
the control commission and renunciation of the minority protection clauses. Nonetheless, he ordered Bárdossy to speak informally
with Comnen.[56] First, Romania agreed, then refused to discuss
any minority issues that concerned Romania and Yugoslavia exclusively. This was a clever Romanian ploy to trick Hungary into
recognizing Czechoslovakia as an equal negotiating partner *in ab-
sentia.* Bárdossy thereupon informed Comnen that Hungary no
longer desired to reach identical minority agreements with all three
Little Entente countries simultaneously.[57]

In effect, Hungary served notice on the Little Entente countries
that it would negotiate individual agreements with each of them
separately, and gain the best possible bargain from each one. The
notion of separate talks was not new. In 1937, Darányi and Kánya
had informed Hitler of such a Hungarian strategy, and to please
the Führer, had pledged to concentrate on normalizing relations
with Yugoslavia, Hitler's and Göring's favorite Little Entente state.
But Hitler had not agreed to this plan. He had merely stated that
loosening the bonds of the Little Entente would be the best possible
policy for Hungary to pursue, and that Czechoslovakia ought to be
Hungary's sole target for isolation and eventual destruction.[58]

By now, however, the situation had changed, owing to the Little Entente's demonstrated solidarity. As a result, the Hungarians
decided to tell a different story to the Germans. On 20 April,
Kánya explained that Hungary would be obliged to reach a joint
agreement with all three Little Entente governments in order to
gain Stojadinović's support. The Hungarian foreign minister hoped
that Stojadinović would abandon his allies and eventually conclude
a separate treaty with Hungary.[59] This was a clever tactic. Kánya
justified in advance Hungary's need for flexibility to negotiate with
the Little Entente countries either jointly, or individually, as the
occasion demanded.

In practice, however, negotiations assumed a different pattern.
The Hungarians demanded separate talks and separate agreements.
This would please Germany and confuse the Little Entente. The
plan succeeded admirably. These unexpected Hungarian demands
caused consternation, extensive debate and disunity in the Little Entente camp. At the 3-5 May Şinaia Conference, the Little
Entente broke ranks on the issue of separate versus joint negotiations. Krofta opposed the Hungarian plan; Stojadinović, encouraged by Italy, supported separate negotiations and individual
agreements; and Comnen reluctantly backed his Yugoslav colleague.

Their communiqué reaffirmed the Little Entente's solidarity, but in fact, this unity was flawed. For example, hitherto Czechoslovakia had used Romania as its surrogate negotiator. Now, the Czechoslovaks lost this advantage. Further, Romania and Yugoslavia pledged to defend Czechoslovakia only against a Hungarian attack, but not against Germany. Similarly, Italy promised not to abandon Hungary if it was attacked by the Little Entente.[60] The Italian pledge to Hungary, however, was just as worthless as the Little Entente's guarantee to Czechoslovakia. Hungary regarded guarantees applied exclusively to unprovoked aggression by the Little Entente as useless. Hungary desired security against retaliation by Romania and Yugoslavia in the event Germany and Hungary launched an unprovoked attack on Czechoslovakia. The Şinaia Conference left both Czechoslovakia and Hungary vulnerable, and solidified the virtual impasse of the past few months. Paradoxically, however, this deadlock hastened further negotiations.

The fourth phase of Hungary's negotiations with the Little Entente commenced on 12 May, when Raoul Bossy, Romania's ambassador in Budapest, handed a message to Kánya from King Carol. The Romanian monarch expected a Hungarian-Romanian agreement soon, even though his government believed that all four parties ought to negotiate simultaneously. He expected a joint agreement as soon as Czechoslovakia had promulgated its long-awaited minority statute, or at the latest by September 1938. Kánya offered numerous reasons for being opposed to Bossy's suggestion.[61] In fact, however, he was ready to negotiate, but only on Hungary's terms, and would wait until he wore down Romanian resistance. Kánya undoubtedly realized that the suggestion to include Czechoslovakia in the negotiation process stemmed from Romania's guilty conscience for having deserted Czechoslovakia at Şinaia. For all practical purposes, however, the Little Entente had been split, and would never be mended. This was a tactical and diplomatic victory for Hungary.

The following weeks demonstrated the Little Entente's vanished unity. The isolated Czechoslovaks had been accusing the Hungarians of trying to separate Czechoslovakia from its allies in order to destroy it.[62] They were absolutely correct. For a while, the Romanians pretended as if the Little Entente's solidarity still existed, but their actions proved otherwise. On 25 May, Bárdossy proposed a negotiating formula that would exclude Czechoslovakia. Comnen did not reject the plan, but merely stipulated suspension of Hungarian revisionist propaganda as the price for Romanian acceptance.[63] An acrimonious Bárdossy-Comnen dialogue eventually paved the way for separate negotiations between Hungary and the individual members of the Little Entente.

Eagerness to resume the dialogue with Hungary on a one-to-
one basis, or in tandem with Romania, also became evident in
Belgrade. On 20 May, the Yugoslav government notified Hungary of its willingness to engage in separate and independent talks
with Hungary.[64] Three days later, Stojadinović repeated the offer
and added that, if Romania and Czechoslovakia failed to join, Yugoslavia would ratify a treaty with Hungary unilaterally.[65] Thanks
to clever Hungarian diplomacy, the three Little Entente countries
were virtually on their own vying for Hungary's favors, and Hungarian statesmen could deal with them singly, in pairs, or jointly,
as they chose.

Part II - The Munich Crisis and the First Vienna Arbitral Award

Between the First Czechoslovak Crisis and Czechoslovakia's dismemberment after the Munich Conference, Hungary further undermined the stability of Czechoslovakia. Hungary aimed at reaching either separate or joint agreements with Romania and/or Yugoslavia. These accords would eliminate the military peril from
the east and south while Hungary engaged in seizing the eastern
portion of Czechoslovakia. However, these negotiating tactics led
to conflict with the Germans, who distrusted the Hungarians, despite their steady reassurances of fidelity. The Third Reich wanted
Hungary to ignore Czechoslovakia entirely, and concentrate exclusively on pacifying Romania and Yugoslavia. Hungarian diplomats
recognized, however, that the road to Bucharest and Belgrade led
not only through Rome and Berlin, but through Prague as well.
The two eastern members of the Little Entente felt obligated to
defend their Czechoslovak ally, but they also wished to postpone
committing themselves to the Western camp, because eastern Europe's power structure might soon favor Germany and its Italian
and Hungarian allies.

The temporary vacuum created by the gradual disappearance
of France as a powerbroker in eastern Europe, and the failure of
Germany and Italy to master the area completely, offered Hungary
the opportunity to assume a regional role before one or more of the
great powers became entrenched once again. This meant fishing in
troubled diplomatic waters, practicing divide and conquer strategies against the Little Entente, and trying to extract the appropriate measure of German support to ensure the success of Hungarian
revisionist diplomacy. These tactics also included threatening the
Germans with possible lack of cooperation should they fail to assist Hungary's aspirations. This latter Hungarian policy proved

counterproductive. Later that year, the Third Reich granted only a fraction of Hungary's territorial demands in the November 1938 First Vienna Arbitral Award.

In the second half of 1938, Hungary's negotiating technique with the Little Entente proved profitable. The Hungarians demanded that the Magyar minority's grievances be rectified as the price of settlement with Romania and Yugoslavia. They also insisted on a separate agreement with Czechoslovakia. The situation there was different than in the other two states, they asserted, and moreover, Czechoslovakia was shortly expected to offer extensive concessions to all its minorities. The other Little Entente countries, however, refused to go that far. Hungary would therefore settle its grievances with Romania and Yugoslavia first, await developments in Czechoslovakia, and if these proved advantageous, the individually negotiated settlements would be amalgamated into an omnibus agreement. Meanwhile, Hungary, by dealing with each country separately, retained flexibility, and patiently labored through difficult, often quibbling and acrimonious, debates with the Little Entente's representatives.

During the fourth phase of negotiations, Romania developed a short-term strategy. The Romanians resolved either to agree with Hungary on every point except minority problems, or to discuss all stumbling blocks to an agreement. The Romanians wished to place the Hungarians on the defensive by forcing them to reject unacceptable Romanian proposals. Romanians recognized the value of not being criticized abroad, especially in Germany and Great Britain, for having failed to reach an agreement. Perhaps equally as important, they wanted to be able to blame Hungary for sabotaging the talks. Romanian foreign policy also had long-range objectives. Romanians feared that if the Little Entente offered unacceptable terms, Hungary might be forced irrevocably into Germany's arms. Should that occur, German troops might someday cross Hungary to invade Romania, especially if the USSR utilized Romanian territory or air space to launch a Czechoslovak rescue mission.[66] These apprehensions tempered Romanian intransigence.

On 12 June, Bárdossy reported from Bucharest that Romania had agreed to grant Hungary military equality and would also conclude a nonaggression pact. No doubt, Bárdossy explained, Romanian negotiators hoped that if Hungary accepted these important concessions, then the minority issue could be shelved. If, however, Hungary insisted on the inclusion of minority issues, then Romania would be justified in blaming Hungary for the failed negotiations.[67] This Romanian tactic succeeded. Within less than two weeks, Hungary moderated its position on the minority issue. On 22 May, Kánya had briefed Bárdossy on Hungary's minimal demands. The minority issue would have to be formally entered in the protocols, either directly, or through some ambiguous circumlocution. Kánya counseled Bárdossy to continue negotiating, but to slow the pace. He also wished to insert a clause that would obligate each Little Entente country to settle the minority issue on a separate and individual basis with Hungary.[68]

Bárdossy either misunderstood Kánya or he deliberately altered his instructions. He presented the Romanians with Hungary's original plan for minority protection and demanded its adoption.[69] King Carol deplored these tactics, whereas Comnen felt offended being confronted with a scheme discarded long ago. "Unsatisfactory" and "disappointing" were some of the milder terms he used to criticize the Hungarian proposal. Eventually, Comnen accepted a formula embracing "separate bilateral minority negotiations" at some future date. He pointed out that Czechoslovakia was determined to participate in a joint Czechoslovak-Romanian-Yugoslav declaration on the minority issue.[70]

This disagreement spurred both Hungarian and Romanian resolve to drive a hard bargain. Bárdossy refused to sign anything until the Transylvanian Magyars' grievances had been addressed, whereas Comnen would not permit minority issues to be inserted in any agreement.[71] By 13 July, the two countries had exhausted all other topics under discussion. All three Little Entente states pledged to honor Hungary's demands on military equality, and they were willing to sign a nonaggression pact. This phase of negotiations now terminated, even though Romania and Hungary still remained far apart on the minority issue. As proof of his good intentions, Comnen announced the creation of a ministerial commission to address minority problems exclusively.[72] But far from being mollified by this gesture, Kánya notified the Romanians that if they persisted in bringing the Czechoslovaks into the agreement, then Romania must offer Hungary the far superior minority concessions that the Czechoslovaks had freely promised.[73]

Upon this impasse, negotiations terminated temporarily. Once again Hungary consulted the Third Reich to discover what, if any, German policy or strategic changes had occurred in the campaign against Czechoslovakia. A Sztójay-Göring conversation on 5 July proved inconclusive, and left the Hungarian government as much in the dark regarding Germany's intentions toward Czechoslovakia as before. Göring was also vague on what Germany expected from Hungary in the projected attack. He offered no hint on possible timetables, spoils to be shared or risks to be taken. Göring warned Hungary, however, not to be hasty. In the event of difficulties, Germany would not pull Hungary's chestnuts out of the fire. He explained that a German assault would materialize soon, but that hostilities would erupt only in response to Czechoslovak provocations. Göring urged Hungary to adopt a similar strategy. In fact, he counseled, Hungary ought to wait a few days after a German attack commenced, and then react to a Czech provocation.

Sztójay was less concerned with Czechoslovak military resistance than with a possible retaliation by Yugoslavia. He informed Göring that if Germany could not or would not protect Hungary against that country, then it was time for Hungary to approach Italy as a possible shield.[74] Göring had always prided himself on having considerable influence in Belgrade. Sztójay's retort affronted him. It was a broad hint that the Third Reich's prestige in the Balkans appeared to be slipping. Germany could not permit a client state such as Hungary to offend a high German official and seek protection from Italy, a junior Reich partner. Here, mutual suspicions and fundamental disagreements clashed head-on, and bred a lack of German-Hungarian cordiality and confidentiality. Sztójay's temperamental outburst symptomatized the deep malaise that plagued the two countries' relationship.[75]

On 18 July, Prime Minister Béla Imrédy and Foreign Minister Kánya journeyed to Rome, where they sought answers to the riddles they had been unable to secure in Berlin. Ciano's and Mussolini's responses would influence the formulation of Hungarian foreign policy toward the Little Entente and Germany in the coming months. The Italians, on their part, appraised Imrédy, who had replaced Darányi as prime minister on 14 May. To the visitors' chagrin, Ciano waxed enthusiastically about Stojadinović as a man in whom the Italian foreign minister reposed supreme confidence. The Yugoslav prime minister had confided to Ciano that if Hungary attacked Czechoslovakia on its own, then Yugoslavia would have to rush to the aid of its ally. If, however, Hungary acted in concert with Germany, then Yugoslavia would remain neutral. If true, this was a major Yugoslav concession. Under the terms of the Little Entente treaty, if only Germany attacked Czechoslovakia, Yugoslavia was not obligated to help its ally. If either Hungary, or Hungary in conjunction with Germany, launched an invasion, then Yugoslavia had to help Czechoslovakia.[76]

The Hungarian visitors dismissed Ciano's praise of Stojadinović as wishful thinking, and Yugoslav pledges as undependable. In fact, Stojadinović had assured Krofta at the Şinaia Conference that Yugoslavia and Romania would help defend Czechoslovakia against Hungary unconditionally. This reiterated a Stojadinović pledge offered during the May Crisis.[77] More recently, Stojadinović had labeled any Hungarian territorial aggrandizement as injurious to Yugoslav national interests. The Hungarian visitors regarded Ciano's rhetoric a poor defense against a Yugoslav attack. They also deplored a growing German-Italian enthusiasm for Yugoslavia, and noted a corresponding disenchantment with Hungary. The frustrated Kánya blurted out: "Hungary's misfortune is that Ciano and Göring are in love with Stojadinović!"[78] The discussions ended in mutual disagreement and bruised feelings. Subsequently, however, Mussolini, who liked the Hungarians better than Ciano did, promised to investigate Yugoslavia's intentions toward Hungary.

The Hungarians were shocked to learn how intimate German-Italian relations had grown. Of course, they favored German-Italian friendship, but feared that German superiority threatened to dwarf Italy's influence. Ciano regarded German-Italian unity as a panacea to the region's ills. Hungary, however, required two evenly matched senior allies. Ciano had abandoned the horizontal axis plan that attracted Hungary and Poland. The Hungarians thought it wise, under the circumstances, to ignore that issue henceforth. Ciano also mentioned that Italian-Romanian relations had deteriorated since Goga's departure. This was a mixed blessing for Hungary. Italy would not abandon Hungary in favor of Romania, but neither could it exert any influence in Bucharest to assist Hungary.

Ciano next stated that the Third Reich desired to attack Czechoslovakia unassisted, and refused to apprise even Italy concerning its strategy and timing. Germany would strike with lightning speed at a moment's notice, and thus prevent Czechoslovakia's allies from launching a timely intervention. Under these conditions, Hungary could not coordinate its attack with Germany's. Göring's recent suggestion, coupled with Ciano's, that urged Hungary to mount its attack on Czechoslovakia a few days after Germany's assault, was worthless advice.[79] In the absence of general staff discussions and without Hungarian awareness of Germany's timetable and objectives, armed involvement in Czechoslovakia by Hungary verged on the suicidal, even without Yugoslav intervention.

The Hungarian diplomats departed Rome considerably sadder but not wiser than they had been before their arrival. Apparently, Italy had become a German satellite. The Yugoslavs had Ciano captivated. Italy had lost its influence in Romania, and Italian leaders had scrapped their horizontal axis plan. Every deterrent to a German eastward sweep had been removed. In fact, since the *Anschluss,* Hungary was no longer in the Italian sphere of influence,[80] but had to take orders from Germany if it wished to survive, let alone prosper. The Italians had lost patience with Hungary. Mussolini disliked Imrédy, whom he termed "a man of bogus energy...typical of the kind of ruler produced by a moribund regime." Kánya he regarded as "an old Habsburg relic." The Hungarian visit had "completely fizzled out," and his faith was "much shaken" in Hungary's future. Following this conference, Ciano switched his preference from Hungary to Yugoslavia. Italy would no longer guarantee Hungary's security and frontier against Yugoslavia, the country that would make possible future Axis control of the Danube Basin and the Balkans. He dismissed Imrédy's and Kánya's diplomacy as "...the political game of these arrogant and petulant Hungarians."

Ciano's judgment was cynical but sound. Since the *Anschluss,* Italy needed Yugoslavia far more than it did Hungary, particularly if it wished to rescue its declining great power status. Ciano wanted to use Yugoslavia's military support and enlist Anglo-French friendship to bolster Italy's sagging position. He tried to reduce Italian dependence on Hitler. This would enable him to become the arbitrator between the Western powers and the Third Reich in the Balkans and in Spain.[81]

By the time the Munich Crisis approached in late summer, Hungary enjoyed less than the half-hearted support of Germany and Italy. Both of them regarded Hungary as a geographical expression, not as a valued, trusted friend. Under these circumstances, Hungary tried for the fifth time that year to reach a settlement with the Little Entente, provided it ensured Czechoslovakia's isolation from Romania and Yugoslavia. For various reasons, the Little Entente was as eager as Hungary to emerge with a signed agreement, even if it proved partial or flawed. As the Little Entente's 21-23 August Bled Conference approached, Romanian statesmen wanted to conclude a Hungarian-Romanian and Hungarian-Yugoslav minority agreement prior to the meeting. The Romanians insisted on minor textual changes. However, these were the very points which Hungary wished to preserve. By then, successive drafts had reduced the protocol to innocuity. The term "minority" had been expunged without a synonym having been substituted. Bárdossy was ill, and in his absence, his subordinates refused to sign the agreement prior to the conference.

During this negotiating phase, Yugoslavia pretended to avoid direct contact with Hungary, and delegated Comnen as its proxy. In fact, however, the Yugoslavs assumed the lion's share in the negotiation process at the highest levels. The Yugoslavs desired an agreement with Hungary in order to please Italy. Even more, they wanted to ingratiate themselves with Germany, since March ensconced on their western frontier. The Third Reich, especially Göring, had been masquerading as an honest broker to reconcile the two hostile neighbors. The Germans boasted of having revived Yugoslavia's economy, as indeed they had, and hence their political demands could not be ignored. Neither could Yugoslavia abandon its chief Western benefactors France and Great Britain. Both of these countries had spent large sums of money in 1938 to bolster Yugoslavia's economy. Yugoslavia also wanted to honor its obligations to Czechoslovakia, but feared incurring the wrath of Germany and Italy. The best Yugoslav strategy appeared to be to reject Hungarian pleas for Yugoslav neutrality in the event of a Hungarian attack on Czechoslovakia.[82] This gesture would please the West and not unduly offend the Axis powers. The Yugoslavs realized that someday they would have to choose between the Axis and the West. Throughout 1938, however, the Yugoslavs straddled the fence. They offended no one, promised nothing of substance to any country, and awaited further international developments, over which Yugoslavia had no control.

Much of the information on Yugoslav intentions reached Hungary indirectly through the good offices of foreign diplomats, who naturally conveyed the "truth" to Hungarian officials to satisfy their own countries' interests. On 22 June, Göring's adjutant, General Karl Bodenschatz, informed Sztójay of a Yugoslav complaint, conveyed to Göring during his recent Belgrade visit. Apparently, Stojadinović had notified the Hungarian government earlier in the year about Yugoslavia's willingness to negotiate directly on border rectification, minority issues and Hungarian rearmament. Four weeks later, Hungary had yet to be heard from. Göring desired a Hungarian-Yugoslav rapprochement, and he urged instant action. Bodenschatz departed Budapest with an evasive Hungarian reply.[83] By itself, this incident was minor, but Germany's sense of urgency and Hungary's attitude that bordered on insolence toward Germany are worth pondering, especially if considered in conjunction with other, similar, episodes.

Ciano also recommended an early Hungarian-Yugoslav pact. In a 25 June conversation with Hungarian Ambassador Villani, Ciano clung to his convictions that Stojadinović was "worthy of the most far-reaching confidence." Ciano also thought that Stojadinović would negotiate separately with Hungary. Stojadinović had convinced Ciano that he disdained the Czechs and hated Beneš whom he accused of conspiring with leftist opponents of Yugoslavia's regime. For this reason alone, Ciano asserted, Yugoslavia would not lift a finger if combined German and Hungarian forces invaded Czechoslovakia. Ciano cautioned, however, that Hungary must be circumspect and not attack Czechoslovakia alone, because Stojadinović would then have to safeguard his own and Yugoslavia's honor by defending Czechoslovakia. Villani assured Ciano that Hungarians were not so insane as to attack Czechoslovakia unaided.[84] Still, Ciano's words had a sobering effect. Apparently, Italy could not help Hungary recapture its lost territories. A successful campaign demanded German good will and cooperation. Furthermore, Hungary feared that Italy's steadily growing pro-Yugoslav orientation might someday imperil Italian-Hungarian friendship.

In his direct conversations with Hungarian representatives, Stojadinović projected a bluff, honest forthrightness. He claimed (untruthfully) that he had always been a pro-Magyar, and hoped that current negotiations between Hungary and the Little Entente would succeed. He also stipulated that any Hungarian-Yugoslav accord be limited exclusively to the healing of major divisive issues. He favored such an understanding, because "our great friends," Germany and Italy, also desired it.[85] Stojadinović's friendly overture seemingly coincided with Hungarian intentions of preferably conducting negotiations with each Little Entente member state separately.

Kánya considered how to respond to Yugoslavia. He sensed that unilateral talks with Yugoslavia would frighten the Czechoslovaks into offering generous minority concessions, and also prod Romania into similar action. The latter development would please Germany and Italy. On 30 June, Baron György Bakách-Bessenyei, Hungary's ambassador in Belgrade, thanked Stojadinović for being cooperative, depicted Hungary's difficulties with Romania, and accepted Stojadinović's suggestions: Hungary would gladly resolve all major outstanding issues with Yugoslavia. At the moment, only one such obstacle barred the road to amity—Yugoslavia's poor treatment of the Magyar minority. Even so, Hungary would not demand instant remedies. For the present, a small corrective gesture to the Magyar minority would suffice. Then, Yugoslavia could decide the tempo of future negotiations. Hungary also pledged not to interfere with Yugoslavia's agreements with other states.[86]

Although these positive developments in Hungarian-Yugoslav relations pleased Göring, he cautioned the Hungarians not to be overly greedy. Should Stojadinović be coerced into granting too many concessions to Hungary, he might be forced out of office by his powerful pro-Czechoslovak and pro-French domestic opponents. Still, Göring asserted, he was now convinced that, if Germany attacked Czechoslovakia in response to provocations, and Hungary joined Germany, Yugoslavia under Stojadinović would remain neutral.[87] The same day in Rome, Villani met privately with Yugoslav Ambassador Kristić, who confirmed his chief's friendship for Hungary and emphasized the Yugoslavs' desire for an agreement. Kristić castigated Czechoslovakia, especially Beneš, as the cause of all the current difficulties in Europe. Stojadinović, Kristić maintained, shared these sentiments.[88]

Within three days of these meetings, Kánya discovered how evasive and noncommittal Stojadinović was. The Yugoslav Prime Minister and Hungarian representatives shared one principal aim: both parties saw the need to procrastinate until the European diplomatic crisis had resolved itself in favour of either the West or of the Axis. Bakách-Bessenyei informed Kánya that his 12 July meeting with Stojadinović had been inconclusive. The Prime Minister sincerely desired an agreement, and eventually would offer "certain modest concessions" to Yugoslavia's Magyar minority; but politically, his hands were presently tied. Stojadinović wanted to "wait and see" how the Little Entente fared before committing himself. The Ambassador counseled Kánya to remain aloof, and cultivate a friendlier atmosphere to be exploited in future negotiations.[89] Apart from a few indirect contacts, this diplomatic impasse largely prevailed until the eve of the Bled Conference.

The Bled Conference, which ushered in the sixth phase of negotiations, accomplished most objectives for which Hungarian diplomats had been striving, but it created new problems with Germany. The three Little Entente states renounced all peace treaty provisions that had curbed Hungary's right to rearm for nearly two decades. The agreement, according to Kánya, was "total" and "self-explanatory."[90] Under a provision that resembled the 1928 Kellogg-Briand Pact, the four states renounced the use of armed force to attain national objectives. The treatment of Magyar minorities would be remanded for later detailed discussions. An understanding in principle on the minority issue with Romania and Yugoslavia was "final," and a "gentlemen's agreement" now bound those two countries with Hungary.[91] On 23 August, Stojadinović on behalf of Romania and Yugoslavia, and Bakách-Bessenyei for Hungary, affixed their respective signatures on the treaty document. Although Hungary and Czechoslovakia failed to sign this portion of the document, they both pledged to be bound by its terms.[92] This contradicted Kánya's earlier statement that Hungary would not enter into a formal agreement with Czechoslovakia until it granted meaningful concessions to the Magyars in Slovakia, and unless these provisions by far exceeded Romanian and Yugoslav minority obligations.[93] The Bled Conference demonstrated the astuteness of Hungarian negotiating techniques. Ciano asserted that Hungary had scored a major victory at Bled. In his view, the Little Entente's unity was shattered, despite alliance menbers' claims to the contrary. Czechoslovakia was effectively isolated from its eastern European and Western allies, and could be dismembered whenever Germany and Hungary chose.[94] The road appeared clear for Hungary to join the Third Reich in mounting a surgical operation against Czechoslovakia without fear of deterrence.

In the case of an attack on Czechoslovakia, Hungarian security would not be as assured, however, as Ciano's superficial interpretation of the Bled agreement implied. Many other considerations combined also to urge caution. The danger of possible intervention by Romania and/or Yugoslavia on Czechoslovakia's side was by no means over, because the new treaty was invalid in case of an unprovoked aggression launched by Hungary on any Little Entente member. Italy would be powerless to deter Romania and Yugoslavia from rushing to the aid of their ally. Active involvement by the Soviet Union on Czechoslovakia's side was possible. French and British condemnation of Hungarian collaboration with Germany in a warlike act gave hawks in Budapest pause for sober reflection.[95] Göring's recent warning that Germany would not rescue Hungary in the event the latter encountered difficulties deterred Hungarian leaders from engaging in overt action on Germany's side. Furthermore, Hungarian military experts regarded the Third Reich as ill-prepared for a major conflict. Germany was only superficially armed, they believed, and the German public opposed aggression. The Hungarian military attaché in Berlin urged his government to exercise extreme caution before lauching hostilities in partnership with Germany.[96] Under these conditions, Hungary feared getting involved in any action that might precipitate a global conflict.

Hungarian determination to shrink from the abyss became evident at the Kiel Conference, where Hungarian leaders met their German counterparts, presumably to plan a war against Czechoslovakia. The Kiel Conference revealed a number of pent-up grievances on both sides, and imperiled German-Hungarian relations.[97] German State Secretary Weizsäcker's impressions about the proceedings, in which he personally participated, are fairly reliable. According to Weizsäcker, the conference showed promise until news arrived of the Bled agreement, to which the Germans reacted with hostility. In the ensuing frigid atmosphere the two sides clashed repeatedly.

In his conversation with Kánya, for example, Ribbentrop branded the Bled agreement as counterproductive. In his view, renunciation of force would sabotage Hungarian objectives. A Hungarian attack on Czechoslovakia would now be unworkable, and this would weaken Hungary's position with Yugoslavia, especially in a future Czechoslovak-Hungarian crisis. Any objective observer, Ribbentrop asserted, would be convinced that Hungary had renounced its revisionist objectives, and that its leaders had distanced themselves from Germany.

Kánya replied that Hungary had to be absolutely certain that Yugoslavia would indeed remain neutral before launching any action against Czechoslovakia. Besides, Hungary had just begun to rearm, and needed one or two more years of preparation to fight a war effectively. Ribbentrop retorted that Yugoslavia and Romania would never risk the wrath of the Axis by attacking Hungary. France and Great Britain would also remain uninvolved. Moreover, Hungary assumed that war was a foregone conclusion. In fact, however, German decision for launching an attack would hinge on Czechoslovak provocations. Kánya refused to be pinned down regarding Hungarian participation in a Czechoslovak campaign. Kánya's vacillation left Ribbentrop frustrated,[98] whereas the Hungarian foreign minister's contemptuous behavior and negative attitude turned Ribbentrop not only against Kánya personally, but against Hungary itself. C. A. Macartney, the distinguished British expert of Hungarian history, believed that the harm caused by the Kánya-Ribbentrop interview poisoned German-Hungarian relations thenceforth.[99]

According to Weizsäcker, the Hitler-Horthy interview created fewer controversies than had the Kánya-Ribbentrop exchange. Unlike his foreign minister, the Hungarian regent favored a joint attack, although he feared British disapproval. Horthy promised, however, that Hungary would participate in the campaign regardless of the consequences. Weizsäcker commented that Horthy's ministers, who were far more skeptical than their chief concerning war, never changed their minds. They all agreed that, in case of a conflict, Hungary courted danger.

By Hitler's afternoon meeting with Imrédy, the Germans had apparently become convinced that the Hungarians were determined to avoid the risks of war at any cost. Imrédy was vastly relieved, Weizsäcker reported, when Hitler pledged that, under the circumstances, nothing would be expected from Hungary. He added, however, that "whoever wishes to dine, must help with the preparations." The Hungarians were so overjoyed at being reprieved from compulsory participation in a war they dreaded that they over-

looked Hitler's qualifying statement. They erroneously believed
that Germany meant to start the war, that Hungary would wait for
about two weeks, then would help in mopping up operations and
still reap its full territorial rewards.[100]

Two additional days of discussions brought the Hungarians under relentless pressure to jettison their fear of taking risks. The
Germans also castigated their guests for having struck a poor bargain at Bled. The Hungarian statesmen yielded ground on some
issues, clung to others, and struck back at the Germans. In his
second conversation with Ribbentrop, Kánya modified his view regarding Hungary's preparedness on the basis of "new information."
Kánya conceded that "to some extent" Hungary would be able to
join Germany in a war by 1 October 1938.[101] But in subsequent
discussions with Göring, Horthy and his ministers begged for post-
ponement of any military undertaking at least until the spring of
1939.[102]

On the question of Hungarian security in the event of an attack on Czechoslovakia, the Hungarians agreed unanimously that
France would not desert Czechoslovakia; that Yugoslavia was unpredictable; and that Italy could not curb that country. Great Britain
had already objected to Hungary's excessive demands, and would
definitely protect Czechoslovakia. In fact, Imrédy told Weizsäcker,
all of Europe, apart from the Axis, would most likely oppose
Hungary.[103]

The Hungarian diplomats tried unsuccessfully to rebut German
allegations that Hungarian negotiators had been incompetent at the
Bled Conference. They argued (inaccurately and unconvincingly)
that the agreement was invalid until Czechoslovakia rectified the
treatment of its Magyar minorities. But Hungarian demands were
so draconian, they explained, that the Czechoslovaks would never
agree to them, let alone fulfill them. In that event, Hungary would
be released of its treaty obligations, would enjoy the moral advantage of having offered Czechoslovakia the opportunity to comply,
and therefore be legally entitled to launch an attack. Moreover,
Stojadinović had signed the agreement only on behalf of Romania
and Yugoslavia, but not for Czechoslovakia.[104] The Germans rejected these explanations, whereas the Hungarians refused to commit themselves to any warlike action. This caused a schism, which
contributed to further misunderstandings shortly thereafter.[105]

Following Kiel, diplomatic exchanges between Germany and
Hungary flagged until the Munich Conference. After the Kiel Conference, Hungarians increasingly questioned German promises of

help. On 14 September, Sztójay handed Ernst Woermann of the German Foreign Ministry a copy of the text circulated among the Western powers, in which Hungary complained that in the course of the big power discussions at Munich, Magyar minority grievances had been totally ignored. If a settlement failed to include the Magyars, threatened the note, Hungary would not accept responsibility for the consequences. Czechoslovakia's Magyars would very likely revolt, and "catastrophic agitations" would erupt in Hungary. This declaration demonstrated Hungary's determination to coerce the German government into championing Hungary's revisionist cause, not just that of the Sudeten Germans, at the Munich Conference.

The German response was negative. The Germans explained that current negotiations focused exclusively on securing equitable treatment for Czechoslovakia's Sudeten Germans via autonomy, whereas Hungary wanted to annex Czechoslovakia's Magyar-inhabited regions. The two cases differed, and hence they ought not to be linked. The Hungarian chargé d'affaires in Berlin dismissed this explanation as "discrimination." Kánya threatened Germany that unless Czechoslovakia's Magyars gained equal status with the Sudeten Germans, the "Hungarian Government would go to the limit."[106] Hungary was apparently bluffing by threatening to invade Czechoslovakia in order to force Germany's support. The Third Reich feared that this impetuous Hungarian action would undermine German prestige, and wreck delicate negotiations then being conducted by Germany and the Western powers.

On that day, Göring summoned Sztójay and berated Hungary for not doing enough to help itself and Germany in the current crisis. Instead of employing the Hungarian press corps to promote pro-Hungarian propaganda, the government was muting it instead. Hungarian envoys in world capitals ought to be acquainting foreign ministers with the Hungarian side of the story, because their Czechoslovak counterparts were successfully swaying world opinion. In fact, Magyar minority leaders in Czechoslovakia and the Hungarian government had never unequivocally demanded acquisition of Czechoslovakia's Magyar-inhabited areas from Prague. These regions were totally calm, Göring asserted, whereas the Sudetenland was seething with discontent. Kánya informed Göring that all his suggestions would be heeded, with one exception. Hungary would demand a plebiscite to be held in Czechoslovakia's predominantly Magyar-inhabited districts. He also inquired whether Hitler would champion the Magyar minority's cause while negotiating with the Western powers on the Sudeten German question. The Germans curtly informed him that the Führer never represented the briefs of non-German ethnic groups.[107]

This rebuff drew two Hungarian responses. One was a terse, cold communication by Horthy addressed to Hitler sometime between 17 and 20 September. The other was a rude letter penned by Imrédy to Hitler on 20 September. The Imrédy letter lacked every vestige of customary diplomatic and social courtesy. The Hungarian Prime Minister complained that the Germans apparently planned to show "the utmost consideration for the interests of the Sudeten German population," whereas the plight of Czechoslovakia's Magyars and other minorities would be totally ignored. Imrédy threatened Hitler that the Hungarian government and public would oppose such a settlement with "the greatest indignation." Finally, Imrédy pledged to resort to measures "outside the diplomatic sphere of action." [108] The Imrédy letter was courageous but foolhardy, and proved counterproductive. Small countries seldom derive profit from threatening large, powerful states from which they hope to secure future benefits.

Imrédy's letter intensified the indignation of German leaders. At a 20 September meeting at Obersalzberg, Hitler let Imrédy and Kánya feel his fury and exasperation. Hitler scorned Hungarian vacillation at a time when he would not hesitate to risk a world war in order to solve the Czechoslovak crisis. Hitler was certain that France and Great Britain would not fight, even though he would demand the cession of all of Czechoslovakia's German-inhabited areas. Now, Hitler asserted, was the last opportunity for Hungary to jump on the German bandwagon, otherwise Germany would cease supporting Hungary's territorial claims. Germany and Hungary ought to liquidate Czechoslovakia jointly. Hitler advised his visitors to demand an instantaneous plebiscite to be held in all of Czechoslovakia's Magyar-inhabited regions, refuse to guarantee Czechoslovakia's borders, and if need be, threaten to resign from the League of Nations. Hitler also urged Hungary to organize and mobilize an army of irregular bands to stir up trouble in Slovakia. Hitler gave Hungary three weeks to reach a decison. After that, he would settle the Czechoslovak issue either with or without Hungary's help. Hitler regarded armed intervention as the only plausible solution to the Czechoslovak problem.

Imrédy professed being shocked by Hitler's breathtaking tempo. He had been led to believe that the Czechoslovak question would not be settled for at least one or two years. In the meantime, Czechoslovakia's Magyars and the Hungarian government would be demanding a plebiscite. Hungary would guarantee Czechoslovakia's borders, but only if the Czechoslovaks accepted all demands for the remedy of the Magyar minority's grievances. All the while,

Imrédy explained, Hungary was hastily rearming. In two weeks' time, however, Hungary would still not be ready to wage a successful campaign. Yugoslavia worried the Prime Minister, because, although its political leadership was weak, the armed forces were pro-French and sufficiently strong to be taken seriously. In his view, only threats and bribery would deter the Yugoslavs from attacking Hungary.[109]

In the final weeks of September 1938, while Germany and Italy negotiated with France and Great Britain on the destiny of the Sudeten Germans, Hungarians engaged in feverish diplomatic activity. They wanted Germany to represent Czechoslovakia's Magyar minorities, and gain the same advantages for them as for the Sudeten Germans. The Hungarians knew that Germany's quest for Sudeten autonomy was a sham. Eventually, Hitler would demand incorporation of the Sudetenland into the Third Reich, and somewhat later, all of Bohemia and Moravia would be annexed. Consequently, the Hungarians, desired, at the very least, incorporation of Czechoslovakia's Magyar-inhabited regions in Slovakia and Ruthenia into Hungary. With Germany's support, they hoped to annex these two eastern provinces of Czechoslovakia entirely. This audacious plan encountered numerous obstacles, and met opposition by nearly every foreign country directly and indirectly involved in or affected by the projected transaction.

Poland proved to be the sole supporter of Hungary's maximal demands. Poland wished to collaborate with Hungary, and wanted Polish aspirations in Czechoslovakia satisfied in a general settlement that would include Sudeten Germans, Magyars and Poles. Poland particularly favored Hungary's seizure of Ruthenia. This would create a common Polish-Hungarian boundary to serve as Poland's sole outlet to the outside world should Germany decide to blockade Poland's Baltic ports.[110] The idea of forming a horizontal axis lived on in Poland.

Italy supported many of Hungary's aspirations. Ciano believed that Germany should not be the only state to profit from the disappearance of Czechoslovakia. Poland and Hungary must also benefit.[111] He advocated the annexation of all Magyar-inhabited areas in Slovakia, but balked at the acquisition of the entire Slovak province.[112] Although more sympathetic to the Hungarian cause than Ciano, Mussolini agreed.[113] Germany promised to support the aspirations of Czechoslovakia's Magyar minority,[114] but only if Hungary promised to invade Czechoslovakia simultaneously with German forces. But German secrecy on the timing of such an attack placed an impossible burden on Hungary. Not surprisingly,

Hungary refused to be drawn into such a conflict.

The Western powers and the Little Entente appeared to wallow in confusion and indecision. Romania and Yugoslavia purposely declined to spell out precisely how much Hungarian aggrandizement they would tolerate in Slovakia and Ruthenia. These two Little Entente countries wanted to keep Hungary in uncertainty as to whether they would fight if Czechoslovakia was attacked. They succeeded in curbing excessive Hungarian ambitions. They let it be known, however, that they would approve if Hungary acquired only Czechoslovakia's overwhelmingly Magyar-inhabited regions. Czechoslovakia's total partition between Germany and Hungary, on the other hand, or unilateral action by Hungary against their ally, would be countered by armed intervention. This position made eminent sense. If Hungary insisted on incorporating Slavic-inhabited areas of Czechoslovakia, then Romania and Yugoslavia had cause for concern. The peace treaty had given both countries a large non-Magyar population. A precedent established in Czechoslovakia would inevitably invite Hungarian claims on all the lands now held by Yugoslavia and Romania, even areas inhabited by non-Magyars.

Czechoslovakia refused to consider Hungarian claims or complaints while the Sudeten issue was being negotiated with Germany. Prague promised to address the question of all minorities afterward. This policy collided with Hungarian demands for linkage of the Sudeten and Magyar issues. France and Great Britain conceded that every non-German minority problem in Czechoslovakia had to be solved, but only after the Sudeten German complaints had been settled successfully, and then only if Hungary remained patient and quiescent while it awaited its turn to be pacified.

Owing to its friends' half-hearted or ineffectual support and thanks to its adversaries' stubborn opposition, Hungary failed to benefit from the negotiations that resulted in the 30 September Munich agreement. This pact ensured the annexation of the Sudetenland by the Third Reich, and signified a total victory for *völkisch* champions in Czechoslovakia and Germany. The conferees ordered Czechoslovakia to settle with Hungary and Poland within one month, otherwise the four great powers (Great Britain, France, Germany and Italy) would impose a mandatory solution of their own. This is precisely what happened. By the end of October, Czechoslovakia and Hungary could not come to terms, and both countries appealed for arbitration. With the grudging consent of France and Great Britain, Germany and Italy accepted the role of arbitrators. Their foreign ministers' decision would be irrevocable and binding on both Hungary and Czechoslovakia. On 2 November, the arbitrators announced their verdict. It was a far cry from the ambitious demands Hungary had lodged originally.[115]

Unfortunately for Hungary, Ciano, one of the two arbitrators, distrusted the Hungarian leaders; Ribbentrop, the other member, also disliked them.[116] Moreover, many other German leaders had by then become disillusioned with Hungary, distrusted Hungary's statesmen and suspected their actions and motives. Evidences of German skepticism surfaced throughout these weeks. On 27 September, Ribbentrop confronted Sztójay with his government's alleged perfidy. Apparently, the Hungarian Foreign Ministry had instructed the Hungarian ambassador in London to reassure the British foreign secretary that Hungary would never attack Czechoslovakia. Sztójay denied Hungary's alleged indiscretion in London. Göring pointed out that in Czechoslovakia's Těšín region, an area disputed by Poland, local Poles were putting up a spirited resistance against Czechoslovak rule, whereas Magyars were quiescent in Slovakia. Göring warned that unless Hungary was willing to fight, the country might be left out in the cold when settlement time arrived.[117]

One month later, the London story was still circulating at the German Foreign Ministry and the press reported it to the German public. This perturbed Sztójay, because German ill will and negative attitudes would harm the Hungarian cause on the eve of arbitration.[118] Only three days earlier, in conversations with Polish Ambassador Józef Lipski, Ribbentrop had alluded disparagingly to Hungarians. The German Foreign Minister threatened to withdraw from arbitration, and to wash his hands of the matter. He cited Hungarian ingratitude, capriciousness and unpredictability as the reasons for his revulsion.[119]

Numerous other signs suggested that, although Germany would support Hungary's territorial claims against Czechoslovakia, the backing would prove minimal. Even this grudging advocacy had a steep price. On 14 October, the day on which Czechoslovak-Hungarian talks held in Komárno (Komárom) broke down, Darányi asked Hitler to support restoration of Czechoslovak territories inhabited by Magyars to Hungary. Hitler replied affirmatively, but asserted that in return Hungary would have to join the Anti-Comintern Pact, resign from the League of Nations, and conclude a ten-year commercial treaty with Germany as the price of support.[120] No sooner did Darányi agree to these terms than the controlled German press terminated its anti-Hungarian rhetoric and treated the Hungarian cause in a somewhat friendlier fashion than hitherto.[121]

Hungarian promises to comply with these German demands proved insufficient, however, and German sympathy for Hungarian aspirations failed to materialize. Göring informed Sztójay that Hungary would not be given the city of Bratislava (Pressburg, Pozsony), because its German inhabitants had no desire to become Hungarian citizens.[122] Subsequently, Ribbentrop confirmed Göring's statement. As arbitrator, Ribbentrop would oppose having Slovakia's German- and Slovak-inhabited areas transferred to Hungary, because Hungary's government mistreated its minorities.[123] The Italian ambassador in Prague confided to his Hungarian colleague that the German government did not support Hungary's claims enthusiastically, and that it did not press Czechoslovakia to improve its offers to Hungary.[124]

This cautionary note proved correct. Ribbentrop told Sztójay that Hungary's territorial demands on Czechoslovakia were unreasonable. If Hungary gained territory in northern Slovakia, then the strategic position of Ruthenia would become untenable.[125] Ribbentrop's statement not only demonstrated Germany's greater concern for Czecho-Slovakia than for Hungary, it also proved indirectly that the province of Ruthenia would not be restored to Hungary at this time. In Rome, Villani found out that Germany so vociferously opposed the creation of a joint Hungarian-Polish frontier that the Italians, who favored such a scheme, conceded the hopelessness of changing the Germans' minds.[126] The Germans were apparently convinced that the Poles and Hungarians would turn such an arrangement against them at the first opportunity.[127]

Thanks to Ciano,[128] encouraged no doubt by Mussolini who desired a strong Hungary, Ribbentrop consented to a number of Hungarian territorial gains that he had stubbornly opposed until the eleventh hour. Bratislava remained part of Slovakia, but Hungary received Košice (Kassa, Kaschau) in southeastern Slovakia, and Užhorod (Ungvár) and Mukačevo (Munkács) in southern Ruthenia.[129] In all, Hungary obtained about 5,000 square miles of territory with a population of slightly over one million. The cession included a broad belt of southern Slovakia and a narrow strip of southern Ruthenia, both of which were largely Magyar-inhabited. Hungarian statesmen realized that in view of German distrust, the arbitrators could not have accomplished more for Hungary than they had. The Hungarians chafed, however, at the "loss" of their former capital, Bratislava, and they felt cheated out of their common frontier with Poland. They thanked their "benefactors," but did so only perfunctorily. The messages were muted, curt, and lacked warmth.[130]

Hungary's economic policies and diplomatic course in 1938 were also influenced by the country's unease about the Swabians, many of whom were turning pro-German. They were exhilarated by the Third Reich's spectacular territorial, diplomatic, economic and psychological triumphs during that year. The German presence astride Hungary's western frontier with former Austria had sent shock waves of *völkisch* enthusiasm through Swabian-inhabited communities all over Hungary. Hungary's economic concessions to Germany promised prosperity and material well-being for the predominantly rural Swabians. Hungary's negative diplomatic posture, however, appeared to them to hinder Germany's eastward progress. This puzzled and dismayed *völkisch* Swabians. Unlike Hungary's non-German citizens, they counted on enhanced German influence in Hungary. They informed the government that they welcomed German pressures on Hungary in support of their autonomist aspirations. The government met this perceived internal and external menace through the twin-formula of promises and dissimulation.

CHAPTER IX

SWABIAN CULTURAL AND EDUCATIONAL
CONTROVERSIES
IN 1938

The growing divergence between government promises and the
actual quality of instruction in the German village schools played
into the hands of the *völkisch* Swabian leadership. By 1938,
the disciplined and indoctrinated *VK* attracted devoted followers among a growing number of Swabians dedicated to National
Socialist-inspired *völkisch* principles. Most of them were disenchanted with their alleged unjust treatment by the Hungarian authorities. The 1938 issues of the *Deutscher Volksbote* (*DV*), the
VK's official monthly publication,[1] offer a reliable guide to *völkisch*
sentiments and aspirations. As a prerequisite for peaceful coexis-
tence with the Magyars, the *völkisch* Swabians demanded that the
German minority's position in Hungarian society be fundamentally
altered. They desired reform of Hungary's minority school system,
and wanted the Swabians recognized as an autonomous corporate
body, with the *VK* to serve as their leader. National Socialist Germany supported these *völkisch* objectives. This intervention exacerbated and complicated the Hungarian-Swabian controversy, poisoned Magyar-Swabian relations and injected a lasting irritant into
German-Hungarian diplomacy.[2]

In 1938, the *völkisch* Swabians faced several difficult tasks. They
had to persuade pro-goverment Swabians that the *VK* merited their
support, and yet they had to proceed cautiously lest they alarm
Hungary's Magyar and loyalist ethnic public, or arouse the suspicions of the Budapest government. At first, the Swabian nationalists suggested ways and means of improving the condition and
quality of Swabian cultural institutions and minority education.
By early 1938, however, the Third Reich had grown strong, having
absorbed Austria in March and established a common German-
Hungarian frontier. Encouraged by these National Socialist successes, the *VK* escalated its demands, and disseminated *völkisch*
propaganda in the pages of the *DV*. Two major themes predominated. In addition to a fundamental reform of the Swabian minority
school system, the nationalists also wished to banish chronic disagreements between the Swabian minority on one hand, and Hungary's government and public on the other hand. Later that year,

they asked the government to permit the Swabian community to enjoy an autonomous constitutional status in Hungary.

In 1938, Swabian experts and publicists in the Third Reich analyzed the ethnic content of official Hungarian population statistics. These revealed that assimilation had enabled the Magyars of Hungary to augment the ranks of their own intelligentsia by draining the demographic pool of the Swabians. The *völkisch* Swabians confronted the *UDV* and government with this evidence. Between 1920 and 1930, they pointed out, the Swabian population had declined by 72,581 (13.2%). The Swabian share in nearly every occupation, except in farming and mining, was lower than the Swabian percentage of the country's inhabitants. [3] Although the Swabians' literacy rate of 83.1% exceeded the general population's ability to read and write (79.3%), the Swabians lacked a vigorous and numerically strong middle class. Nearly every Swabian student entering the exclusively Magyar-language middle and higher educational establishment had to become formally "Magyarized." In 1930, for example, only 7,005 Swabians (1.5% on a proportional basis) possessed any type of educational training above elementary school level. This meant that in the first decade of Trianon Hungary about 1,000 well-educated Swabians had become Magyarized. Also in 1930, only 118 students professing to be Swabians attended university; 933 frequented middle schools; and 103 were enrolled in teacher training institutes. In 1935, only ten Swabians (about 10% of those enrolled) graduated as elementary school teachers. The matriculation ratio for Swabians at non-elementary educational levels was correspondingly low. As a result of these poor showings in educational preparedness, in 1935, only 95 Swabian elementary school teachers were employed in all of Hungary (0.5%), compared with 232 Swabian instructors in 1920 (1.2%). The vast majority of Swabian teachers were situated in Hungary's non-Swabian areas.

One result of poor-quality German education was that Hungary's Swabian population diminished steadily, and that the number of intellectuals and professionals who declared themselves Swabians declined. In 1930, according to official Hungarian statistics, proportionately more Swabian pupils had a six-year elementary school education than did Magyar children. This was due to the fact that Swabians were overwhelmingly rural dwellers, for whom the sixth grade represented the final year of formal education. The percentage of Magyar pupils exceeded the Swabian rate at every higher educational level. (See Table 1) The same sources also reveal a shortage of Swabian middle class individuals engaged in various occupations. (See Table 2) Apart from being petty business entrepreneurs, Swabians reached or exceeded their percentile occupational ranking in Hungary's population only in the following, mostly agricultural or humble, occupations: land owners (below 50 yokes between 5.6% and 9.4%); land owners in general 7.8%; mining operators 6.6%; mining employees 5.9%; miners 11.5%; and laborers 6.7%).[4]

Official Hungarian statistics thus verified charges brought by *völkisch* Swabians that Hungary's minority school system served as a Magyarizing agent for the country's minorities, particularly Swabians. Swabian children below school age accounted for 5.5% of the German-speaking population. Between the ages of six and nine, their proportion rose to 7.5%, most likely because many rural Swabian children who initially enrolled in minority schools declared themselves as Germans. Between the ages of ten and eleven, the share of professed Germans declined to 3.4%, and between twelve and fourteen amounted to only 2.3%. Apparently, after the third or fourth grade, talented Swabian students transferred to Magyar schools, where they were obliged to declare themselves as Magyars. Between the ages of fifteen and nineteen, however, the proportion of professed Germans rose again, and peaked between the ages of twenty and twenty-nine (7.9% and 16.6%, respectively). These increases resulted because most superficially Magyarized Swabian youngsters stopped attending school after the age of fourteen, whereupon they almost invariably reverted to being Germans. Of course, these figures also demonstrate that the Swabians had a relatively low birth rate.[5] (See Table 3)

Statistics such as these convinced the *VK* that without the benefit of an intelligentsia, the Swabians faced a slow but inexorable ethnic extinction.[6] Nationalistic Swabians therefore argued that rescuing their intelligentsia from oblivion, or "denationalization," was the *sine qua non* for the resurrection of the Swabian *Volk*. The *VK* proposed to attain this objective by re-Germanizing renegade Swabians, especially those on middle and higher educational levels. They also wanted to terminate the alleged insipid, harmful pseudo-minority B-type rural elementary schools that sentenced Swabian children to a life of permanent toil as struggling peasants. In these institutions, the children allegedly learned neither German nor Magyar properly. Gifted Swabian pupils wishing to become professionals had to be educated exclusively in Magyar, declare themselves as Magyars, and by the time they graduated, some of them were in fact thoroughly Magyarized, and presumably lost to the Swabian *Volk*. As more and more Swabians became aware and proud of being Germans, the *UDV*, with its government-approved program of cosmetically improving the quality of the existing minority school system while achieving no real gain in fact, gradually lost many disenchanted followers to Basch's dynamic *völkisch VK* organization.[7]

The *VK* maintained that all Hungarian minority school types, including the new bilingual ones, were pedagogically absurd.[8] They were not minority schools at all, the nationalists asserted. The government allegedly exploited these facilities as indirect instruments for assimilating Swabian children.[9] These institutions seldom engaged competent German pedagogs. They employed Magyar teachers who had only a smattering of German. Moreover, the few teachers who advocated German education risked being censured by school officials, or were punished by being transferred to Magyar regions. Most instructors also encountered obstacles when they attempted to order German texts.[10] From the *völkisch* perspective, bilingual minority schools violated the essence of *Volkstum*. The Swabians required pure German schools. Here Magyar would be taught by Magyar teachers on a daily basis, but only as a second language. Georg Goldschmidt, editor of the *DV*, explained that pure German schools, even if taught by qualified non-Germans, were not truly German.[11] Education, he believed, was holistic. It was futile if pedagogs merely taught children various subjects, even if instruction was efficient and conducted in the native tongue; students had to be instructed in perfect German by *völkisch* instructors, and indoctrinated in the *völkisch* spirit. Swabian pupils had to be acculturated in the German *Volksgeist*, taught Magyar only as a second language, and encouraged to become Hungarian patriots in a polyglot country.[12]

As much as the *VK* disliked bilingual education, it claimed to be willing to let the system prove its merit. In this respect, the *völkisch* Swabians asserted, they were disappointed. The *DV* published varied complaints regarding alleged violations in the Swabian minority school system. Unsympathetic Magyar and Magyarized teachers, clergymen and administrators had thoroughly infiltrated the rural educational system, the newspaper claimed. In some localities teachers punished Swabian pupils for speaking German after school hours. In more than one Swabian community, school authorities disregarded the Swabian public's demands to have school prayers and other religious services conducted in German.[13] The *DV*'s survey of several purely Swabian and mixed Magyar-Swabian villages disclosed a pattern of minority school violations. In nearly all the communities canvased, clerical teachers refused to offer German instruction. They either ignored parental groups' decisions to adopt bilingual instruction, or they sought to persuade parents to abolish

all German content and establish Magyar institutions. In a few
places, the clergy or school authorities forbade parental groups to
assemble; in others, the gendarmerie scared the unsophisticated villagers into choosing Magyar-language schools for their children. In
a few instances, officials threatened parents with economic reprisals,
and forced them to endure other forms of subtle or overt pressures.[14]
In most of these villages, functionaries either overruled or indefinitely postponed Swabian parents' efforts to introduce bilingual
instruction in the schools.[15]

At one point, Goldschmidt suggested safeguards to ensure the
unhindered functioning of bilingual instruction. A clause in the
school law stipulated that if at least forty parents petitioned the
school authorities in writing and demanded minority education
for their offspring, then the officials had to comply with parental
wishes. Under this system, hostile functionaries were not permitted to thwart parental desires.[16] Goldschmidt suggested, therefore,
that in reaching decisions on the choice of bilingual versus Magyar-
language schools, the authorities should consider only the evidence
of parental written appeals. [17] Nothing ever came of Goldschmidt's
recommendations.

This critique of Swabian minority education and the *VK*'s condemnation of alleged abuses must be cast into a proper perspective.
The *DV* published massive and persuasive documentation attempting to prove nationwide and pervasive persecution of Swabians by
local officials. The *VK*'s objective was to extract farreaching educational and other concessions from the government. Budapest
tried to avoid the embarrassment of having the *völkisch* Swabians
air their grievances in Berlin. Hungary wanted to preserve amicable relations with Germany, and this necessitated the avoidance
of contentious issues that might blemish Hungary's image in the
Third Reich. Most of the alleged violations were true in a literal
sense. The abuses, however, were not universally applied. In some
minority regions rural functionaries did obey the regulations. Furthermore, the Hungarian government, as much as it disliked alien
cultures, never condoned harassment of non-Magyars as a matter
of official policy. Ever since the 1867 Compromise, when Hungary
gained control over its internal affairs, the rule had almost always
been to eschew force, intimidation, or threats of economic depriva-
tion as a means of influencing the behavior of non-Magyar citizens.
But after the war, many functionaries in Swabian regions became
embittered by the defection of most of Hungary's minorities. They
abandoned friendly persuasion in their eagerness to vanquish the
völkisch Swabian menace, which they believed to be nourished by

German culture, the German language, and later on by the dreaded Third Reich. In a simplistic fashion, these patriotic, overzealous officials sought to eliminate the alleged Pan-German peril by attempting to eradicate the *völkisch* Swabians' two most conspicuous external symbols, the German language and culture.[18]

These sporadic, thoughtless actions perpetrated by the relatively few unsophisticated Magyars provided the *VK* with the perfect pretext to unleash propaganda designed to extract ever more educational and other concessions from the Hungarian state. The *VK* charged that petty obstructionism in the schools had caused German minority education to deteriorate steadily. In February 1938, Goldschmidt complained that the problem in the German school system was more serious than ever before. The 1935 school law had first roused, then disappointed, the hopes Swabians had of securing improved German educational facilities for their children. Hostile administrators, who cleverly manipulated the local school systems, made it impossible for Swabian parents to obtain bilingual schools or to seek redress for their grievances. When faced with obstinate parents, officials would appeal to the county authorities, and persuade them to override parental wishes by authorizing the establishment of Magyar-language institutions. Instead of assisting the aggrieved Swabians, the *DV* charged, the central government aided and encouraged the opponents of minority education. A 15 December 1937 decree [19] ordered 400 minority schools located in Swabian and mixed villages to choose bilingual education at once, or nine months ahead of the previously stipulated deadline. The alternative was that these facilities would be transformed automatically and immediately into Magyar-language institutions. Moreover, the change would be permanent and could not be appealed.[20]

Notwithstanding these anti-Swabian measures, the central government insisted that it favored minority education in the spirit of the 1935 school law. After 15 December 1937, however, rural school administrators indubitably found it far easier than before to persuade Swabian parents to accept Magyar-language schools for their children on a permanent basis. In October 1938, Heinrich Mühl complained that the 1 September 1938 deadline for institutionalizing the 1935 school law had just elapsed, but that bilingual education was still a distant goal.[21] It is true, of course, that many Swabian parents voluntarily chose Magyar-language institutions for their children, in order to avoid the confusing bilingual curriculum in the B-type schools, as well as to evade the stigma of being charged with unpatriotic behavior by the authorities.

After March 1938, the *DV*'s campaign against alleged minority school violations reached a new stage. The Third Reich had seized Austria, and now shared a common frontier with Hungary in the western part of the country, where in some areas the Swabian population predominated. The *VK* now wished to abolish the 1935 school law by discrediting the concept of bilingual education on practical and ideological grounds. The *völkisch* Swabians wanted to prepare the ground for an entirely new approach to minority instruction. One month before the *Anschluss*, the *DV* was still campaigning vigorously to promote bilingual education. It had dispatched well-trained agents bearing printed petition sheets to Swabian and mixed-language villages in hopes of persuading parents to sign the documents in support of bilingual minority education. At the time, Goldschmidt had branded anyone obstructing this plan "not only an opponent and an enemy, but an irresponsible scoundrel."[22]

By May, however, Goldschmidt sang a different tune. He condemned the Hungarian government for having sabotaged the 1935 school law. In the same breath, he spurned the ordinance because many of its provisions allegedly violated Hungarian law, and because parental groups lacked the power to ensure its proper implementation. The minority school impasse would remain unresolved, in his view, until the government permitted Swabians to send their children to pure German schools. Goldschmidt solemnly pledged not to rest until the Swabians had attained this objective.[23]

In July, the *DV* temporarily moderated its educational demands, but only because Minister of Education Count Pál Teleki delivered a stern warning. He would satisfy only legitimate non-Magyar cultural and ethnic aspirations, but combat any attempts aimed at endangering Hungary's security under the pretext of obtaining minority rights for the Swabians. All people, in his view, had the right to speak their mother tongue and to practice their ancestral customs and beliefs. Non-Magyar pupils desiring minority education in the spirit of the 1935 school law would therefore be accommodated, but only if their parents approved, and then only if the government considered such instruction necessary. Moreover, in Swabian-Magyar villages, Magyar pupils would have to be taught exclusively in their mother tongue. Teleki believed that these measures would satisfy legitimate Swabian educational aspirations, and he ordered all further *völkisch* agitation to cease.

Goldschmidt agreed to abide by the Teleki plan, but only if Magyar-language schools enrolled Magyar children exclusively. Currently, Swabian rural pupils lacked guarantees of receiving a German education, even if they or their parents desired it. Indeed, he asserted, assimilation of Swabians by Magyars, or vice versa, via the school system, should be outlawed. Furthermore, in the bilingual schools German subjects should be taught only by *völkisch* German teachers selected by the *VK*.[24]

In early November, the Third Reich enhanced its prestige and influence in Hungary when the First Vienna Arbitral Award restored a portion of southeastern Czechoslovakia to Hungary. About 1,060,000 jubilant Magyars and 14,000 considerably less enthusiastic Germans returned to the mother country. [25] This new evidence of German might emboldened the *VK*, and prompted its spokesmen to become indiscreet.[26] Heinrich Mühl revealed that the Swabians had doubted the effectiveness of Hungary's minority school system and laws as far back as 1923, because the Hungarian authorities had never taken minority education seriously. They had designed minority schools to be instruments of assimilation, rather than to have them serve as institutions groomed eventually to become unilingual German schools. Only Swabian autonomy, with the *VK*-led German-speaking *völkisch* community serving as a corporate structure, could remedy the current educational impasse. Barring a solution along these lines, a Hungarian-Swabian rapprochement was out of the question.[27]

The evidence respecting the quality of Hungarian minority education is ambiguous. (See Table 4) For a small country with limited resources, Hungary conscientiously maintained a minority school system at considerable financial sacrifice, even though most Magyar-speaking citizens rejected the concept of educating ethnic minorities in their own mother tongue. Moreover, the government, although it subsidized these establishments, wielded little direct control over them, because the ecclesiastical authorities in charge of most rural institutions enjoyed considerable operational autonomy, provided they lived up to minimal national norms and standards established by the Ministry of Education. The *VK* did have certain legitimate grievances regarding the administration of German minority education in Trianon Hungary. The lack of teachers who spoke German fluently constituted the most obvious obstacle to genuine effectiveness. The number of such teachers seldom exceeded one-hundred at any given time, because the government refused to establish teacher academies for the training of German pedagogs. Candidates had to attend vacation and part-time courses, so that a meaningful numerical rise of German teachers was out of the question. Official Hungarian statistics also reveal that year after year, Magyar-language schools had better pupil-teacher ratios than their German counterparts. Moreover, whenever economic adversity prompted the government to adopt economizing measures, the Swabian schools always bore the brunt. The government preferred funding state-run Magyar-language elementary schools, which the Ministry of Education controlled fully, in order to entice Swabian and other minority pupils from their own underendowed and poorly-equipped institutions.

The most puzzling element these statistics reveal was the considerable annual fluctuation in the number of elementary school pupils with German mother tongue. Every year after 1931–1932 the number of German pupils declined from a maximum of 59,751 to a ten-year minimum of 50,633 in 1937–1938. This demographic trend had two possible explanations. Jewish pupils professing German background protested National Socialist anti-Semitism by switching their allegiance to the Magyars. Far more vital from the *völkisch* Swabian perspective was the fact that throughout the 1930s, Swabian pupils became increasingly the targets of the Hungarian government's Magyarization drive, a campaign pursued with great vigor in the country's schools. The process of "robbing the Swabian cradle" constituted one of the *völkisch* Swabians' most worrisome concerns. This government policy literally decimated each annual crop of Swabian youngsters by luring the most talented among them into the Magyar-language school system. This practice imperiled the long-range survival of the Swabian *Volk* by depriving it of its incipient intelligentsia.

The *VK*'s principal objection to the Swabian school system was its ethnic Magyar and Magyarized proponents' ideological divergence from everything the *völkisch* Swabians valued. One such fundamental difficulty, which perennially troubled Hungarian-Swabian relations, was the fact that most Hungarians, particularly ethnic Magyars, disagreed with the *VK*'s view on the meaning and significance of such concepts as "nation" and "state." The *völkisch* Swabians were partially deterministic. They regarded "nation" and "state" as two distinct concepts. Descent exclusively determined a person's membership in the nation, whereas individuals voluntarily chose their membership in the state. *Völkisch* Swabians regarded nationality as a divinely ordained, exclusive, impenetrable corporation, which linked kindred individuals by language, race, culture and historical continuity.[28]

In contrast, the Swabians belonging to the *UDV* favored a "sliding-scale" position. Gustav Gratz explained that some Swabians were "German-Hungarians" ("Deutschungarn"), while others were "Hungarian-Germans" ("ungarländische Deutsche"). The choice of these terms depended on whether the individual desired to stress his status as a Hungarian citizen of German background ("Volksstamm"), or as a member of the global German community ("Gesamtdeutschtum") who happened to be a Hungarian citizen. In either case, Gratz asserted, the Swabians were merely a minority in a Magyar-dominated Hungarian state. By implication, therefore, Gratz rejected the concept of a Swabian or German *Volk* on Hungarian soil.[29] On a different occasion, Gratz told a Swabian student group that Hungary's Germans were "a people with two souls," who served their *Volk* and their fatherland with equal fidelity, and who knew how to unite these two duties in full harmony.[30]

Ethnic Magyars, who considered themselves Hungary's dominant people, expected to assimilate resident aliens (*i.e.*, non-Magyars) through their own voluntary acceptance of the allegedly superior Magyar culture and language. According to Professor Faluhegyi, director of the Minority Institute at Pécs University, the Magyars of Hungary and their expatriate brethren in the Successor States were a "nationality" imbued with a strong national sentiment, whereas Hungary's other peoples, including the Swabians, were "minorities" who had lost, or never possessed, a feeling of belonging to fellow-nationals across Hungary's frontiers.[31] To a true Magyar, the Magyar nation and the Hungarian state mutually overlapped and harmonized.[32] This explains why Magyars could not agree with or fully trust even Swabians who were government loyalists such as Gustav Gratz and other *UDV* leaders. This prejudice and suspicion prevented the Hungarian government from fully utilizing the *VK-UDV* schism by supporting the latter's relatively modest and limited cultural and educational desires wholeheartedly. Such a policy might have been useful. The *VK*'s philosophy posed a mortal danger to the Hungarian state, whereas the *UDV*'s did not, and the government needed a credible counterpoise to combat the *völkisch* Swabians.

If nation and state were indeed two distinct concepts that need not necessarily harmonize, then National Socialist logic demanded that one state should be permitted to intervene in the affairs of its *Volksgenossen*, even if they were citizens of another state. Numerous declarations issued by the *VK* and various Third Reich officials which affirmed the feasibility of arrangements of this type made most Magyars suspect the *völkisch* Swabians' loyalty to the Hungarian state. Heinrich Mühl proposed, for example, that the Swabians' economic and cultural affairs be "regulated among the three parties [*i.e.*, the *VK*, the Hungarian government and the German regime] to their mutual benefit and satisfaction."[33] Ägidius Faulstich insisted that, unless the Swabians maintained psychological and intellectual contact with their "ancestral culture [*i.e.*, National Socialism in the Third Reich], they would perish as a people."[34]

Hermann Göring amplified these views. He explained that minorities residing abroad must serve as peaceful mediators between their host countries and Germany. He insisted, however, that, although Germany would never intervene in the internal affairs of any other country, the Reich would nonetheless guard and protect all Germans residing abroad, to the extent of helping them preserve their *Volkstum* and ensuring that their living conditions were secure.[35] The *DV* also tried to soothe Hungary's suspicious public. Hitler merely wished to protect Germany's national interests and the welfare of Germandom without, however, compromising the independence of foreign countries, the newspaper claimed. The *DV*'s February 1938 banner headline, however, quoting a slogan derived from Hitler's 20 February 1938 Reichstag speech, conveyed more than a subtle threat to countries with German minorities: "We are all sons of the German Volk, no matter where our cradle is rocked."[36]

Shortly after the *Anschluss*, Gustav Gratz attempted to effect a reconciliation with the *VK*, in response to widespread appeals for Swabian unity. Gratz stipulated only one precondition for a rapprochement. The *VK* must cease accepting funds from abroad (*i.e.*, from Germany) to finance its political activities. The *völkisch* organization must reject this secret subsidy, because it was endangering its unsuspecting patriotic followers, whom the Hungarian authorities suspected of treason by association. By living off the proceeds of funds procured from a foreign government, *völkisch* leaders were practicing corruption, and showed a poor example to those who truly cared about the welfare of Hungary's Germans.[37] The *VK* was stung to the quick by Gratz's "peace conditions." The *DV* accused Gratz of inciting the Magyar public against the *VK* on the grounds that it was a treasonous organization. It received foreign funds and defied the Hungarian state. The publication defended the action of the *völkisch* Swabians. They were not traitors, nor did they pursue political goals; but they *were* Germans, and this distinction was precisely what differentiated them from Gratz and his followers.[38]

The *DV* issued a lengthy list of its own reconciliation demands. The *VK* would not make peace with the *UDV* until its leaders recognized the Swabians as a "Volksgemeinschaft," and acknowledged the principle of "Volkspersönlichkeit." They must agree to solve the minority school problem without recourse to decisions by school boards or parents' conferences, accept bilingual education as merely a transitional phase that must soon yield to unilingual German instruction, approve separate German teacher academies, German textbooks, as well as pure German education from kindergarten through middle schools. The *UDV* must also advocate the unimpeded publication of German dailies and weeklies, foundation of autonomous German clubs, associations, a political party, and at least one German seminary, compulsory German church services, and other facilities.[39] Of course, the *VK* had no intentions of reconciling with the *UDV*. The *völkisch* leaders knew that the *UDV* would not be permitted to bless a program that was virtually a declaration of independence from Hungarian state control.

The standards of loyalty that bound the *völkisch* Swabians to the Hungarian state appeared so ambiguous, if not tenuous, that the *VK* leaders had difficulty persuading the public that their followers were trustworthy. After the *Anschluss*, Franz Basch begged the "Germanophobe Magyar middle classes" to abandon their "psychotic fear of Pan-Germanism and National Socialism." His appeals made no impact. He succeeded even less in reconciling the public to tolerate Swabian power nurtured by German unity. Magyar nationalists, Basch admonished, must realize that the era of rampant assimilation was over. The Swabians were caught up in the same process of *volksbewusst* devotion to the German *Volk* that had gripped Germans everywhere. But Magyars ought to be of good cheer, because the *völkisch* Swabians' projected role in Hungarian society harmonized with the provisions of the Hungarian constitution, and because none of the Swabian demands clashed with Hungarian laws. Basch concluded that Swabians would always be Hungarian patriots, even as they would also remain devoted champions of the German *Volk*.[40]

These loyalty pledges to the Hungarian state coincided with negotiations involving the *VK*'s attempt to persuade the government to grant the Swabians collective status. The *VK* would determine who belonged to the Swabian *Volksgruppe* and who did not, on the basis of racialist principles adopted from National Socialist practice. The *DV* warned that Hungary could not permanently deny the aspirations of the Swabians to regulate their own affairs,[41] and threatened that a people too long thwarted in the pursuit of its *völkisch* ambitions could easily become radicalized.[42] The July issue of *DV* prominently featured Béla Imrédy's 2 June speech, in which the Hungarian Prime Minister pledged to honor Swabian demands, even while he ridiculed local officials who sabotaged the minority laws for having "regressive minds."[43]

It was around this time that the formerly Anglophile Imrédy lost confidence in Great Britain. He inaugurated a pro-German course of action, and hence his pledges to remedy the *völkisch* Swabians' grievances were to some extent sincerely meant. Within nine months, however, Imrédy had to resign his portfolio as prime minister because Hungary's traditionalist-minded political establishment, led by such statesmen as the former prime ministers Count István Bethlen and Count Pál Teleki (the latter soon to be Imrédy's successor as prime minister) wished to steer Hungary on a cautious middle course between the Rome-Berlin Axis and the Western powers. In the Swabian districts, Imrédy's "permissive" minority policy had loosed a storm of indignation among the officials whom he had ridiculed. Imrédy's attempts to chastise the rural intelligentsia and local functionaries, the most formidable and effective foes of Swabian cultural development and German education, thus failed.

In addition to praising Imrédy's pro-Swabian speech, the *DV*'s July issue also featured, for the first time, a tentative listing of *völkisch* Swabian demands. These included the right to choose a Swabian leader; solution of the school problem; freedom to organize social, professional and political associations; and "permission to live according to the laws of the state and the eternal laws of nature" (*i.e.*, devotion to the *Volksgeist*).[44] In August, Goldschmidt published a detailed, definitive eight-point program.[45] It urged recognition of the Swabian *völkisch* community as a corporate body; solution of the school problem in the spirit of the 1868 nationality law, under which, according to Goldschmidt's erroneous interpretation, bilingual schools would be gradually transformed into German institutions, German teachers and school texts would be made available, and all types and grades of German educational institutions would be created, except universities. Under these proposals, Swabians would be able to publish newspapers and magazines unfettered by governmental restrictions, found autonomous clubs and associations, launch financial drives, conduct church services exclusively in German, and organize a Swabian political party. This program, which Goldschmidt labeled the *VK*'s maximum demands, the government totally rejected,[46] even though the *DV* had pledged earlier that a Swabian political party would limit itself strictly to internal matters relating to ethnic concerns, and would never interfere in the conduct of the country's foreign policy.[47]

The government's rejection of Swabian demands angered Goldschmidt. He accused Budapest of hypocrisy, because the government demanded similar rights for Magyar expatriates in the Successor States.[48] Hungary could not expect the Czechoslovaks, Romanians and Yugoslavs to treat their Magyar minorities with consideration, he exclaimed, as long as the Magyars of Hungary abused their own non-Magyar national groups. Moreover, Hungary would never be able to wield influence in the Danube Basin, unless the region's varied nationalities could anticipate membership in a future Hungarian empire that would grant autonomy to all non-Magyars.[49]

Spurred by gratitude for the Third Reich's assistance in the acquisition of parts of southeastern Czechoslovakia in early November, on 26 November, the Imrédy government authorized the establishment of the *Volksbund der Deutschen in Ungarn (VDU)*, a *völkisch* organization with Franz Basch as its leader. The government did not, however, disband the *UDV* or curtail its activities or jurisdiction, much to the *VDU*'s chagrin.[50] In other respects, as well, the new organization disappointed *völkisch* Swabian expectations, because the *VDU*'s jurisdiction was strictly cultural, and the government moved slowly in approving the creation of local chapters. Moreover, the *VDU* could not commence operations until the Ministry of the Interior activated the law through an enabling decree. In his inaugural speech before the *VDU* founding assembly, Franz Basch overlooked these deficiencies, ignored the government's and public's misgivings about the presence of an alien autonomous body on Hungarian soil, and exulted in the *völkisch* Swabians' hard-fought triumph. Of course, the Hungarian government had no intentions of permitting the *VDU* to function as a genuinely self-governing association, even within its designated narrow cultural matrix. By lodging extravagent claims on behalf of the *VDU*, Basch virtually ensured that his organization would have its activities severely curtailed and monitored by the government.

Basch asserted, for example, that the *VDU* had the right to pass legislation for all members of the Swabian *Volk*, and that its regulations were binding on everyone, including even those who had deserted the *Volk*, but who wished to be reinstated. He declared that in all Swabian villages, the schools, churches and administrative bureaus existed to serve the German *Volk*. The *VDU* would permit only members of the *Volk* to serve as Swabian leaders, because aliens would mislead the people. Basch pledged allegiance to the German *Volksgemeinschaft*, but acknowledged that the Swabians also owed fidelity to the Hungarian state. Basch contradicted his loyalty to Hungary by claiming extraordinary jurisdictional scope for the *DVU*. This included poor relief, preservation of folk customs, creation of economic institutions, establishment of all types of schools, the foundation of museums, libraries and cultural courses, the sponsoring of musical performances and plays, sports events, and organizing study trips at home and abroad. Basch's roster implied that the *VDU* had gained full administrative self-government, not merely cultural autonomy.

Basch conceded that the Hungarian government's and the public's mistrust of the Swabians posed a serious and difficult problem for the *VDU*. He expected these impediments to cease, principally because Hungary's diplomatic interests demanded pacification of the *VDU*. Basch expected the prime minister to order the provincial and local authorities to stop sabotaging the school laws, and he was convinced that they would obey instantaneously. Genuine pacification would fail without a fundamental improvement in the government's treatment of the Swabians. He warned the government that, as much as the Swabians considered Hungary their fatherland and were faithful patriots, nonetheless, true love and concern depended on reciprocity. The Hungarian government and the Magyar people would have to demonstrate their good will. Finally, Basch offered to make peace with Gratz's *UDV* and return to the fold, but only if that group accepted the *UDV*'s conditions.[51]

At the end of 1938 Hungary wallowed in a state of confusion and flux. The country's leaders had been coerced by Germany and the *völkisch* Swabians into granting farreaching concessions, but they struck back. In the economic realm, Hungary had no intentions of granting Germany's grandiose food delivery demands. Diplomatically, Hungary had scuttled Hitler's plans of mounting a simultaneous German-Polish-Hungarian dismemberment campaign in Czechoslovakia. The *völkisch* Swabians celebrated their "autonomy" prematurely. To their dismay, they enjoyed fewer, not more, privileges after passage of the autonomy legislation. As Europe drifted toward armed conflict, the gulf between the Hungarian government and most citizens, including the moderate Swabians, on one hand, and the Third Reich and the *völkisch* Swabians, on the other hand, widened. For Hungary, the year 1939 portended more strife with its German ally, and augured reduced amity with its German minority. The possibility of losing Germany's support without gaining the approval of the Western powers loomed as a distinct and frightening possibility.

TABLE 1

Education in Hungary in 1930

Educational Level	Total Number	% of Swabian Population	% of Magyar Population
University Education	1,562	0.3	1.0
8-year middle school	5,443	1.1	2.3
6-year middle school	3,288	0.6	1.0
4-year middle school	15,368	3.1	5.7
6-year elementary school ..	236,009	48.0	34.8
4-year elementary school ..	85,403	18.4	23.0
Can read and write	50,422	10.5	10.7
Can only read	3,891	0.8	0.8
Can neither read nor write	77,044	17.2	20.7
a - children under 6 years	52,790	11.0	11.2
b - persons over 6 years .	24,504	4.7	9.3

Source: Franz Schittenhelm, "Das ungarländische Deutschtum in Zahlen," *Nation und Staat*, XI (1937-1938), 162-171.

TABLE 2

Category	Total Number	% of Swabian Population
'otal Swabian Population	478,630	5.5
;ommercial entrepreneurs	3,584	4.3
;ommercial employees	1,018	2.5
;ank owners	10	3.1
;ank officials	303	1.7
;ank employees	89	2.6
;usiness entrepreneurs	13,148	6.7
;usiness officials	1,790	4.1
;usiness employees	34,485	5.4
;overnment employees	149	0.9
;ounty employees	15	0.6
/unicipal employees	72	0.7
;ommunity and county notaries	20	9.5
udges and government attorneys ...	17	0.9
,awyers	30	0.5
'hysicians	96	1.1
/eterinarians	3	0.3
;ngineers	50	4.5
ournalists	24	1.6
'riests and ministers	91	1.9
;indergarten teachers	12	0.8
;lementary school teachers	95	0.4
Jrban school teachers (polgáriskola) .	16	0.5
/iddle school teachers (gymnaziums)	45	1.3
Jniversity teachers	6	1.7

»urce: Schittenhelm, "Das ungarländische Deutschtum in Zahlen," *Nation und Staat*, 162-171.

TABLE 3

Age Distribution of Swabians and Magyars in Hungary in 1930

Age Range	Number of Swabians	% of Swabians	% of Magyars
Under 3 years	26,089	5.5	7.0
3 - 5 years ..	26,681	5.6	6.9
6 - 9 years ..	35,729	7.5	9.1
10 - 11 years .	17,430	3.4	4.2
12 - 14 years .	10,678	2.3	3.3
15 - 19 years .	37,662	7.9	10.2
20 - 29 years .	80,503	16.6	18.6
30 - 39 years .	69,274	14.5	13.9
40 - 49 years .	56,220	11.9	10.1
50 - 59 years .	52,000	10.8	7.4
60 - 69 years .	39,751	8.3	5.4
70 - 79 years .	20,986	4.4	3.2
80 - 89 years .	4,318	0.9	0.7
Over 90 Years	222	.04	.03

Source: Schittenhelm, "Das ungarländische Deutschtum in Zahlen," *Nation und Staat*, 170.

TABLE 4

Minority Education in Hungary 1923-1938

(Selected years)

Academic Year	Pure German Schools A-Type	Number of Pupils in A-Type Schools	Mixed Language Schools B- and C-Types	*Number of Pupils in B- and C-Type Schools	Pupil-Teacher Ratio in Minority Schools	Pupil-Teacher Ratio in Magyar Schools	**Number of German Elementary School Teachers	***Number of Elementary School Pupils with German Mother Tongue
1923-1924	9	239	250	28,061	43:1	40:1	96	48,596
1926-1927	48	4,115	415	45,670	43:1	41:1	83	40,825
1937-1938	47	6,146	391	60,033	54:1	47:1	Unknown	50,633

Source: Magyar Királyi Belügyminisztérium, *Magyar statisztikai évkönyv és jelentés* (Budapest, 1924-1939).

*Many pupils in these school were Magyars or members of other nationalities.

**Most of the teachers with German mother tongue did not occupy positions in Swabian regions, but were dispersed throughout Hungary's other regions.

***Pupils were queried each year to declare the language in which they felt most fluent and at ease.

CHAPTER X

THE DIPLOMATIC PICTURE - EUROPE IN 1939

For Hungarians, the year 1939 brought disappointment and disillusionment tempered only by modest territorial gains. Hungarians had expected the restoration of a good portion of their former possessions held by the three Successor States, but had to settle for meager territorial acquisitions in Czechoslovakia alone. They lost confidence in the desire and ability of France, Great Britain and Italy to arrest or challenge the headlong thrust of German power, became more hostile to Yugoslavia and Romania, bemoaned the loss of Poland, a cherished friend, and dreaded the revivified Soviet Union. Hitler's diplomatic "masterstroke," the Russo-German pact of August 1939, enabled Germany to launch the Polish campaign without fear of intervention by the Western powers. By German invitation, the Soviet Union thus advanted into eastern Europe. As most informed Hungarians realized at the time, the Soviets were not likely to leave the region voluntarily. Hungary warned Germany that, sooner or later, the Soviet Union would force Communism upon the region, and revive Pan-Slavism in the people of the Slavic states which Germany wished to dominate (Bohemia-Moravia, Slovakia, Yugoslavia, Bulgaria, and Poland, not to mention the Slovaks, Serbs, Croatians, and Ruthenians residing in Hungary). These admonitions fell on deaf ears in Berlin.

In order to prevent being victimized by the Third Reich's opportunistic foreign policies that apparently ignored the national interests of Germany's allies, Hungary persisted, as it had in 1938, in playing Machiavellian politics with Germany and in deceiving the Swabians in Hungary. When Prime Minister Imrédy became overly friendly with Germany, and when he grew too permissive with the Swabians, Hungary's traditional élites, led by Counts Bethlen and Teleki, arranged Imrédy's political demise by publicizing the Prime Minister's remote Jewish ancestry. On 15 February 1939, Imrédy resigned under a cloud.

Pál Teleki, the new prime minister, immediately suppressed all Hungarian National Socialist parties and organizations, seized their funds (mostly obtained secretly from the Third Reich), and had their leaders arrested. On 24 February, before Hitler had time to lodge a protest, Teleki cleverly shepherded Hungary into Hitler's favorite organization, the Anti-Comintern Pact, to which Italy and Japan also belonged. On 15 March, Hitler "rewarded" Hungary by allowing the occupation of Ruthenia, the easternmost and poorest province of the defunct Czecho-Slovak Republic. On 11 April, Teleki withdrew Hungary from the political branch of the League of Nations, and on 3 May, he legislated the anti-Jewish measures that had already destroyed the careers of two previous prime ministers.

Teleki proved adept at duping Germany. He curtailed the influence, albeit temporarily, of Hungary's nativist Nazis. Simultaneously he introduced a number of pro-German and anti-Semitic measures. This soothed Germany's Nazi leaders. They preferred dealing with a "reliable" and cooperative Hungarian government, rather than with inefficient and squabbling pro-Nazi factions, howevermuch they admired the Third Reich and followed its orders.

Teleki also tried to outmaneuver Hungary's *völkisch* Swabians. He made many promises, fulfilled only a few, complained to the Third Reich about the *Volksbund's* disloyalty, and set Hungary's *völkisch DVU* and the loyalist *UDV* at each others' throats. In this manner, he weakened Hungary's Swabians, and reduced the risks of a unified Swabian confrontation with the Hungarian state.

Teleki additionally attempted to prevent a National Socialist triumph at the polls in the parliamentary election of 28 May. In order to soothe the Swabians and the Third Reich, he introduced various measures that pleased Nazi Germany. These policies also served to regain the allegiance of some of the Hungarian Nazis, and to pacify the government's own restless ultraright wing. Teleki's stratagem partially succeeded. Without these ploys the government party might have been defeated by an extreme right-wing—National Socialist coalition. Instead, Hungary's right-wing elements remained divided and temporarily harmless.

These election results greatly influenced the course of Hungarian foreign policy. The Western allies were made to see that in a free franchise, Hungary did not succumb to National Socialism. The Third Reich gathered much the same impression. Of course, Hitler would not hesitate to utilize the strengthened Nazi parliamentary contingent to embarrass, even threaten, the government, should the latter fail to cooperate with Germany. Hereafter, Hungarian cabinets had to be sensitive to the Hungarian ultraright. Collusion between the *völkish* Swabians and domestic Hungarian Nazis, both groups covertly assisted by the Third Reich, became a perennial danger that the government tried to avert by a "divide and conquer" policy.

In view of Hungary's precarious situation in 1939, the government intensified its opportunistic diplomacy toward Germany. Promises to improve the condition of the Swabian minority became more frequent, but these pledges were seldom kept. Hungarian declarations vowing unlimited economic cooperation and full support for Germany's war efforts remained mainly paper promises. For example, Hungary refused to assist Germany in the Polish campaign, which drew the disapproval of the Third Reich's leaders and strained relations between the two countries.

Hungary's relationship with Czechoslovakia had never been cordial, but at least the two countries had maintained diplomatic relations and preserved a degree of common courtesy. This was far from being true for Slovakia, the only surviving semi-independent rump of the former First Czechoslovak Republic. Hungary wanted to occupy all of Slovakia in 1938, but direct negotiations with the Slovaks had proved fruitless. After numerous border clashes, Germany and Italy designated a new frontier on 2 November 1938. The fact that numerous ethnic Magyars remained in Slovakia exacerbated Hungarian resentment. Hungary refused to make peace with Slovakia, rejected pleas for badly needed economic aid, and several times threatened aggression in response to largely imaginary Slovak provocations. The exasperated Germans constantly had to keep their two troublesome "allies" from attacking each other.

Relations between Hungary and Romania were also poor. In the late summer of 1938, Hungary, Romania, Czechoslovakia and Yugoslavia had reached a virtual accord at the Bled Conference on the matter of the treatment of Magyar minorities, and on Hungary's right to rearm. Czechoslovakia's destruction a few weeks later rendered the treaty useless for the surviving parties. Throughout most of 1939, Romanian fascism flourished, which manifested itself in the refusal of Romania to accommodate Hungary on a number of burning issues. Responding to persistent rumors of German ultimatums being served on Romania, Great Britain and France guaranteed Romanian independence after March 1939. In fact, however, Romania accommodated both hostile camps, and remained a bone of contention.

The Third Reich regarded a German-Romanian agreement as a major coup. It ensured the delivery of huge quantities of food and oil supplies from Romania to Germany. In contrast, Hungary's resources were far more humble, and Hungarians had refused to share some of them with Germany. But hereafter, Germany could bypass Hungary as a military and political ally and as a major economic resource and utilize Romania instead. Hungary tried to depict the Romanians as unreliable double-dealers in Berlin, but to no avail. Hungary's worst fears came to pass in 1940, when Romania was swept completely into the Axis orbit.

Hungary's relations with Yugoslavia were only slightly better than with Romania. After World War I, Hungary had not relinquished nearly as much territory or populations to Yugoslavia as either to Czechoslovakia or Romania, nor did Yugoslavia overtly persecute its Magyar minorities. In 1938, Hungary had been reluctant to join Germany and Poland in a joint attack on Czechoslovakia, because Hungary's leaders feared retaliation by Romania and Yugoslavia. Italy and Germany tried fruitlessly to reassure Hungary's leaders that Romania and Yugoslavia would not dare offend the Axis by attacking Hungary while it incorporated eastern Czechoslovakia. It was no use. The Hungarians were cautious to a fault, and would rather forfeit territorial gain than possibly risk destruction in a losing war. As a result of this apparent timidity, Hitler dismissed the Hungarians as cowardly and lost confidence in their pro-Axis rhetoric.

Whether Romania and Yugoslavia would have attacked Hungary in the fall of 1938 is conjectural. The Yugoslavs emulated Romania's example. Both countries tried to maintain a balance between the West and the Axis. Invading Hungary would have antagonized the Axis without gaining favor in the West. In order to please its Western benefactors, on 26 August 1939, Yugoslavia reestablished democratic government and held secret elections. A fundamental reorganization scheme remedied interethnic strife, and offered the Croats cultural and economic autonomy. When Germany attacked Poland, Yugoslavia remained neutral for over one year. All this time, however, Hungary tried and failed to restore normal relations with its southern neighbor, because the Yugoslavs refused to relinquish even a token portion of Magyar-inhabited territory. Their stubbornness contributed to the destruction of Yugoslavia in 1941. In this campaign, Germany tempted and coerced Hungary into participation by promising to permit all of Yugoslavia's Magyar-inhabited areas to be annexed by Hungary.

Ever since its reconstitution after World War I, Poland and Hungary had been devoted friends. Poland ardently supported Hungary's territorial demands against Czechoslovakia, and, to a lesser extent, against the other Little Entente countries as well. Hungary reciprocated by trying to dissuade Germany from waging war against Poland. The German-Polish crisis began in March-April 1939, immediately after Germany's seizure of western Czecho-Slovakia. Germany had been tricking the Poles into a false sense of security by promising peaceful future relations. In fact, Germany merely awaited the favorable resolution of the Czecho-Slovak crisis before striking. The Germans were so secretive about the invasion that the Poles were unable to obtain timely warning from their Hungarian friends. On 31 March, the British and French pledged to defend Poland, but the offer was strategically unviable, and thus failed to deter Germany. On 28 April, Germany denounced the German-Polish Nonaggression Pact of 26 January 1934, accused the Poles of persecuting their German minority, and tendered unacceptable territorial demands that would have violated Polish sovereignty.

Hungarians deplored the breakdown in Polish-German relations. Not only was a valued friendly country's survival at stake, but Hungarians also feared that, if they failed to support Hitler, Germany's "friendship" for Hungary might turn into enmity. Although defying Germany seemed foolhardy, the Hungarian government and public ostentatiously cheered Poland. Nothing infuriated the Germans more than Hungary's fraternization with Poland. Germany lodged protest after protest in Budapest, but to no avail.

Next to Poland and Austria, Italy had been Hungary's most faithful ally and commercial benefactor. By 1939, however, Italy had lost its economic and political influence in eastern Europe and became a virtual German satellite. In January 1939, Count Ciano established intimate political, cultural and economic ties with Yugoslavia, and attempted to persuade Hungary to join the alliance. By then, Hungary no longer trusted Italy. The invitation aroused suspicions in Budapest. Italy might either be trying to lull Hungary into a false sense of security vis-à-vis Yugoslavia, or worse still, Italy and Yugoslavia might be plotting against Germany, and wanted to involve Hungary. Hungary had thus far rejected German demands to adopt policies that would benefit the Third Reich. By the same reasoning, Hungarian leaders refused to let Italy exploit Hungary in a hopeless cabal directed against the Third Reich.

Events in the next few months demonstrated Hungary's wisdom in steering clear of Italian schemings. In April, Italy invaded and conquered Albania, and in May, Mussolini concluded a political and military alliance with Germany. It may have been true that Mussolini tried to deter Hitler's aggression in Poland in order to avert a global conflict, and Italy did remain neutral when the war broke out. From Hungary's viewpoint, however, Italy could no longer defend Hungarian interests. Its preoccupation had shifted mainly to Africa and the Mediterranean basin, and Hungary had been clearly placed outside of Italy's sphere of influence. Since the First Vienna Arbitral Award, Hungary's survival depended exclusively on

Germany's "good will." The era of Italian economic influence and political effectiveness in eastern Europe was over, even though Italy tried in vain to recover its prestige on a few occasions in 1939.

Ever since Admiral Horthy rode into Budapest at the head of his army in 1919, Hungary remained one of the most fervent anti-Bolshevik states in the world. This preoccupation at first attracted many members of the Hungarian government and the conservative élite to the rising National Socialist movement in Germany. By 1933, the Third Reich's National Socialist anti-Bolshevik mission served as a potent common cause that bound Hungary to Nazi Germany. They were determined to launch a Christian crusade to vanquish the scourge of Communism. In late August 1939, the Soviet Union and Nazi Germany shattered this ideological illusion by concluding a trade pact, followed by a nonaggression treaty. The repercussions of this perceived betrayal were keenly felt in Budapest. Hungarian leaders had believed that, come what may, the Third Reich would always defend their country against the Bolshevik menace. Now even this certainty vanished.

When Germany declared war on Poland, the Soviet Union at first remained neutral. Then, on 17 September, the Red Army swarmed across the Polish frontier, and linked up with the Germans at Brest-Litovsk two days later. On 29 September, the two allies partitioned Poland. Hungary now had the Soviet Union as a close neighbor. It was scant consolation to Hungary that Romania was also imperiled by the Soviet Union, which had been demanding Bessarabia and parts of Bukovina since the end of World War I. Hungarians erroneously believed that the embattled Romanians would become more coopeerative on Transylvania, the treatment of Magyars, and other Hungarian grievances.

Indeed, the Romanians were caught between the Germans and the Russians, and had to please both. In June 1940, Romania had to surrender Bessarabia and northern Bukovina to the Soviet Union, and in August, under pressure from Berlin and Rome, Romania yielded a portion of Transylvania to Hungary. This windfall was less a reward for faithful Hungarian service than German dislike for King Carol, whom Hitler wanted to force out of office. He succeeded. Within a week the King fled, having been replaced by his son, Michael V. In fact, however, Romania came under the domination of General Ion Antonescu, an Iron Guard sympathizer, who was congenial to Hitler and Mussolini. Far from being a thoroughly happy occasion for Hungary, the acquisition of Transylvania was an unsubtle reminder that the Rome-Berlin Axis dealt ruthlessly with uncooperative "allied" leaders. Furthermore, Hungary was forced to grant the *Volksbund* unconditional autonomy, so that the Swabian *Volksgruppe* became a state within a state.

Until June 1941, when Germany invaded the USSR, Hungary felt apprehensive about the negative repercussions of the Soviet presence near its frontier. Hungary feared the spread of Pan-Slavic propaganda among its Serbs, Ruthenes and Slovaks, but also among the Slovaks of Slovakia, now a German protectorate, which Hungary hoped to annex someday. Germany, on the other hand, refused to take the Pan-Slav menace seriously.

Hungary also feared that Communist propaganda would subvert the country's landless rural masses and seduce the impoverished urban proletarians into revolutionary action. Since the Communist party was outlawed, the Hungarian National Socialist parties attracted these two disaffected groups like a magnet. Hungarian leaders expected the country to be struck by disaster if extreme right-wing and left-wing forces became sufficiently powerful and polarized. Should the government prove unable to curb the extremists, Hungary would succumb either to the Nazis or to the Soviets. Similarly, if Hungary became embroiled in the current war, the outcome would be quite predictable. Hungary would turn either Communist or National Socialist. Both alternatives would terminate Hungarian independence.

The loss of Austria, Poland and Italy as allies, the removal of Czechoslovakia as a buffer against Germany, Romanian and Yugoslav enmity, the acquisiton of two additional potential foes— Slovakia and the Soviet Union—combined with the realization that Germany would prove a slender reed upon which to lean in troubled times, prompted Hungarian policymakers to keep the country's lifelines open to the West. All but the most ardent Hungarian Germanophiles hoped for a compromise in the current war. They desired to return to equitable and friendly great power competition in eastern Europe, where Hungary might regain all the Magyar-inhabited areas by international consent. Only then would Hungary be able to fulfill its traditional role as middleman and conciliator between East and West. In Hungarian fantasies, the Soviet Union would be pushed vaguely back "to the east," where it would obediently remain, obeying the wishes of a reconciled and powerful Western European family of nations.

Reality, however, confounded Hungarian expectations. The Hungarians, for example, believed that the British, having mistakenly punished Hungary after World War I for its alliance with Germany, had experienced a change of heart, and now would help restore its proper dominant position in east-central Europe. According to this Hungarian scenario, the British apparently realized belatedly that Trianon had been an error that must be rectified. Hungarians gathered these impressions from intensive exposure to the rhetoric of a handful of Magyarophile British politicians and publicists. Press barons such as Lord Rothermere convinced many Hungarians that the British government and public stood resolutely behind Hungary. Rothermere raised unrealistic expectations and caused a great deal of harm. Prime Minister Imrédy, for years an enthusiastic pro-Briton, eventually discovered this deception, and became an outspoken pro-Nazi enthusiast. For a long time, even the pragmatic and experienced Count Bethlen believed that Great Britain would someday help remedy the injustices of Trianon, and restore Hungary to its former splendor.

In fact, however, the British had little time, energy or resources to waste on Hungary between the wars. Most Britons believed that Hungary wanted to discard the hated Trianon Treaty by force rather than engage in negotiations or settle grievances through compromise. They saw Hungarians supporting disreputable fascist revisionists. A case in point was Nazi Germany. Hungarians were fawning over the Third Reich, even though its system and philosophy offended the parliamentary principles Hungarians proclaimed proudly as precious. And they gratefully accepted, via German auspices, shares of Czechoslovakian soil under circumstances that were legally questionable, and morally and ethically reprehensible. Later on, Hungary acquired territory from Romania and Yugoslavia, again with German assistance. As the British perceived the situation, Hungarian sense of justice appeared to be selective. The ends, it seemed, justified the means. As a result, the British cast Germany and Hungary into the same mold as troublemakers. Already in 1938, Great Britain and France dismissed Hungary as a country that was definitely lost to the Nazi cause. Thereafter, they concentrated their efforts and few available resources to keep Poland, Romania, Yugoslavia, Greece and Turkey out of Nazi clutches. By 1939, whether rightly or wrongly, Hungary's image as the unredeemable Axis satellite dominated British and French thinking.

In view of its total isolation, Hungary had to depend entirely on the wits of its leaders to preserve what could be salvaged of its national sovereignty. Hungarians exploited every plausible opportunity to postpone taking unpleasant steps. They made numerous promises to Germany, kept very few of their pledges, and when the German-Polish war erupted, Hungarian leaders expressed their displeasure over the conflict in no uncertain terms.

CHAPTER XI

HUNGARY'S ECONOMIC DILEMMAS IN 1939

By 1939, Germany dominated the economy of the Danube Basin.[1] The Third Reich had replaced Italian influence, and relegated its junior ally to an as yet undefined Mediterranean presence.[2] The Third Reich regarded economic hegemony east of Germany as an indispensable feature of its Four-Year Plan.[3] The countries of eastern Europe were to become cogs in a complex German economic wheel. Ultimately, the area would become an agricultural hinterland that would help the Third Reich extend its economic influence as far as Baghdad.[4] Germany planned a permanent *Lebensraum* and *Grosswirtschaftsraum* reserved for Germans only. In 1938, Hungarians still hoped that a Greater Hungary would eventually become the Third Reich's regional agricultural agent. In 1939, however, these illusions vanished. Hungary's leaders realized that their country was merely one of several weak, vulnerable and mutually hostile agricultural states competing for German favor. (See Table 1) Germany would treat none of them considerately, but rather play one country off against another to achieve its own economic objectives.

By late 1938, Germany's economic grip on the small eastern European countries was sufficiently tight to foil any resistance. The Third Reich altered the satellites' standards of payment and redefined the terms of transacting trade with Germany. For example, Germany raised prices on export items destined for eastern Europe's agricultural states; qualities of German manufactured goods deteriorated; and German suppliers deliberately delayed deliveries of essential commodities in order to destabilize their trading partners' economies. Germany also increased the proportion of armaments these small countries, but especially Hungary, had to purchase if they desired to retain the Third Reich's custom for their food staples. Most of the weaponry sold under these agreements was obsolete. Germany thus not only discarded old arms, but the proceeds helped to finance its own rearmament at a relatively low cost, while Germans were being kept well-fed at bargain rates. Additionally, Germany gradually raised the Mark, which increased export prices and decreased the Third Reich's costs of agricultural purchases.[5]

These strategies enabled Germany to assume undisputed economic control in eastern Europe by 1939. German firms owned about 14% of Hungary's mining and industrial enterprises. This exceeded 50% of all such foreign investments, including 25% of all Hungarian businesses in foreign hands.[6] By the first quarter of 1939, Germany was buying 95% of Hungarian slaughtered meats, 88% of live hogs and 75% of all grains.[7]

In the early autumn of 1938, Hungary appeared ready to terminate its ambitious industrialization program and offered to sell its entire food production to Germany on a long-term basis. But the gesture was a ruse. The Hungarian government wanted to gain Hitler's confidence and good will, in order to ensure that Hungary shared in the territorial spoils when Czechoslovakia disintegrated. The Hungarians discovered to their chagrin a few months later that the Third Reich had taken their tactical gesture seriously. On 12 January 1939, Ribbentrop had his staff summarize these Hungarian proposals in preparation for his 6 February conference with Count István Csáky, Hungary's recently appointed foreign minister.[8]

The Csáky-Ribbentrop encounter, which covered numerous topics, proceeded under a pall. Just before the meeting, Hitler had berated Csáky for Hungary's alleged ineptitude and disloyalty during the Munich Crisis. Because of Hungarian bungling, Hitler had raged, Czechoslovakia still survived, and as a result, Hungary could no longer hope to seize any more Czechoslovak territory. On the contrary, Hitler asserted. Henceforth, he would promote the interests of the Third Reich exclusively, and let Hungary fend for itself. Hitler perceived a shadow darkening German-Hungarian relations, and he refused to tolerate such a situation. He was also furious because many Hungarians blamed him personally for their country's insignificant territorial gains in Slovakia and Ruthenia. This attitude he considered a "tremendous betrayal and ingratitude, which offended the entire German people."[9] Csáky had tried to soothe Hitler. Having learned the lessons of Munich, Csáky assured Hitler, Hungary now rejected the romantic adventurism that sought to expand the country in all directions simultaneously, even if these territorial acquisitions meant the absorption of large numbers of non-Magyars. Hungary realized that the presence of many aliens would merely weaken the national fiber.[10]

Ribbentrop reiterated Hitler's list of grievances regarding Hungary's recent deplorable behavior and attitudes, but he offered to let by-gones be by-gones. He wanted to start a new happy chapter in German-Hungarian relations, based this time on far closer political, ideological and economic cooperation than had been the case hitherto. Csáky assured Ribbentrop that Hungary desired to collaborate with Germany in every possible way, and did not object when the Germans placed the scheme calling for a ten-year German-Hungarian commercial pact and joint economic planning on the agenda.[11]

Alfred Nickl, head of Hungary's economic delegation, feared the consequences of a long-range German-Hungarian commercial agreement. He warned Csáky that the Germans planned to relegate Hungary to the level of a humble supplier of raw materials.[12] Nickl had ample cause for concern. The Germans had adopted the original Hungarian suggestions for a long-term agreement as a bona fide proposal for Hungary's voluntary reduction to colonial status. Nickl's German counterpart, Emil K. J. Wiehl, demanded a detailed outline from Hungary on how the plan would function. Nickl replied that Germany's share of Hungary's exports had recently risen to 48%. More than two-thirds of Hungary's agricultural production now went to the Third Reich. (See Tables 2 and 3) Under these circumstances, Nickl asserted, any further increases would be difficult to manage. In fact, Nickl considered a ten-year German-Hungarian commercial agreement far too ambitious. Even a five-year treaty would be excessive. If Germany truly insisted on concluding a ten-year trade pact with Hungary, then either party ought to be able to revise the treaty on short notice. This limitation, of course, would have destroyed the effectiveness of such an agreement for Germany.

Instead, Nickl offered Wiehl his own vaguely structured version of a German-Hungarian agreement. (See Table 4) He informed Wiehl that Hungarian agriculture could accommodate Germany's needs, but not if it meant that his country's economic infrastructure would have to be transformed to suit Germany's specific requirements. Under impending Hungarian land reforms, planners anticipated the planting of new types of crops that Germany might need. But Nickl thought that German exports to Hungary were insufficient to balance German indebtedness. By mid-1939, Hungarian exports to Germany would exceed German imports by 50 million Pengő and hence Hungary had little incentive in catering to Germany's agricultural requirements. If Hungary increased its export volume beyond the present scope, then by 1940 Germany's debit would rise to 100 million Pengő. Such a debt would be excessive, Nickl asserted, because the various consumer items and machinery that Hungary needed from Germany cost only 20 million Pengő. Nor did Hungary expect to purchase any additional military hardware from Germany in 1939. Nickl suggested that Germany might reduce its indebtedness by selling the German-owned coal mines located near Pécs to Hungary for 20 million Pengő. The proceeds would be applied to Germany's overdrawn clearing account with Hungary.

Nickl also dispelled any German illusion that Hungary would curtail industrialization. Hungary's growing population could not survive on agriculture alone. On the contrary. Hungary had to reduce its dependency on industrial imports. Nickl cautioned that if Germany forced Hungary and the other southeastern European countries to abandon manufacturing, then the entire world would discover that the Third Reich practiced economic repression and colonialism. In Nickl's view, the less said regarding this topic the better, for Germany's sake.

Wiehl's report to the German Foreign Ministry betrayed profound disappointment regarding the first day's negotiations. In Wiehl's view, Nickl had reiterated well-worn Hungarian arguments and themes. Wiehl particularly criticized Nickl for reneging on Hungary's earlier deindustrialization promises. The following day's talks proved equally fruitless for Germany. The Third Reich's leaders were greatly concerned about Germany's oil shortage. Consequently, they sought opportunities to explore oil and natural gas sites in friendly countries. Romania had a large-scale agreement of this type pending with Germany. Hungary's oil deposits were far more modest than Romania's, but some locations promised to yield commercially viable quantities of fossil fuels. German State Secretary Wilhelm Keppler proposed joint German-Hungarian exploration of all these sites. Nickl, however, would allow the Germans to investigate only the least promising locations at their own expense, whereas Hungary would retain exclusive rights to explore and exploit the most promising sites. Nickl informed Keppler that Hungary had offered exclusive exploration rights on the very best locations to an American company. Although these concessions were renewable in September, Nickl cited "a high Hungarian source" that the American concession would not be revoked.

The German negotiators demanded that Hungary terminate the American concession, and insisted on joint German-Hungarian exploration and exploitation of all Hungarian sites. Nickl tried to minimize the problem, whereupon the Germans refused to consider selling the Pécs coal mines, and became uncooperative on discarding other lucrative and desirable German properties located on Hungarian soil that the Budapest government wished to purchase at low prices.[13] The Germans regarded the Hungarians as opportunists who refused to accommodate Germany on vital products such as oil, while Germany was paying Hungary 20 Pengö per quintal for wheat at a time when in Rotterdam grain of that quality sold for only 8-10 Pengö.[14]

Later that day, Wiehl responded to Nickl's "extremely disappointing suggestions." Apparently, at this point, the Germans decided that exerting excessive economic pressure on Hungary was counterproductive. Germany, said Wiehl, would prefer to have Hungary draft a detailed German-Hungarian coordination plan devoid of the customary tired old arguments. If, however, Hungary rejected intensive bilateral cooperation with Germany in favor of exploiting its own resources, then Germany would not object at this time. Both parties would have to recognize, however, that negative Hungarian attitudes had produced a new situation in German-Hungarian relations. The two countries would have to employ different methods henceforth to achieve fruitful results. Possibly, negotiations might once again proceed through regular channels, notably, the permanent German-Hungarian trade commission that normally met twice annually, and was scheduled to gather in Munich and Budapest, respectively, in the near future.

Wiehl treated Nickl's individual proposals with restraint. He conceded that a five-year commercial agreement would be more than adequate to serve the two countries' needs. Delivery quotas ought to be fixed in advance, Wiehl thought, but price structures should be adjusted biennially. Wiehl rejected Nickl's proposed increases in cattle shipments as excessive, but demanded lower prices. Germany would not purchase more hogs, unless the volume of maize used as feed also rose proportionately. Salami imports had to pass stringent German hygienic regulations, and Hungary would have to meet these standards. The Germans had not yet utilized their current quotas of Hungarian quality wines, nor did they intend to stock up in the future. Germany would scrutinize Nickl's proposal on tobacco exports, consider concluding agreements on a number of new food items and fodder, and would inform Hungary regarding Germany's decisions as soon as possible. Wiehl considered Nickl's proposal concerning the transformation of Hungarian agriculture to suit Germany's needs far too tentative to merit a response. He urged German and Hungarian experts to study the suggestion thoroughly. He believed that Hungary's five-year rearmament plan harmonized admirably with the two countries' requirements. Hungary's arsenal would be modernized, whereas Germany's huge clearing debts to Hungary would be diminished.

Wiehl addressed the question of German exports to Hungary. He conceded that German shipments of certain consumer items and raw materials to Hungary ought to be increased, but he flatly rejected the export of certain commodities that Hungary badly needed, notably timber, crude iron and machine tools. In general, he considered Hungarian import regulations so complex that they impeded the flow of many German export items into Hungary. He urged the Hungarian government to review its import regulations, and to lower certain tariffs. Nickl rejected the latter two proposals as "impractical."

Wiehl condemned Hungary's change of heart regarding deindustrialization. Abolishing superfluous Hungarian industry was an absolute, unavoidable necessity, upon which successful German-Hungarian relations depended. Hungary would be foolhardy to create new industries for which raw materials were unavailable domestically, and which Germany would refuse to sell. Hungary, he conceded, was a sovereign state, and hence had the right to make economic decisions; yet he counseled the Hungarian government to submit this burning issue to bilateral discussions.

Nickl responded that a deindustrialized Hungary could easily find itself in a precarious position. Germany might refuse to sell Hungary badly needed manufactured goods, while it purchased Hungarian agricultural products selectively. Even now, he complained, Germany demanded all of Hungary's grain, but on one pretext or another, refused to buy various types of meat products. Should Hungary decide to deindustrialize, then at the very least, Germany would have to pledge not to leave Hungary in the possession of unmarketable agricultural products. Nickl wanted the two countries to remand the deindustrialization problem to cabinet level negotiations, and leave the less controversial issues to the economic experts.[15]

A few days later, Admiral Horthy reneged on still another promise that Hitler regarded as the litmus test of Hungarian loyalty. In his 5 March 1938 speech, Darányi had pledged speedy legislative action to curtail the economic power of Hungarian Jewry. Although at that time Darányi enjoyed an overwhelming parliamentary majority, his Jewish legislation (Law XV) suffered defeat. It passed the Lower House on 18 May, and the Upper Chamber six days later, but Darányi himself was forced to resign on 13 May, and the law remained still-born. His successor, Béla Imrédy, who also wielded a comfortable majority, submitted the law for passage to parliament on 23 December 1938, but before legislation could be enacted, Imrédy had to resign in disgrace due to his own alleged distant Jewish ancestry. Anti-Jewish legislation in Hungary had destroyed the political careers of two prime ministers who tried to introduce it.[16]

Horthy had never tried to conceal his anti-Semitism. He disliked Jews, but he resented even more Hitler's attempt to create a racial

problem in Hungary that he regarded strictly a domestic socioeconomic question. Yet Horthy did deplore Hungary's allegedly excessive economic dependence on Jews. Most of all, Horthy considered
German interference in Hungary's Jewish "question" an effrontery,
a vulgar imposition, and an unwonted interference with Hungary's
sovereign rights. Horthy, of course, could not voice his displeasure
over German meddling in the Jewish problem officially. He chose an
informal occasion to rebuke Hitler. At a diplomatic dinner recep-
tion in Budapest, Horthy told German Minister Otto Erdmannsdorff that he entertained serious misgivings about implementing
radical anti-Jewish legislation in Hungary too suddenly. Horthy
professed being an avid anti-Semite who believed that Hungary's
Jewish question would have to be solved eventually, but presently,
he regarded Jewish economic power and professional skills as an
indispensable Hungarian asset. If Germany desired effective Hungarian support, then Jewish economic power would have to remain
in force for the time being. Hungarian society lacked suitable personnel to replace Jewish experts, many of whom wielded "positions
of extraordinary influence." Horthy characterized Hungary's Jews
as "milch cows." It would be counterproductive to slaughter them.
If the Jews were removed, Hungary would lose its major sources of
income at a time when the country desperately needed more money
to finance its rearmament program.[17]

Horthy evidently tried to postpone the day when Hungary would
have to bow to German demands and dismiss Jews from public and
business life. Horthy knew that when that occurred, Hungary's
sovereignty would be a dead letter. Horthy had cautiously chosen a
social occasion on which to protest the German leadership's interference on the Jewish question. It was a futile gesture. Before long,
Horthy had to swallow his pride, set Hungary on an anti-Semitic
course, and weaken Hungarian sovereignty. Anti-Jewish legislation
came into effect shortly before parliament recessed on 4 May 1939.
The statute was Teleki's gift of gratitude to Hitler, who had granted
Hungary permission to annex the rest of Ruthenia in the middle of
March.

By the end of June, Sztójay perceived the gathering of war
clouds in Berlin. Although he assured the Hungarian foreign ministry that German intentions were as peaceful as Hungary's, Sztójay
felt uneasy because Hungary and Germany might blunder into
an armed conflict involuntarily, if conflicts could not be rectified
through normal diplomatic channels. He strongly urged the creation of joint German-Hungarian economic contingency plans to go
into effect in the event of a conflict. He believed that Hungary ought

to have a military-economic exigency plan in conjunction with Germany and Italy, in order to forestall misunderstandings and avoid bruised feelings among the Axis allies should war erupt. Italian military authorities had already raised the issue of coordinating the military economies of Germany and Italy. Sztójay urged his government to conduct similar negotiations with the German military leadership. For the time being, he preferred these discussions to be held in secret, and the decisions to be non-binding. Sztójay also counseled Csáky to reassure Germany and Italy that Hungary would not deliberately embroil its two allies in a war against their will.[18]

The Third Reich refused to invite Hungary to participate in ongoing German-Italian military-economic negotiations. Germany had no faith that Hungarians would keep military secrets, and therefore, the latter were kept in the dark with vague promises that discussions would follow in the near future.[19] The Germans had other reasons for not wishing to share their military and economic plans with Hungary. Hungary was an avid supporter of Poland, Hitler's next victim. Prime Minister Teleki's twin letters of 24 July, addressed simultaneously to Hitler and Mussolini, definitively terminated any German desire to confide in Hungary. Teleki's first letter announced Hungary's wish for closer cooperation with the German-Italian committee dealing with military-economic matters. The second letter, citing "present circumstances," declared that Hungary would not cooperate with Germany because of its hostile intentions against Poland.[20] This was Teleki's way of protesting Hitler's imminent Polish campaign.

Hitler was outraged. He cancelled all military staff talks and suspended military collaboration with Hungary. The German foreign ministry informed Sztójay that Teleki's second letter had severely injured German-Hungarian relations. Three days earlier, he was told, Germany had been on the verge of including Hungary in German-Italian military-economic talks.[21] One week later, Sztójay was informed that unless Hungary's pro-Polish public posture ceased, the Third Reich would retaliate by suspending all further vital arms shipments. Sztójay's protestations that Hungary was pro-German carried no weight. On one pretext or another, Germany refused to resume weapons shipments to Hungary for a while.[22] When war erupted on 1 September, Hungarians were relieved to learn that, "for the moment," Germany did not require them to provide armed assistance of any kind.[23] The government, however, placed the Hungarian economy on a war footing. On 2 September, Teleki requisitioned certain raw materials, temporarily tightened workplace regulations, and introduced price controls.[24]

Far more aggravating and unwelcome for Hungary was the fact that, at German insistence, Hungary had to render economic aid to the hated Slovak government. Slovakia urgently needed 25,000 tons of coal and 150 wagonloads of fats. Germany was unable to provide these necessities, but German officials knew that Hungary could. Sztójay condemned Slovakia for seeking help from Hungary, even as its officials publicly insulted their would-be benefactor. Sztójay had no choice but to promise the Germans that he would submit the Slovak shopping list in Budapest, but he predicted that his superiors would not deal with the Slovaks unless their anti-Hungarian rhetoric ceased.[25]

Worse still, on 9 September, Ribbentrop demanded German use of the Hungarian railway system leading to the southern Polish frontier. Germany wanted to exploit Hungarian neutrality to transport troops and war material into Poland in perfect safety through Hungary.[26] This request confronted Hungary with a dilemma. Large-scale German military traffic would interfere with Hungary's transportation system at harvest time, force Hungary to betray its Polish friends, and jeopardize Hungarian neutrality. Count Csáky rejected Ribbentrop's demand, because it was incompatible with Hungarian national honor, and because ultimately it would harm the German war effort. Compliance would embroil Hungary in the war, and because the country was totally unprepared, Germany would not only lose Hungary's economic and other support, but ultimately would have to rescue Hungary from a military disaster. Csáky was pro-German, yet he threatened to resign if Germany insisted on injuring Hungary's economic, military and national interests in this manner.[27]

Ribbentrop deplored Csáky's negative response. He reminded Csáky that Hungary controlled the railway lines in question only because Germany had helped Hungary acquire them.[28] The Germans were not likely to forgive this perceived injustice. The Germans had long memories, he asserted. They would neither forget nor forgive Hungary's rejection. Some day, he predicted, the Hungarians would have to pay the price for their non-cooperation.[29] Hungary also refused to permit German troops to set foot on Hungarian soil, but only consented to transport German war material in sealed, unescorted boxcars.[30] Hungary withdrew even this minor concession when Slovakia also clamored for transport privileges on Hungarian soil for its troops and weapons. Csáky threatened that any Slovak troop movements near the Hungarian frontier would be considered a warlike act, and vowed that Hungary would respond accordingly. Hungary thereupon rushed troops to the Slovak border, which caused a considerable stir and extreme annoyance in Berlin.[31]

Incidents, misunderstandings and mutual resentments became exacerbated and poisoned German-Hungarian relations after the outbreak of hostilities with Poland. These controversies not only soured routine diplomacy, they placed Hungary's economic relations with the Third Reich at risk. During a conference with Carl von Clodius, deputy head of the economic branch of the German Foreign Ministry, Prime Minister Teleki sought to clarify and defuse a number of vexing economic issues that had plagued the two countries' relations even before the outbreak of German-Polish hostilities.

The question of Ruthenia's economic exploitation proved one of the major problems between Germany and Hungary. Germany had informed Hungary that the former Czechoslovak province could be seized only if the Third Reich would be permitted to exploit the economic potentials of the area, especially its natural wealth. Hungary promised to grant this privilege, but then reneged on its pledge. Germany offered to withdraw its claim in return for gaining a free hand in the exploration and exploitation of the province's oil resources. Teleki denied that Hungary had ever renounced its sovereign rights over the territory's natural wealth. Moreover, Hungarian pride was hurt. Hungary possessed perfectly competent geologists who were capable of surveying the area without the benefit of German experts, Teleki informed the Germans. Hungary might, however, consider permitting Germany to participate in the exploitation of Ruthenia's oil resources at some undefined future date. Clodius rejected Teleki's response as insolent and unacceptable, whereupon Teleki promised to emerge with an improved proposal. He never did, and there the matter rested.

Another source of German-Hungarian tension was Hungary's refusal to normalize commercial relations with Germany's Slovak protectorate. Slovakia urgently needed Hungarian agricultural products and fats on an ongoing basis. Teleki repeatedly refused to deal with the Slovaks until they ceased transmitting anti-Hungarian propaganda and stopped persecuting their Magyar minorities. Clodius reminded Teleki that Germany had no desire to get embroiled in Hungarian-Slovak squabbles. Slovakia was a valuable German ally in the fight against Poland, whereas Hungary was not. It was Hungary's duty to aid Germany by assisting its confederate. Refusal to help Slovakia would sabotage the German war effort. Teleki grudgingly agreed to release the desired goods, but he refused to ship the goods to Slovakia. He dispatched the cargo to the Third Reich, and told the Germans to do with it as they pleased. By using this approach, Teleki avoided having to deal directly with Slovakia, and he salvaged a shred of tattered German-Hungarian relations. Germany shipped 30-40 wagonloads of fats to Slovakia from its own supplies, which Hungary duly replaced.

The third major source of contention that poisoned German-Hungarian relations involved Hungary's decision to devalue the Pengő against Western European currencies by about 11% when war broke out. Through this deft action, Hungary indirectly devalued not only the Pengő but the German Mark, and thus exploited war conditions to profit handsomely at the Third Reich's expense. (See Tables 5A and 5B) The Germans were furious. Teleki feigned a lack of expertise in complex fiscal matters. He urged Clodius to discuss the problem with Lipót Baranyai, president of the Hungarian Credit Bank, who had introduced these currency changes. Baranyai explained that the new rates were essential, because they made Hungarian exports competitive in Western European countries. Clodius ordered Baranyai to restore the Pengő to its prewar value. Baranyai would not yield, and dared Clodius to demand his ouster. Clodius then realized that this action was part of a carefully devised stratagem, and that Baranyai had the upper hand, because he enjoyed the Hungarian government's enthusiastic support. Clodius lodged a sharp protest and pledged to resume the struggle on behalf of the Mark at a later date.[32]

German-Hungarian discussions thus broke down in nearly total disagreement on three substantial and symbolic points. Each outcome left the Germans more disgruntled than before. Hungary had reneged on its economic promises in Ruthenia, refused to deal with Germany's Slovak protectorate, and virtually pirated an 11% profit on all commercial transactions with Germany. At the same time Hungary exploited its neutral status to improve trading with Germany's enemies.

One month later, while sojourning in Budapest on an eastern European factfinding tour, Otto Braun, director of Transdanubia, a German export-import firm, asserted that by this time most German officials had come to take Hungarian duplicity for granted. According to Braun, the Hungarian government engaged in questionable practices and deceptions designed to injure Germany's vital interests. The Budapest government used the Germanophile diplomat Count Csáky as a "frontman" to issue reassuring pro-German statements. This was meant to lull the Third Reich into a false sense of security. In the meantime, Hungary was secretly undermining Germany's hegemony in the Balkans. He discovered, for example, that Tibor Eckhardt, the noted anti-German Opposition leader, had recently visited Belgrade and planned to travel to Rome on a secret Hungarian government mission. Eckhardt admitted to reporters that his task was to explore the possibility of creating a presumably anti-German three-power bloc composed of Italy, Yugoslavia and Hungary. He was to report directly to the Hungarian prime minister upon his return. Braun regarded Hungarian foreign policy as insincere, and was convinced that it would remain so. The emergence of a faithful pro-German government in Budapest was unlikely. For Germany, he asserted, the situation in Hungary was deteriorating from day to day.[33]

Extreme German pessimism regarding Hungarian behavior, lack of faith in Hungary's desire to aid the German war effort, and the belief that Hungary disregarded Germany's economic welfare, soon became the leitmotifs of the Third Reich's diplomatic approach to Hungary. In the long-run, German lack of confidence in Hungary, its aims and its leaders, would prove to have disastrous consequences for that country.

TABLE 1

German Exports and Imports in Eastern Europe 1938-1939

Country	% of Total Exports to Germany		% of Total Imports from German?	
	1938	1939	1938	1939
Bulgaria ..	63.5	71.1	57.8	69.5
Hungary ..	50.1	52.4	48.1	52.5
Romania .	37.1	43.1	49.9	56.1
Yugoslavia	49.9	45.9	50.3	53.2
Greece ...	36.7	30.0	31.9	32.1

Source: Basch, *The Danube Basin*, p. 218.

TABLE 2

Comparative Growth in German-Hungarian Trade 1933 and 1938

German Exports to Hungary	
1933	1938
38 mill. Marks	110 mill. Marks plus 36 mill. Marks from Ostmark and Sudetenland

Hungarian Exports to Germany	
1933	1938
34 mill. Marks	110 mill. Marks plus 76 mill. Marks to Ostmark and Sudetenland

Source: Ránki, *A Wilhelmstrasse*, Item 207C.

TABLE 3

German-Hungarian Exports and Imports 1937-1940

Year	Imports from Germany		Year	Exports to Germany	
	Mill. Pengö	%		Mill. Pengö	%
1937	212 (87)	43.9 (18.0)	1937	230 (99)	40.8 (16.8)
1938	171 (47)	41.6 (11.5)	1938	238 (95)	45.7 (18.3)
1939	237	48.3	1939	304	50.4
1940	319	58.0	1940	251	51.0

For 1937 and 1938, Austrian figures are in brackets. The 1938 figures also include the Sudetenland.
Source: Jócsik, *German Economic Influences*, p. 25.

TABLE 5A

Price of Hungarian Exports to Selected Free and
Exchange-Control Countries and Germany

	(Average Prices in Pengö in Quintals)							
Commodity Exported	1931	1932	1933	1934	1935	1936	1937	1938
Dressed Poultry								
Great Britain	185.7	117.7	113.4	97.8	85.9	84.6	N/A	N/A
Germany	194.0	143.8	122.3	109.2	122.1	126.5	N/A	N/A
Butter								
France 1931-33)								
Great Britain)	280.7	160.8	135.5	65.0	109.9	114.4	135.0	135.9
1934-38)								
Germany	276.0	199.9	157.4	203.0	197.9	204.4	211.0	204.7

Source: Statisztikai Havi Közlemények, XXXVI-XLI (1931- 1938), *passim.*

TABLE 5B

Price of Hungarian Imports from Selected Free and
Exchange-Control Countries and Germany

	(Average Prices in Pengö in Quintals)							
Commodity Exported	1931	1932	1933	1934	1935	1936	1937	1938
Raw Coffee								
Great Britain	140.0	155.0	130.0	121.1	78.9	78.1	91.2	67.2
Germany	140.0	180.0	145.7	121.1	85.2	106.5	126.1	128.9
Anthracite Coal								
Poland	3.50	3.50	3.50	2.78	2.57	2.56	2.30	2.30
Germany	3.50	3.51	3.48	2.96	3.10	3.08	3.05	3.19
Cocoa Beans								
Great Britain	N/A	N/A	N/A	44.2	43.0	53.0	74.4	50.3
Germany	N/A	N/A	N/A	44.2	43.0	51.0	88.0	62.2

Source: *Statisztikai Havi Közlemények,* XXXVI-XLI (1931-1938), *passim.*

The German-Hungarian-Swabian Triangle

TABLE 4

Nickl's Proposal to Wiehl, 6 February 1939

Commodity	Current Annual Volume	Projected Annual Volume	Price
Wheat	2 mill. metric tons	2.5 mill. metric tons	current
Maize	not mentioned	no change	not mentioned
Rye	not mentioned	no change	to be adjusted
Other Cereals	not mentioned	no change	to be adjusted
Cattle	30,000 head	40,000 head	current (6.8 mill. Pengő to 9.3 mill. Pengő)
Hogs	240,000 head	300,000 head	not mentioned
Bacon and Fats	not mentioned	15% to 20% rise	not mentioned
Tobacco	not mentioned	rise to accommodate Ostmark needs	not mentioned
Salami	not mentioned	rise to accommodate Ostmark needs	not mentioned
Quality Wine	not mentioned	special quota to be established	not mentioned

Source: Compiled from Ránki, *A Wilhelmstrasse*, Item 188.

CHAPTER XII

SWABIAN CULTURAL AND EDUCATIONAL DIFFICULTIES IN 1939

On 26 November 1938, the Imrédy government granted the *Volksdeutsche Kameradschaft* (*VK*) permission to establish the *Volksbund der Deutschen in Ungarn* (*VDU*). The new "völkisch-cultural organization"[1] would be allowed to compete with the government-controlled *Ungarländischer Deutscher Volksbildungsverein* (*UDV*), heretofore the only nationwide Swabian cultural organization authorized to function in Trianon Hungary.[2] For nearly five months the *VDU* languished in limbo, while its leaders anxiously awaited having their organization validated by the Ministry of the Interior.

In the interim, however, the *völkisch* leaders were confident that, at last, their long-standing grievances would be remedied. They were convinced that the government would transform B-type bilingual and Magyar-language elementary schools located in purely Swabian villages into German institutions, *volksbewusst* German teachers and acceptable textbooks would become available, and that all types of German schools, with the exception of universities, would be allowed to operate. Swabians would be able to launch financial drives, conduct church services in German, organize their own political party, establish autonomous clubs and associations, and publish German newspapers and magazines unfettered by government regulations and supervision.[3] In fact, however, the government created the *VDU*, and allowed the monthly *Deutscher Volksbote* (1935–1938) to be transformed into the weekly *Deutscher Volksbote, Wochenblatt für Kultur, Politik und Wirtschaft* (*DVW*), only because the Third Reich forced Hungary to act.[4]

By early 1939, fundamental and irreconcilable differences in practice and philosophy had nearly led to a rupture in Hungarian-Swabian relations. More than ever before, the dominant Magyars, avidly supported by Magyarized superpatriots, demanded undivided devotion to Magyar culture from all Hungarian citizens. According to this view, a person's membership in the Hungarian nation demanded a voluntary acceptance of Magyar cultural and political norms. This standard clashed with Swabian *völkisch* principles, which required devotion to the Hungarian state, unless this fidelity conflicted with the demands of the German nation. The Third Reich expected every member of the German *Volksgemein-schaft*, regardless of citizenship, place of residence or birthplace, to be a faithful member of the German *Volk*. National Socialist philosophy demanded that duty to the German nation must overrule legal responsibility to the demands of the political state. This had frightening implications for Hungary, which harbored about half a million Swabians, many of whom resided in strategically vulnerable frontier locations. Swabians imbued with this spirit might easily betray Hungary, because they regarded nation and state as two distinct concepts.

According to Ägidius Faulstich, a *VDU* stalwart, *Volk* was a natural phenomenon based on common blood and language that blended in an intimately shared *völkisch* essence. This bond was not the accidental product of peculiar circumstances, but obeyed eternal immutable laws, and unified its members psychically and spiritually.[5] A person's membership in the nation thus hinged on native attributes, whereas affiliation with the state was a matter of personal choice. Therefore, a Swabian citizen of Hungary could be simultaneously *volkstreu* to the German *Volksgemeinschaft* and *staatstreu* to the Hungarian political state, but only if the latter allegiance harmonized with the demands of his primordial duty to the German *Volk*. This meant that a Swabian citizen of Hungary might desert his country if the state violated his *völkisch* sensibilities. The bitter controversy and misunderstandings that poisoned Swabian-Magyar and German-Hungarian relations during this time may be seen as both cause and product of this unbridgeable philosophical gulf.[6]

Hungarian Prime Minister Béla Imrédy's Christmas message of 25 December 1938 betrayed unease with the promises tendered to the *völkisch* Swabians one month earlier. The government realized that the preoccupation of the non-Magyar minorities with maintaining their ethnic consciousness was "an affair of the heart." But this did not mean that these peoples should be permitted to make light of Hungary and regard the country as merely their place of residence. They must learn to love Hungary as their fatherland. He hoped that mutual trust and good will would eventually prevail and all divisive problems would cease. In order to dampen *völkisch* ardor, Imrédy promised to launch an ambitious reform program that would gradually transfer arable land from large estates into the hands of landless peasants and small farmers,[7] including Swabians.

Imrédy's rhetoric failed to sway the *völkisch* Swabians. An interview with the Prime Minister three days later convinced *VDU*

leader Franz Basch that the Swabians' grievances would not be settled promptly.[8] His earlier optimistic expectations had been premature. The question of the Swabians' loyalty to the Hungarian state
(*Staatstreue*) thereupon became a vitally important issue that the
volksbewusst Swabian leaders had thrust upon them by a skeptical
and hostile Hungarian society.

The *völkisch* Kurt Gündisch protested when the Hungarian government urged Swabians to demonstrate their trustworthiness by
acknowledging that their national interests harmonized with Hungary's political aspirations. Gündisch accused the government of
reverse reasoning. Citizens' rights had to be unconditional, whereas
the recipients of these benefits had to be loyal to the state. Only if
the Swabians ceased being patriotic would the government have the
right to withdraw privileges enjoyed by everyone else. Indeed, the
authorities were dutibound to grant the Swabians their *völkisch*
rights, Gündisch maintained. He ridiculed the government's demand that Swabian goals be coopted with Hungarian aspirations.
This, he believed, was a covert plan for Magyarizing the Swabians.
Gündisch promised to encourage Swabians to promote Hungary's
welfare, but he would do so only if the establishment heeded St.
Stephen's advice to medieval Magyars to safeguard the rights of
Hungary's non-Magyar citizens.[9]

In an interview with *8 Órai Újság*, Franz Basch agreed with
Gündisch's views. The *Volksbund*, he boasted, currently represented
80% of Hungary's German population, but, he assured Hungarians,
they had nothing to fear, because his organization was loyal and legal. Furthermore, the *volksbewusst* Swabians would never challenge
Magyar hegemony in Hungary. The Swabians, however, deserved
being designated a nationality (*Volksgruppe*), instead of merely a
minority. They also needed their own representatives in the Hungarian parliament, creation of a state secretaryship for Swabian affairs, *völkisch* teachers in Swabian schools, and the right to establish
völkisch social organizations. Basch pleaded for the Magyar public's
sympathy and trust, and swore that the Swabian connection with
the Third Reich was not political, but strictly cultural and spiritual. These non-threatening contacts need not be renounced, he
argued, because they would never conflict with the Swabians' traditional Hungarian loyalties. Indeed, Swabians were eager to serve
Hungary, for example, by acting as intermediaries in the settlement
of growing German-Hungarian controversies.[10]

The boast that the *Volksbund* represented four out of five Swabians was certainly an exaggeration and the public knew it, but

Basch's swaggering alarmed people. The *VDU*'s numerical follow-ing was conjectural, but in at least one Swabian community the *Volksbund*'s own documentation contradicted Basch's claims. In Bataszék, 406 Swabian parents had to decide which type of school-ing to adopt for their children. Only 100 parents chose the bilingual B-type school; the remainder favored a Magyar-language institu-tion, provided it offered a certain amount of German reading and writing instruction.[11]

The Basch interview unleashed a storm of protest in Hungarian public life and in the Magyar-language press. Almost to a man, Hungary's influential traditionalist opposition members, notably an informal assemblage composed of Count István Bethlen, Gyula Kornis and Tibor Eckhardt, assailed both Swabians and the govern-ment. The group's 14 January memorandum urged Regent Horthy to dismiss Imrédy from office. The Prime Minister had allegedly harmed Hungarian security by placing the *völkisch* Swabians un-der the jurisdiction of treasonous ethnic leaders. Sooner or later, these "pied pipers" would incite the Swabians and the Third Reich against Hungary.[12] Some newspapers assailed Basch as an insolent fellow for proclaiming the Swabians a nationality; others dreaded the consequences of growing Swabian independentmindedness, and feared that the Swabians might eventually achieve corporate or au-tonomous status in Hungary. Indeed, the *DVW* did advance the claim that the Swabians ought to gain collective status as a "le-gal personality" (*Rechtspersönlichkeit*) in all aspects of community life. Their culture, economics, politics and *Weltanschauung* must become *völkisch*.[13] This was a thinly disguised bid for autonomy, a claim which most Hungarians regarded as a provocation.

A casual observer might have argued that in his various pro-nouncements Imrédy had suggested a somewhat similar solution. In a January speech delivered in Budapest, Imrédy had reasserted the government's obligation to protect the "non-Magyar minori-ties," because they had shed their blood for the Hungarian father-land just like its other children. They belonged to the Hungar-ian political nation, but were also "devoted guardians of their na-tional characters, language and customs."[14] But Imrédy had in fact merely reiterated Hungary's traditional willingness to permit indi-viduals to practice their ethnic peculiarities, whereas the *völkisch* Swabians desired their people to enjoy collective national privileges. *Völkisch* Swabians regarded the Prime Minister's declarations as opportunistic. Imrédy, in their view, only wanted to humor Hun-gary's recently acquired non-Magyar citizens, some of whom were Germans. He hoped to convince these people that Hungary treated its non-Magyars magnanimously, in order to encourage other former subject peoples to rejoin the Hungarian fold. And, of course, Imrédy also wanted to convince Berlin that Budapest had undergone a change of heart in the much-criticized treatment of ethnic, especially Swabian, minorities.

The *völkisch* Swabians assailed the government on still another thorny issue. The *DVW* complained that currently barely fifty schools remained in the country's 400-odd Swabian communities in which reading, writing and arithmetic were still being taught in German. About 200 institutions had been transformed into Magyar-language facilities. Three out of four Swabian parents surveyed by the *DVW* had criticized the government's handling of the minority school problem. The *DVW* asserted that Swabian parents desiring German schools encountered subtle and persistent opposition and obstruction by the secular and ecclesiastical authorities, who defied the Prime Minister's solemn Christmas pledge that German children must have access to German schools.[15]

In the Hungarian Parliament resentment against Swabian assertiveness intensified. On 18 January, several deputies, including the Speaker of the House, reproved the Hungarian National Socialist deputy Count Sándor Festetich for implying that the police harassed *VDU* members for no other reason than that they were Germans.[16] One week later, a Member reported that his constituents in a Swabian village located near Budapest had lodged a complaint because the authorities introduced a "German" (*i.e.*, bilingual B-type) elementary school against parental wishes. He claimed that these Swabian parents desired Magyar-language instruction exclusively for their children. Another Member cited similar examples from his constituency in Pest County. He denounced the *völkisch* Swabians for demanding special rights, criticized Prime Minister Imrédy for having given the *Volksbund* permission to operate, and condemned him for dignifying its leaders by negotiating with them. He would much rather see these Swabian malcontents emigrate to Germany.[17]

Minister of Education Count Pál Teleki's speech in Parliament reiterated the government's position on the minority issue. Teleki discouraged any Swabian hopes for a radical change in the way the minority school system was being administered. Any alterations conceived in haste or introduced under duress would be forbidden, Teleki announced. Most importantly for the *völkisch* Swabians, Teleki spurned any school plan that would be organized on the basis of collective Swabian representation. On the contrary; the government would consider Swabian complaints and suggestions only if they were indisputably lodged by individual parents, and reject petitions obviously solicited collectively by the *Volksbund*.[18]

The *DVW* disputed Teleki's basic premises regarding nationality rights and minority education, and especially scorned the government's determination to regulate school language on the basis of individual parental choice. The newpaper wanted this issue determined by the "eternal standards of Volkstum." Any other solution would produce a tug-of-war each school year, and expose Swabian children to the constant danger of being assimilated. The burning question remained whether Hungary in fact desired to Magyarize the Swabians. The *DVW* believed that Teleki's scheme would definitely ensure the eventual absorption of the Swabians into the Magyar ethnic stream.[19]

By late winter, the *Volksbund* regarded the consensus as being so overwhelmingly anti-Swabian that any plans for Swabian corporate status would have to await more auspicious circumstances. On 15 February 1939, Count Teleki replaced Imrédy as prime minister. *Volksbewusst* Swabians viewed the change with consternation. Imrédy had been a pro-Swabian champion compared with Teleki, whose outspoken anti-Swabian public record spanned two decades. At a 4 March *Volksbund* rally, Basch warned his followers that the new government would soon revoke Imrédy's concessions, persecute Swabian *Volksgenossen*, particularly in Hungary's western and southern border regions, where Swabians were densely concentrated, and encourage the anti-Swabian hate campaign orchestrated by the Jewish-dominated Magyar-language press.[20]

The Third Reich cautioned the *Volksbund* to moderate its attacks on the Hungarian government. Germany desired tranquility in the Danubian region because within one month Hitler planned to annex western Czechoslovakia, and later that year he expected to draw Poland into the Third Reich's sphere of influence. Both of these operations required Budapest's tacit cooperation and good will.[21]

The *Volksbund* brashly disregarded these instructions. Its officials continued pressuring the Hungarian government on a range of issues, but they did change tactics. The *DVW* began demanding a new nationality law that would enable Hungary's Swabians to enjoy a special position just short of corporate status. The editor blamed Swabian difficulties on the absence of foolproof constitutional provisions to ensure the welfare and protection of minorities. Georg Goldschmidt explained that Hungary's current minority legislation, the still valid 1868 Nationality Law, might theoretically protect non-Magyar language rights, but noted that continual violations by the government had discredited the statute. In view of the prevailing juridical vacuum, the Swabians required a new fundamental law. Nothing short of comprehensive legislation respecting the "eternal right" of each nationality to function according to its own cultural standards would ever pacify the Swabians.[22]

The *Volksbund* mobilized its most persuasive spokesmen to persuade the nervous Hungarian public that the *völkisch* Swabians had not ceased being faithful to the Hungarian state. They claimed that they did not challenge the right of ethnic Magyars to be the masters of Hungary, nor did they dispute the Hungarian government's determination to eradicate political philosophies regarded as alien and harmful. *Völkisch* Swabians regarded National Socialism as neither alien nor harmful. The patriotic protestations of the *Volksbund* were therefore sincere. These Swabians insisted that they had no desire to interfere in the conduct of Hungary's internal affairs, insofar as they concerned the ethnic Magyar population. On the contrary. They urged that Magyars and Swabians be permitted to conduct their own national affairs without interfering with one another. They perceived no contradiction between professed fidelity to the Hungarian fatherland and simultaneous devotion to the German motherland. As long as Germany and Hungary remained friends, they argued, no quarrel could possibly poison their relationship.[23]

This reasoning prompted Georg Goldschmidt, who was also the *Volksbund*'s deputy leader, to challenge Reformed Bishop László Ravasz's Szeged speech of 11 March 1939. Ravasz explained that all the minorities must be assimilated. After all, the Magyars were hemmed in between the rivers Tisza (Theiss) and Duna (Danube). They had no choice. Alien peoples must not proliferate in Hungary. On the contrary, the Magyar stock must be numerically augmented. Goldschmidt argued that Ravasz's rhetoric harmed the *völkisch* Swabian cause precisely because the Bishop was an enlightened and influential member of the Magyarized intelligentsia. Goldschmidt feared that not only Magyars but ethnic waverers would heed the Bishop's advice, and accused Ravasz of having declared a virtual ethnic war against Hungary's non-Magyar nationalities.[24]

On 15 March 1939, Germany annexed Bohemia and Moravia; Slovakia became a German protectorate, and the Reich gave Hungary permission to seize Ruthenia. These events intensified the *völkisch* Swabians' expectations for reform. The *Volksbund* knew that after accepting its new acquisition from Germany, Hungary would be more obligated to the Third Reich than ever before. But, as Georg Goldschmidt astutely observed, Swabians who anticipated a change of heart in the hostile attitudes of the Magyar-language press and Hungarian public were doomed to disappointment. Goldschmidt wanted the minorities to receive tangible concessions, not the vague government press releases that promised the newly incorporated non-Magyar nationalities better treatment than they had received in the "old days" of the Habsburg era. He deprecated Prime Minister Teleki's announcement that Hungary would hereafter abolish the discredited nationality policies associated with the liberal era and adopt St. Stephen's traditional methods of true toleration. Goldschmidt had been convinced that Teleki would introduce national autonomy statutes for the Swabians, resembling those the Transylvanian Saxons and the Croatians had enjoyed in the vanished Habsburg Empire. He noted that, whereas most Hungarian newspapers advocated granting various rights to the recently incorporated Slovaks and Ruthenes, they ignored Hungary's far more numerous and better-educated German-speaking people. Some papers depicted the Swabians as a menace to Hungarian security, and urged ethnic Magyars in mixed nationality areas, especially in the German-inhabited counties adjoining former Austria, to assist their localities to launch vigorous name-Magyarization campaigns in order to counteract the Swabian birthrate that allegedly outstripped Magyar fertility.[25]

With the annexation of Bohemia and Moravia, and the acquisition of Slovakia as a protectorate, Germany strengthened its strategic grip on Hungary. The Hungarian public and the Magyar-language press responded to this danger by intensifying their attack on the *völkisch* Swabians. Magyars and Magyarized individuals nearly unanimously condemned the *völkisch* Swabians' insistence on preserving the German language and culture. Aurél Kern of *Szabadság* wrote that the *Volksbund*'s solution of the Swabian ethnic problem would injure Magyar interests. He urged Hungarians of every political affiliation to join the struggle against the "radical" Swabians.[26]

Another influential writer published demographic data to document the alleged Swabian menace. József Ambrus, president of *Turúl*, the Hungarian Student Association, deplored the Swabians' numerical increase, especially in Hungary's vulnerable western border regions. Out of 224 Magyar villages averaging only one child per family, 192 were situated in this sensitive area endangered by the Third Reich. In a few counties, the higher Swabian birthrate had produced a 13% population gain for the German-speaking inhabitants since the war. Ambrus urged that energetic Magyar peasant stock be transferred into areas where Hungary adjoined the Third Reich in order to bolster the ethnic Magyar strain.[27]

On the eve of Czecho-Slovakia's demise, István Morvay, editor of *Magyar Út,* also foresaw the German danger, and insisted that the western part of Hungary be settled by ethnic Magyars through the application of liberal land reform, so that Germany would be unable to claim the region on *völkisch* grounds. He realized that Hungary would have to accommodate and soothe Germany, but the important western frontier region must be Magyarized, even if the action meant risking the Third Reich's displeasure.[28]

Hungarian fears of the perceived Swabian menace occasionally created strange bedfellows. At the end of March 1939, for example, *Törzsökös Magyarok,* an ultra-right-wing anti-Semitic and racist Magyar organization, informed the Hungarian Upper Chamber of its opposition to Hungary's proposed anti-Jewish laws. The organization believed that these regulations would ultimately harm Hungary, because if choice positions were taken from Jews, these would not be given to ethnic Magyars, but to Aryans (*i.e.*, Swabians), whom *Törzsökös Magyarok* considered a far more dangerous foe than the Jews. Swabians practiced "dissimilation" and advocated alienation from Hungary, the organization charged, whereas the Jews were eager to assimilate into the Magyar mainstream.[29]

Reports in the Magyar-language press aggravated the *völkisch* Swabians' disenchantment with the public's sentiments concerning Swabian rights. On 5 April, *Magyar Nemzet* editorialized that what the country needed was not a new nationality law, but the honest application of existing regulations. This, of course, implied retention of traditional individual ethnic rights and maintaining the discredited 1935 school law. By now, the *völkisch* Swabians firmly rejected both approaches.

The 9 April issue of *Új Magyarság* advocated territorial autonomy, but only for the Ruthenes of the Carpatho-Ukraine (formerly Ruthenia). On the same day, *Esti Újság*'s editor, Member of Parliament János Makkai, emerged as the lone Hungarian pro-Swabian dissenter. In his view, Hungary's Magyars must henceforth draw exclusively on their own stock for replenishment and strength, and cease Magyarizing Hungary's minorities as a means of reinforcing Magyardom. The country's various ethnic groups must be granted autonomy and offered the opportunity to develop their own unique leadership and intelligentsia. He considered such an accommodation the only solution to achieve harmony in Hungary. Right after the war, Hungary was virtually a nation-state, he asserted, but it had once again become a nationality-state that required a more flexible approach to the treatment of minorities.[30]

Makkai's plea was a voice in the wilderness. Most influential Hungarians rejected the idea. The government's recently revivified and immensely popular name-Magyarization campaign proved the point. Since 26 November 1938, the *VDU* leaders had been hoping to regain some of the ground they had lost in the minority schools, and they planned to launch re-Germanization drives among Magyarized Swabians. But the establishment appeared equally intent on further eroding the Swabian ethnic base. On 15 January 1938, the Mohács chapter of the Hungarian War Veterans' Organization had urged all minorities to Magyarize their foreign-sounding names, so that their patriotism would be deemed above reproach.[31] In a convention speech at the end of March 1939, Dr. József Ambrus of *Turúl* urged all non-Magyar students to Magyarize their names within a stipulated deadline. This announcement, the government's official newspaper *Hétfő* reported, the assemblage greeted with enthusiasm and thunderous applause.[32]

The evolution of what appeared to be a concerted anti-Swabian campaign at the highest and most influential levels of Hungarian public life perturbed the *völkisch* leaders. Georg Goldschmidt deemed the situation particularly aggravating because according to a manifesto issued by Regent Horthy, the relatively underdeveloped Carpatho-Ukraine was soon to receive administrative autonomy. Goldschmidt thought it outrageous that the literate and culturally developed Swabians, with their proven fidelity to Hungary, had to have their rights to self-government constantly barred.[33] In his Easter message, Prime Minister Teleki reiterated that Hungary must readopt the nationality policies of St. Stephen, in order to ensure the country's smooth development. But he totally ignored the Swabians.[34]

By now, Basch had become thoroughly exasperated. The Hungarian government's failure to expedite the country's existing nationality laws was bad enough. Failure to introduce new statutes to satisfy the *volksbewusst* Swabians' aspirations for autonomy he deemed inexcusable. Teleki and Csáky were Berlin-bound on an official visit. Basch wished to inform the appropriate Reich authorities beforehand that the "outwardly pro-German, and inwardly anti-German orientation" of the present Hungarian regime was a painful reality. Early in April, Basch appeared in Berlin for talks with German leaders. Upon his return, he threatened the government that unless the Swabians were granted "total mobility," the Third Reich would apply potent remedies to compel Hungary to act. Henceforth, he stated, Hungary would have to conduct unambiguously pro-German policies, introduce effective anti-Jewish laws and allow Swabian peasants to participate proportionately in a thorough land redistribution program.[35]

Basch gambled that his aggressive tactics and strategic timing would scare the Hungarian government into offering concessions as a means of creating a congenial atmosphere when Teleki and Csáky consulted with Reich officials in Berlin. Considering the Hungarian public's hostility to past Swabian assertiveness, and in view of the government's customary reluctance to yield under pressure, it struck everyone as a tremendous surprise when on 13 April 1939, Minister of the Interior Ferenc Keresztes-Fischer released the enabling decree that enshrined the *Volksbund* as the *volksbewusst* Swabians' legal cultural organization, and granted the new association the right to establish local chapters.

The initial reaction of the Basch group was to rejoice. The leaders thought that the *Volksbund* would at last replace the government-sponsored and subsidized *UDV*. When this failed to materialize immediately, the *Volksbund's* optimism became dampened. The *völkisch* Swabians thought they had ample reason to be skeptical, as the Hungarian government had disappointed them before. At best, the Teleki regime regarded the *Volksbund* as nothing more than a negative carbon copy of the *UDV*, and occasionally "attempted, with some success, to play the two organizations off against each other."[37] Ägidius Faulstich hoped that the government would permit the *VDU* to operate freely, and not tolerate local officials to hamper its operations.[38] Georg Goldschmidt was more optimistic. He considered 1939 the year when Swabians might expect a favorable change, thanks to an "organic process," through which the Hungarian government had finally recognized the Swabians as a *bona fide* nationality.[39] In fact, however, the government had done nothing of the sort. It had legitimized the *Volksbund* only to express its appreciation to the Third Reich for having granted Hungary permission to occupy Ruthenia, and to avoid the embarrassment of having the frustrated *völkisch* Swabian leaders venting their spleen in Berlin against the glacial progress of their cause in Hungary.[40]

To their dismay, the initially euphoric *völkisch* Swabians soon discovered that, from their perspective, the new autonomous status left a great deal to be desired. They failed to acquire the fundamental freedoms they coveted. The key word in the regulation was "cultural." The Minister of the Interior stripped all the currently tolerated non-cultural activities from the *Volksbund's* range of control,[41] and changed the designation of *Volksgruppe* (national group) to "Hungarian citizens of German nationality."[42] But for a brief moment, the *Volksbund* celebrated its "victory" as a vindication of its unity, determination, persistence and fidelity to *völkisch* principles. Its officials formally thanked the government for its vote of confidence that defied "the vicious anti-Swabian press campaign." Many Swabian demands remained unfulfilled, the *DVW* conceded, but the government's courageous action augured happier days for the Swabians. The *VDU* thereupon reiterated its devotion both to the German *Volk* and to the Hungarian fatherland.[43]

The Hungarian election of 28-29 May 1939, the country's first postwar franchise conducted nationwide by secret ballot, enabled the Hungarian government to offer the *völkisch* Swabians an eagerly sought political accommodation that might have been significant. Instead, the Swabian gain was inconsequential. As an alternative to letting the *völkisch* Swabians form a political party, a notion the Hungarian government rejected, the Third Reich suggested a compromise solution that would permit three *Volksbund* candidates to stand for election on the government party (MEP) ticket. The Teleki government adopted this proposal, but was aware of the perils of sponsoring what might turn out to be a *völkisch* Swabian electoral triumph in predominantly German-inhabited regions. Such success would escalate nationalistic prestige and encourage increased demands. According to Hungarian law, any political association which had at least 20,000 members and four deputies serving in parliament could proclaim itself a national political party, and enjoy all the privileges that status entailed. By late 1939, the *Volksbund* numbered between 20,000 and 22,000 members, and was growing rapidly, despite various hurdles erected by the local authorities.[44] This explains why the government secretly hindered the electioneering activities of the three *Volksbund* candidates, Dr. Heinrich Mühl in Bonyhád, Dr. Konrad Mischung in Mohács, and Jakob Brandt on the Bács-Bodrog list, on the eve of the election. The government deemed it wiser to forfeit a few seats than to strengthen the *völkisch* Swabian contingent within the government party.

The *DVW* angrily accused the MEP of sabotaging the *Volksbund's* political opportunity by intimidating Swabian voters and by unleashing the police at political rallies.[45] In many instances, the government apparently assisted the election of what the *Volksbund* regarded as the common enemy, the Hungarian National Socialists. Undoubtedly, the government feared the racists of the Hungarian Nazi Party far less than it did the Swabian *Volksbundists* who were running on the MEP ticket. In view of these actions, one Swabian candidate, Dr. Mischung, lost the election by an embarrassingly wide margin to Dr. Anton Keck, a Magyarized Swabian of Hubay's Arrow Cross Party, who captured more than 50% of the electoral district's Swabian vote.[46] The other two Swabian candidates won by comfortable margins.

The election results, and particularly the MEP's shabby treatment of the Swabian candidates, exasperated the *Volksbund*. It felt equally out of sorts with the Third Reich, which seemed quite unconcerned with the humiliation of a Swabian *Volksbund* candidate. In fact, the German government had not yet committed itself to any specific Hungarian pro-German group, whether Magyar or Swabian, but rejoiced at the success of any parties of the extreme Right at the expense of the Hungarian Left and Center. For the time being, the Third Reich preferred dealing directly with the Hungarian government, although clandestinely, all anti-government right-wing groups received German subsidies regardless of their ethnic status. Publicly, however, Nazi Germany hailed the Hungarian election results as a victory for its *Weltanschauung* in general, and for the *Volksbund* in particular.[47]

The Hungarian government may have won the election by a handsome margin, but in the process, Teleki learned a number of disturbing lessons about the Swabian electorate. Only two years earlier, the *völkisch* Swabians represented the extreme right wing in Hungarian political society; now, they had been shunted closer to the political center in view of the emergence of the even more radical Hungarian National Socialists, who captured sizeable numbers of Swabian and Magyar votes. The government's preferred domestic Germans, represented by the *UDV*, were rapidly melting into numerical insignificance.[48] The popularity of the Hungarian Nazis with Magyars and Swabians alike particularly worried the government. The only consolation was the apparent splintering of the Swabian electorate into at least three major mutually antagonistic groups—the loyalist *UDV*, the *völkisch DVU*, and the Swabian supporters of the Hungarian Nazis. After this election, the Hungarian regime was suspended between two hostile domestic fires, the pro-Nazi Hungarian National Socialists, its ranks riddled with Magyars, Swabians, and Magyarized Swabians, and the pro-Nazi *völkisch* Swabians, who openly supported the Third Reich.[49]

The presence of *völkisch* Swabians in the MEP coalition seemed to imply that the government sympathized with the autonomist views of these new members. Whereas the nationalistic Swabians were pleased with this strange marriage of convenience, most Hungarians rejected their government's public plea that Hungary must make the Swabians feel at home. The central government, local officials, and the people of Hungary must honor the language and customs of their non-Magyar fellow-citizens, and cease persecuting them, Foreign Minister István Csáky asserted, adding that Hungary's plans for ensuring a better future depended on the success of a benevolent minority policy. Hungary could either restore the country's historic grandeur by gaining the allegiance of the ethnic minorities still languishing under alien rule, or be relegated to oblivion.[50] In an earlier speech at Sopron, Csáky and Teleki tried unsuccessfully to persuade the audience that the country had nothing to fear from Germany, and, borrowing a *Volksbund* notion, urged Hungary's Swabians in the western counties to serve as middlemen to promote German-Hungarian friendship. Csáky blamed the chauvinistic Magyar-language press and public for imperiling Hungary's brilliant future. Teleki vowed to vanquish the opponents of his fair-minded nationality policy.[51] These, and other similar statements, however, were merely propaganda designed mainly for consumption in the Third Reich and to soothe Swabian indignation with the government's assimilationist policies.

Hungary's public had no way of knowing that the government merely pretended to please the Swabians and soothe their supporters in Germany. Most Hungarians rejected the government's pleas to treat the Swabians with special consideration, and vilified the Swabians for exposing Hungary to the perils of Pan-Germanism. On this subject, nearly everyone in Hungary, from the left-wing Jewish press to the Hungarian National Socialist newspapers, agreed. Dezső Szabó, a noted populist writer-propagandist and an exponent of Magyar racist nationalism, asserted that the government's new permissive minority policy endangered the survival of the numerically weak ethnic Magyar middle classes. If treated benignly, the Swabians would become powerful, until they excluded Magyars from top positions in Hungarian society. Szabó resented the fact that these Swabian "foreigners" had been appropriating choice middle class positions in Hungarian society for years, and had usurped the bulk of the country's best soil. He cautioned "these aliens" that the land did not belong to them, but to the indivisible Hungarian nation. If the Magyar language did not please these malcontents, they should emigrate.[52] A provincial newspaper asserted that a person could not be simultaneously a Hungarian and a German, as the *Volksbund* claimed. Hungary's population consisted of Hungarian Magyars, Hungarian Swabians or Hungarian Germans, but the country had no use for a German *Volk* or a German *Nation* within its midst.[53]

Throughout the summer of 1939, the Magyar-language press intensified its attacks on Swabians, and was joined by some of the pro-government Budapest newspapers. István Milotay, Member of Parliament and editor of *Új Magyarság*, considered the Swabian "radicals" a security risk, because they were Pan-Germans, and because they conducted pro-German agitation in Hungary. He suspected that a covert connection existed between these Swabian "radicals" and official German circles, which, notwithstanding their reassuring rhetoric, endangered the survival of Hungary. He predicted that, inevitably, most Swabians would abandon Magyardom spiritually, culturally and politically, and sooner or later betray Hungary to National Socialist Germany.[54]

The provincial press embroidered Milotay's statements. It printed horror stories concerning those Swabian villages where the *Volksbund* had permission to conduct membership drives for local chapters. In Moson County, for example, *Mosonvármegye* reported, five high-echelon *Volksbund* functionaries had recently harangued the Swabian masses. Not once did they use the Magyar language or refer to the Magyar names of the villages they visited. They were greeted by indoctrinated mobs of children who howled "Sieg Heil!," sang the Hungarian national anthem halfheartedly, but enthusiastically belted out *reichsdeutsch* songs and marches. The speakers made flattering allusions to German greatness, complained about the predicament of Hungary's Swabians and offered the crowds autonomist panaceas. The visitors boasted that they belonged to the 70-million-strong German *Volk* centered in the Third Reich, and inflated the number of Hungary's Swabians from the official census figure of 478,000 to 700,000 souls. These "commotions" scandalized Moson County's ethnic Magyars and Swabians, most of whom were sober and patriotic Hungarians,[55] the newspaper reported.

The ultra-right-wing Magyar-language press, including those representing the various factions within the Hungarian National Socialist movement, joined the anti-Swabian chorus. This antipathy to the *völkisch* Swabians was surprising, because the Hungarian Nazis agreed with the National Socialist *Weltanschauung*, admired the Third Reich, and venerated Hitler. But the Hungarian Nazis promoted the "Turanian" (Finno-Ugric) brand of racial purity. Zoltán Meskó, Member of Parliament and a prominent Hungarian Nazi, urged that under a projected land reform bill, only "racially pure Magyars" be eligible to obtain land in predominantly non-Magyar-inhabited parts of the country. To qualify, even racially pure Magyars would first have to abandon foreign-sounding names.[56] *Nemzeti Figyelő* believed that assimilation into the Magyar majority was an honorable way for people to demonstrate their Hungarian patriotism; nobody had the right to discredit or criticize Magyarization, least of all the non-Magyar ethnic leaders, who lived on Magyar bounty as Hungary's guests.[57]

Pro-Hungarian Swabians also assailed the *Volksbund.* A self-professed "patriotic German" resident of Pécs was up in arms because the *Volksbund* enjoyed great success in his region converting Swabians to *völkisch* extremism. He urged the government to grant individuals such as himself and similarly-minded patriotic Swabians the right to organize countermeasures against "these Pan-Germans."[58] Writing in *Neuer Sonntagsblatt,* the *UDV*'s official weekly newspaper, Hans Rippel accused an unidentified *Volksbund* agent of recruiting Swabians for the "radical" organization in the Bakonyság region, fostering tension and causing fraternal rifts among Swabians.[59]

In the late summer of 1939, the Hungarian university students' official newspaper strongly condemned the *Volksbund*'s activities, and criticized the government for having permitted the *völkisch* Swabians to re-Germanize Hungary's assimilated Swabians, even those whose forebears had become Magyarized centuries ago. The editor asserted that, if minorities desired to assimilate their adopted country's culture and language, then governments had no right to stop them. Governments must extend only such rights and privileges to their minorities that would encourage assimilation.[60]

In the weeks prior to the outbreak of World War II, the *Volksbund* gained only scattered public approval among Hungarians. An editorial in the newspaper of the ultra-conservative former Prime Minister István Friedrich was one of a few to suggest a favorable disposition of the Swabian problem. It urged the government to establish clear guidelines within which Hungary's Germans would be able to function freely. These concessions must match those that the Hungarian government urged the Successor States to adopt in the treatment of their Magyar minorities. Finally, the government must transform the nationality program from paper fiat into genuine freedom of action for the Swabians. Saboteurs of this law should be punished, and the Hungarian government must educate the public to cease obstructing the laws.[61]

Professor Ödön Polner adopted a curiously ambiguous position, certain aspects of which even the *DVW* found overly daring. Polner asserted that membership in the nation did not depend so much on transmitted physical and spiritual peculiarities as on a people's adoption of variously acquired characteristics. He cautioned that the concepts of "state" and "nation" did not necessarily correspond. The Hungarian nation, for example, contained both native linguistic Magyars and non-Magyars who had voluntarily adopted the Magyar tongue. Hence, Hungarian citizens who spoke non-Magyar languages could become members of the Hungarian nation, but only if they adopted its aims and purposes, and provided they became emotionally involved in its vital concerns.[62]

This thesis placed the *Volksbund* in an awkward position. Polner's implication that Hungary's non-Magyars who refused to become Magyarized in the orthodox sense might still be accommodated within the Hungarian political nation was a trap. If Hungary adopted such a scheme, non-conformists would automatically become exposed to intense Magyarization pressures by nationalists. Moreover, the *Volksbund* would be forced to betray basic principles in order to accept acculturation or voluntarism as a means of promoting membership in the Hungarian nation. Goldschmidt commented that Polner had apparently misunderstood the constitutional limitations that Hungarian jurisprudence imposed on nationality. The still valid 1868 Nationality Law regarded all Hungarian citizens, notwithstanding national origin, mother tongue or personal sentiment, as members of the indivisible, unitary Hungarian nation. Hungary's King St. Stephen had urged Magyars to cultivate multilingualism and to share their rights equally with non-Magyars, in order to ensure Hungary's future prosperity. Goldschmidt also cautioned that in Hungary the terms "Nation" and "Volk" had different meanings. "Nation" embraced all citizens regardless of nationality, whereas "Volk" expressed the peculiarity of each of the Hungarian nation's ethnic or national members.[63]

Between 13 April, the date on which the Hungarian government officially recognized the *Volksbund*, and 1 September, when World War II erupted, the *völkisch* Swabians burned with indignation because of the virulence of the public's ill will toward those Swabians whose aspirations supposedly menaced Hungary's security. As a rule, the Basch group remained prudently on the defensive, but occasionally lashed out in frustration against its domestic tormentors. Unfortunately for the *völkisch* Swabians, however, on these few occasions the overzealous *Volksbund* exercised poor judgment and even less tact. Its undiplomatic rhetoric and thoughtless deeds frightened and offended the public. One issue of the *DVW*, for example,[64] featured a large portrait of Adolf Hitler on the front cover, alongside a panegyric entitled "Zum 50. Geburtstag des Führers 20. April 1939." A paeon lionized Hitler as history's most distinguished German leader, a hero who had restored German pride and self-respect.[65] The publication of such provocative copy exacerbated the public's resentment, animosity and apprehension of all Swabians.

Moreover, the *völkisch* Swabians sought to establish their national distinctiveness in apparent defiance of the government's and public's determination to achieve Magyar homogeneity. The *DVW* pressured the government to clearly establish the vital needs of the country's Magyars, and identify those of Hungary's Swabians and other national groups. Such guidelines, the editor believed, would prevent the eruption of interethnic conflict. The *DVW* particularly detested its arch-critic Anton Klein, a Magyarized Swabian Member of Parliament for the opposition Smallholder Party. Klein had defeated Georg Goldschmidt in the 1938 parliamentary election by capturing 50% of the Swabian vote and sweeping nearly the entire Magyar electorate in a district where Swabians outnumbered Magyars three to one. Klein infuriated the *DVW* for claiming that he represented all the Swabians in his electoral district. Goldschmidt branded Klein a traitor to the German cause because he rejected the idea that a non-Magyar nationality could legally function in Hungary.[66]

The *Volksbund* also criticized Magyar-language newspapers for publishing provocative "Letters to the Editor" that attacked the *völkisch* Swabian philosophy. *Magyar Nemzet* carried this practice one step further by utilizing a letter written by a loyalist Swabian in the paper's editorial column. Dr. Paul Drescher joyfully announced that he had decided to Magyarize his name. He wanted to become a Magyar because "the Germans have never contributed significantly to [Hungarian] culture in the past, and were incapable of doing so today."[67] *DVW* castigated *Magyar Nemzet* for exploiting Drescher's letter, and for using it as shabby propaganda to promote the newspaper's Magyarization campaign.[68]

Derogatory newspaper copy such as this prompted Johann Kuhn, a *Volksbund* supporter, to declare that, as everywhere in nature, so too in nationality affairs, the weak succumbed and only the strong survived. The German nationality struggle must therefore be vigorously pursued in Hungary. Nationalities had but two alternatives: they could assimilate, or they could fight for the well-being of their *Volk*.[69] The *UDW* castigated a *Pesti Hírlap* editorial for asserting that the position of Hungary's Swabians was entirely satisfactory.[70] It was wrong and presumptuous for a Magyar-language newspaper to pass such a judgment on behalf of an alien *Volk*. Only nationality leaders had the right to determine the status of their people and speak up on their behalf.[71]

By the end of July 1939, constant sniping had worn *Volksbund* leader Franz Basch's patience thin. Basch accused the "sensationalist" hostile Magyar-language press of twisting and misreading his speeches in order to mislead the presumably naïve public. Basch condemned the biweekly *Nagymagyarország* for allegedly falsifying his recent lecture before the Association of Hungarian University Students (MEFHOSz), which had invited Basch and Hungary's Slovak and Ruthenian minority leaders as speakers. *Nagymagyarország*'s reporter Pusztay-Popovits charged that the presentation expanded Basch's well-known 1938 seven-point program to thirteen. Not so, Basch retorted. He had merely analyzed and amplified his original seven points in response to queries from the audience. The *DVW* complained because even the respectable *Nemzeti Újság* and other decent Magyar papers were behaving no better than the "irresponsible" *Nagymagyarország*. All of them sensationalized the alleged "German menace" without offering any proof, and they all overdramatized the Swabians' "new demands."[72]

About this time, Johann Kuhn tried to clarify the *Volksbund*'s thinking on the nature of Hungarian patriotism. Patriotism did not demand Swabian assimilation into the Magyar ethnic and cultural stream, as Anton Klein claimed. Klein was understandably popular with the Magyars. He and his sort of assimilants had repudiated their German origin and culture, and persuaded ethnic Magyars that fidelity to any non-Magyar *Volk* was a treasonous act that betrayed an absence of Hungarian patriotism. Kuhn cited a recent incident in Parliament to demonstrate that this line of reasoning was erroneous. Klein had verbally assaulted Dr. Heinrich Mühl of the MEP. Foreign Minister Csáky ruled that Klein's outburst had violated Hungary's interests. Kuhn inferred that Klein was being unpatriotic, whereas Mühl, who was an avid admirer of National Socialism, was a Hungarian patriot. Kuhn reasoned as follows: The Third Reich demanded that would-be friends, such as Hungary, show sympathy for the National Socialist system. Hence, Hungarians had to learn to appreciate National Socialist philosophy. By instructing Hungarians how to gain Germany's favor, the *Volksbund* and men such as Mühl were Hungarian patriots providing an essential service in the Hungarian national interest.[73]

Dr. Heinrich Neun, another *Volksbund* enthusiast, amplified Kuhn's views. Only the *Volksbund* had the capability to organize Hungary's Swabians to be true to their Hungarian fatherland, he asserted. The *Volksbund* had demonstrated its ability to maintain superb discipline even when *völkisch* Swabians had to face provocateurs. Law and order always prevailed during *Volksbund* rallies and membership drives, even though nearly everywhere the Magyar and the Magyarized village intelligentsia thwarted the *völkisch* organization's aspirations. Neun deplored the hostile attitudes of the inflammatory provincial press, which regarded all *Volksbund* activities as dangerous and anti-Magyar.[74]

The *Volksbund* also crossed journalistic swords with an old enemy, Gustav Gratz, who had recently resigned as president of the *UDV* and became chief editor of *Pesti Napló*, an anti-Nazi Jewish-oriented Budapest daily. Gratz's 30 July article, as well as another one published a few days earlier,[75] accused the *völkisch* Swabians of being unpatriotic, particularly because the *Volksbund* accepted illicit funds provided by Germany. This made the organization a foreign agent subject to German control and therefore treasonous, Gratz maintained. The *DVW* and Basch admitted accepting Reich funds earmarked strictly for cultural purposes; this, however, according to the *DVW*, was an irrelevant issue. Since Germany and Hungary were allies, their aims harmonized perfectly. Hence, Germany, as a matter of common sense, could not possibly order the *Volksbund* to perform treasonous acts against Hungary.[76]

On the eve of World War II, the *DVW* accused some of the anti-Swabian Magyar-language press, notably *Magyar Nemzet, 8 Órai Újság* and *Az Est*, of indiscriminately attacking everything that was German, including the Third Reich. These papers supported Great Britain and France, the two countries sworn to the destruction of the Rome-Berlin Axis and the mortal enemies of National Socialism, which Germany and the *Volksbund* cherished. This misguided, unpatriotic press, the Swabian newspaper complained, regarded the very notion of blood community and race as sheer madness and an affront against the Hungarian fatherland.[77]

When the war began, the government could not afford to offend the Third Reich and its Swabian protégés. It eliminated the *Volksbund*'s journalistic critics by implementing a January 1939 press decree that curtailed the publication of frivolous, useless or harmful copy. *Az Est*, and the group of papers under its control, had their licenses revoked. *Pesti Napló* became another casualty, and even Gustav Gratz's presence as chief editor could not save it. *Magyarország* "cleansed" itself of Jewish personnel, changed editorial course, and reappeared as the press organ of cabinet minister Andor Jaross.[78] These actions demonstrated the Hungarian government's apparent zeal to pacify the *Volksbund* and please Germany. The government ordered the press to praise the Swabians and Germany, mainly to reassure the Third Reich and the *Volksbund* that Hungary had turned over a new leaf, and desired German-Hungarian friendship and Swabian amity. Its basic opposition to both parties, however, remained steadfast.

CHAPTER XIII

HUNGARY'S DIPLOMATIC ATTEMPTS TO RESOLVE THE SWABIAN PROBLEM IN 1939

The Hungarian government tried to pacify Germany by assuming a pro-Swabian posture. In practice, however, it accommodated the anti-Swabian national consensus. The hatred and contempt the *völkisch* Swabians evoked among most Hungarians demonstrated the public's revulsion with ethnic non-conformism. Had the Third Reich not intervened on behalf of the *völkisch* Swabians, Teleki probably would have outlawed the *Volksbund* and interned its leaders, as he had disbanded the Hungarian National Socialist and Hungarist Parties on 15 February.[1] Teleki's diplomacy with the Third Reich thus became inseparable from the Hungarian government's Swabian policy. Teleki wanted to avert intervention by Germany in Hungary's internal affairs by placating the disgruntled *völkisch* Swabians.[2] He decided to resolve Hungary's security problems by launching an opportunistic foreign policy that had Hungarian diplomats "dancing at the edge of the knife."[3] Teleki also hoped to reduce *völkisch* Swabian influence by preventing Germany from exercising hegemony in Hungary as well as in other parts of eastern Europe.[4]

The Hungarian government's difficulties with the *völkisch* Swabians spilled over into the diplomatic arena. During his 16-17 January Berlin visit, Csáky promised his hosts that the Hungarian government would soon remedy the Swabian school problem, especially in the confessional institutions, where presently the minority school laws did not legally apply. Csáky also lodged a complaint against the appearance of "unwelcome symptoms in certain Swabian circles" (*i.e.*, the *Volksbund*). Csáky saw a *völkisch* Swabian conspiracy being hatched against the security of the Hungarian state. This threatened to undermine the centuries'-long Hungarian-Swabian amity, Csáky exclaimed. Moreover, he faulted the Third Reich for these disturbances. The Germans denied their involvement in anti-Hungarian plottings with the Swabians, and demanded proof that German governmental agencies had interfered in Hungarian internal affairs.[5]

Franz Basch sought to discredit these complaints by appealing directly to the people of the Third Reich. In the February 1939 issue of *Volk und Reich* Basch characterized the nationality problem as one of Hungary's gravest difficulties. He believed that only a truly resourceful and fearless Hungarian statesman could resolve this crisis. First, however, the Magyars of Hungary would have to abandon erroneous notions and shed ancient anti-German prejudices. Presently, the 1935 school law had yet to be implemented to the satisfaction of Hungary's Swabians. They still lacked genuine representation in the Hungarian Parliament, and many of his *Volksgenossen* had to accept alien spokesmen (*i.e.*, pro-Hungarian Swabian assimilants), who invariably spurned *völkisch* principles. Basch criticized the Hungarian regime for not having fulfilled its promises. Such neglect bitterly disappointed the Swabians. In his view, the regime pursued divisive policies by utilizing the services of Magyarized village officials, whom the central government incited to undermine the *völkisch* Swabians' morale. This approach was no longer effective, Basch asserted, because the assimilationist era was at an end. The Swabians of Hungary were caught up in a strong and irreversible *völkisch* renaissance. [6]

The German government thereupon became publicly embroiled in the Hungarian minority rights controversy. In a presentation prepared for diplomats and the foreign press, Minister of the Interior Wilhelm Frick reiterated the official National Socialist position that all expatriate Germans, including citizens of other states, belonged to the indivisible German *Volksgemeinschaft.* He stressed, however, that fidelity to the latter need not conflict with the devotion a German individual owed to the state of which he was a citizen. Frick explained that in the Third Reich all ethnic minorities enjoyed farreaching rights. None of them, including some 10,000 ethnic Magyar peasants who resided in former Austrian Burgenland, had Germanization forced upon them. Frick threatened, however, that the Hungarian government's failure to improve the condition of the Swabians might have unpleasant consequences for the Magyars living in Germany.[7]

In mid-March of 1939, Teleki perceived an excellent opportunity to drive an advantageous bargain with the Third Reich. Ever since the 1938 Munich Conference, Hungary had been seeking Germany's permission to recover Ruthenia, a prewar Hungarian province and currently the easternmost part of the crumbling Czecho-Slovak state. Its acquisition would offer Hungary a chance to establish a common frontier with friendly Poland. With the discreet help of Italy, these two countries still hoped to forge a north-south defensive shield to block Germany's eastward penetration.[8] At first, Germany regarded Hungary's occupation of Ruthenia as too risky for German security. After considerable prompting by the Axis powers, Hungary signed the Anti-Comintern Pact on 22 February,[9] permitted a purged Hungarian National Socialist Party to reorganize itself on 9 March, and promised to assist the *völkisch* Swabians.[10] The Germans, however, would not reveal the date of their projected invasion of Czecho-Slovakia, yet ordered Hungary to be on the alert. On 15 March, Germany invaded Bohemia and Moravia and simultaneously unleashed Hungary.[12] Hungary had to renounce commercial exploitation rights in Ruthenia in Germany's favor and pledge not to interfere with German rail traffic in the conquered province. Hungary agreed, but within six months reneged on both promises.[13]

To "reward" Germany for the Ruthenian acquisition, Hungary hastened to be the first country to congratulate Hitler on the invasion of western Czecho-Slovakia, and applauded its incorporation into the Third Reich.[14] True to his promise, on 13 April 1939, Teleki ordered the release of the enabling decree that empowered the *Volksbund* to represent Hungary's *völkisch* Swabians. This, however, was a largely ineffectual gesture, if not a retrograde step for the Swabians. The disappointed *Volksbund* gained only cultural, but not political, rights; it still had to seek the government's permission to organize each new local chapter; but most importantly, the government intensified its moral and financial support of the rival *UDV*,[15] and considerably expanded the financial resources of Magyar-dominated religious and rural associations in predominantly Swabian-inhabited areas.[16] The *Volksbund,* which had expected to replace the *UDV,* condemned these measures as a severe disappointment. In contrast, the Third Reich seemed surprisingly content with the *Volksbund's* glacial progress.

Grandiloquent but meaningless Hungarian gestures to Germany proliferated. On 25 March, Csáky relayed a secret offer from Horthy to Hitler. If he agreed, the German Chancellor would have a Hungarian regiment named in his honor, a reward only former German President Paul von Hindenburg and Italy's King Victor Emmanuel III had ever received. As Hitler had yet to accept any honors or decorations from a foreign power, this offer proved a safe and empty gesture.[17] On 12 April, Csáky informed Germany that his country's resignation from the League of Nations the previous day proved Hungary's extraordinary fidelity to the Rome-Berlin Axis, and demonstrated Hungary's courageous acceptance of the international risks entailed in the action. This effusive gesture lacked substance and significance. Hungary remained a full participant in the League's non-political activities, and would not renounce the authority of the World Court at The Hague.[18]

Germany's forbearance in the face of Hungarian *Realpolitik* demonstrated Hitler's excellent sense of timing. The German Chancellor was undeterred by temporary obstacles and humiliations while trying to achieve distant goals. For Hitler, Hungary served merely as a convenient strategic launching pad from which the eventual exploitation of Romania and points east might follow. Until Germany secured Romania as an ally or as a satellite, Hungary had to remain pacified at all cost. Unfortunately for Germany's aims and purposes, Romania remained volatile and unpredictable throughout most of 1939.[19]

Hungarian diplomats exploited unsettled conditions in Romania, and disparaged that country in talks with their German counterparts. Sztójay harangued a German colleague on the Romanians' numerous "sins." On 13 April 1939, Romania had accepted an Anglo-French guarantee. It stubbornly clung to the 15 January 1931 Polish-Romanian defense treaty, and adhered to the military terms of the 9 February 1934 Balkan Pact. Romania's current negotiations with Great Britain, France and the Soviet Union, which had commenced at the end of March 1939, imperiled Germany. A pact would sweep Romania into the Western camp should war erupt. As a consequence, Hungary feared that the Soviet Union would occupy Romania and render inconsequential Hungary's Carpathian defense shield.[20]

Sztójay's forewarning contained a veiled threat. The Germans were not immune to a two-pronged Soviet attack through Poland and through Romania and Hungary, Sztójay hinted. Therefore, the Third Reich ought to support Hungary's territorial demands against Romania, and stop weakening Hungary's national fiber through National Socialist subversion. The Germans ridiculed this pessimistic projection. A few months later, however, Romania was still unstable. After another conversation with Sztójay, Weizsäcker advised his superiors that Romania was indeed so unreliable that all further German munitions shipments to that country ought to be suspended.[21] Until Germany remedied this awkward strategic situation, Hungary had to be humored, to the chagrin of *völkisch* Swabians, who suffered the consequences of a temporary German-Hungarian mutual dependency. Germany's strategic weakness in southeastern Europe partially explains the Third Reich's leniency with Hungary, and the decision later that year to conclude a nonaggression pact with the Soviet Union.

In the interim, the Third Reich's strategic disadvantage encouraged Hungary to defy a number of German demands and to challenge certain actions by the Third Reich it deemed harmful.[22] For example, Germany urged Hungary to introduce effective anti-Jewish laws without further delay. Horthy explained to Germany's Budapest envoy Count Erdmannsdorff that Hungary could not afford to disrupt the economic activities of Hungarian Jewry overnight. In any event, he would permit only slow, gradual and "humane" deju-daization. Horthy preempted anticipated stiff German protests by angrily denouncing the Hungarian National Socialists, who were supported by the Third Reich, as a dangerous pack of "discontented, radical, and frequently Communist," elements.[23] Within two days of this conversation, the newly installed Teleki government outlawed all German-supported parties in Hungary, interned their leaders and confiscated their organizational funds.[24] Yet neither of these unfriendly acts deterred Germany from permitting Hungary to incorporate Ruthenia less than a month later, nor from letting the government present only token solutions to the *völkisch* Swabian problem.

Other crises complicated German-Hungarian relations. On 11 February, for example, Hungarian border guards arrested and jailed a German police officer named Niko for attempting to smuggle a large cache of Nazi propaganda leaflets from former Austria into Hungary. The incident caused an uproar among Hungarians. The government tried Niko, but released him as a political good-will gesture to Germany shortly after the annexation of Ruthenia.[25] This incident further eroded the public's confidence in the benevolent intentions of the Third Reich. Had the Hungarian government sincerely tried to persuade the public that the German menace was a mere figment of some alarmist people's imagination, it would have kept the Niko incident out of the limelight.

The case of the "green books" and the "rolling Marks" precipitated a far more serious scandal than the Niko incident. The foreign bureau of the Reich-subsidized Hungarian National Socialist Party, headquartered in Berlin-Charlottenburg, published a 32-page propaganda booklet that calumniated Hungary, its institutions and people. On 17 May, the Party sent 100,000 copies of this "green book" to various Hungarian news media and prominent personages, and also dispatched a large sum of money, reputedly about one million Pengő, to a clandestine German agent somewhere in Hungary.[26] These mailings coincided with the parliamentary election campaign then being waged. The reorganized Hungarian National Socialist Party hoped to attract dissidents, especially among Hungary's depressed urban and rural masses. The "green book" publicity served as an effective grist for the Nazi propaganda mill.

In Erdmannsdorff's view, the "green book" incident seriously impaired Germany's credibility in Hungary. Moreover, the Minister asserted, it made no sense for the Third Reich to strengthen the Hungarian National Socialists at the expense of the *völkisch* Swabians, or of the Hungarian government. The Teleki regime and German Foreign Minister Joachim von Ribbentrop identified the culprits involved in this caper as the same insubordinate Viennese Nazis earlier implicated in the Niko affair.[27] The Hungarian Nazis denied any complicity in these actions, and repudiated the authors of the "green book," whoever they were. They also disclaimed having any knowledge of the one-million Pengő subsidy. But apparently the Hungarian Nazis did receive some of these, or other, funds, because they mounted a costly and highly effective election campaign, directed against everyone, including the government and its hand-picked *völkisch* Swabian candidates.[28]

The most vexing controversy to envenom German-Hungarian relations on the eve of World War II involved Hungary's demonstratively pro-Polish public posture. As the German-Polish crisis intensified during the summer of 1939, Hungarians ostentatiously demonstrated their fraternal bonds with Poland, and the government issued defiantly pro-Polish official pronouncements. As a result, on 19 July, Weizsäcker informed Sztójay in Berlin that German-Hungarian relations had reached rock bottom. He faulted Hungarian tourists, Polish educational institutions and their Hungarian counterparts, and professional and social organizations in both countries for flamboyant Polish-Hungarian fraternization. Meetings between Poles and Hungarians reportedly turned into anti-German demonstrations. Germany expected these provocations to cease, but Hungary refused to comply.[29]

No less contentious was the incident caused by Prime Minister Teleki's two identical pairs of letters, slated for simultaneous delivery to Hitler and Mussolini on 24 July. In the first letter, Teleki stated that, in the event of an armed conflict, Hungary would dutifully stand by the Rome-Berlin Axis. In the second letter, Teleki explained that under present circumstances, Hungary could not participate in an attack on Poland in the event a German-Polish conflict should erupt.[30] The second Teleki letter loosed a storm of indignation in Germany. Hitler expressed his "outrage" to Csáky at Teleki's ingratitude. After all, Hungary had gained considerable territory in Slovakia and Ruthenia recently, and Hungary owed these acquisitions exclusively to Germany. After this intolerable affront, Hitler fumed, Hungary could no longer depend on further German aid to regain lost Hungarian soil. Hitler reminded Csáky that, should Germany suffer defeat, the victorious Western powers would not hesitate to dismember Hungary to please their east-central European allies.[31]

Within two weeks of this Hitler-Csáky encounter, the Germans politely begged Hungary to deny worldwide rumors that German-Hungarian relations were tense. Weizsäcker explained to Hans Georg von Mackensen, Germany's ambassador in Rome, why the Third Reich needed at least the semblance of amicable German-Hungarian relations. Germany's grievances with Poland had reached the breaking point. Poland would be smashed unless it yielded to German demands.[32] Hitler required a publicly unified phalanx of the Axis Powers, Hungary included, with which to confront Poland and the Western powers. Germany also needed assurances that Hungary would not obstruct the *Wehrmacht*'s operations against Poland.[33]

Teleki ignored German pleas for a declaration of formal support. He still hoped to prevent a German attack on Poland. In the meantime, Hungarians disregarded the gathering war clouds. On 28 August a Hungarian soccer team played a match in Warsaw,[34] while the orchestrated Hungarian press churned out endless pro-Polish copy. Tibor Eckhardt, the internationally respected Opposition leader, issued a Hungarian neutrality statement, most certainly with the government's permission, if not approval.[35]

To the dismay of the Germans, Count István Bethlen, an Anglophile former prime minister and respected elder statesman, journeyed to the French and British capitals for discussions with Western leaders. Germany retaliated against Hungary by suspending the shipment of certain types of essential weaponry. [36] On 1 September, the day on which German-Polish hostilities began, Ribbentrop wired Erdmannsdorff in Budapest to seek promises of Hungarian support. He was to reassure Csáky that, for the moment, the Third Reich did not expect Hungary to intervene actively in the struggle against Poland, but he was to urge Hungary to refrain from issuing a neutrality statement.[37]

That same day, Hungary appeared to relent and obliged Germany by pledging not to issue a neutrality statement in the German-Polish conflict.[38] In fact, Teleki threw Hungary's frontiers wide open to receive fleeing Polish refugees, and he offered sanctuary to defeated units of the Polish armed forces. They were accommodated handsomely in Hungary, and the government assisted numerous Poles who wanted to reach France, where they continued the struggle against the Third Reich.[39] This action, however, constituted the last major opportunity for the exercise of Hungarian independentmindedness. The Soviet-German nonaggression pact of 23 August 1939, the attack of these two powers against Poland, and the rapid disintegration of the latter, destroyed Hungary's advantageous strategic position in the Carpathian Basin by surrounding

Hungary with an iron ring of hostile powers. Germany no longer had to tolerate Hungarian obstreperousness in silence.

CHAPTER XIV

CONCLUSION

Toward the end of the Gömbös era Hungarian diplomacy emerged with three major objectives. Hungary wanted to revise the Treaty of Trianon at the expense of the three Little Entente states; avoid war, if possible; and hand in hand with Italy, prevent the evolution of exclusive German domination in eastern Europe. Hungary lacked both strength and influence to bend events to suit its requirements, and Italy was on the verge of being placed in a similar predicament. As long as Austria survived, Hungary could use its own favorable strategic position to good advantage. Should Austria fall, however, Hungary would become vulnerable to German encirclement and aggression. Routine Hungarian diplomacy, which had sufficed in ordinary times to ensure the country's security, would thereafter be insufficient to protect Hungary's independence. Hereafter, the socioeconomic problems plaguing most eastern European states, combined with their mutual hostility, required more than conventional wisdom and diplomatic prowess to guide Hungary into safe channels. Hungary would have to combine caution with craftiness in order to survive.

Internally, too, Hungary faced seemingly insoluble problems. With the premature death of Gömbös, Hungary lost a resolute and versatile leader, who successfully combined anti-Swabian policies with demands for German diplomatic and economic assistance. The late prime minister had encouraged a schism between Swabian moderates and nationalists. After Gömbös's passing, the rift became irreversible. National Socialist influences flourished among *völkisch* malcontents. The government increasingly wondered how to reconcile its fear of the dissident Swabians and their Nazi German supporters with the objectives of creating a homogeneous Magyar society. The Hungarians also affected to satisfy the Third Reich's minimal demands for Swabian reform in return for German economic support, and also wished to enlist Germany in the task of recovering Hungary's lost territories. In 1936, it was by no means absolutely certain that Germany would support Hungary's territorial claims against the Successor States. Hitler might well decide to abandon Hungary and assist whichever east-central European or Balkan state best promoted Germany's own expansionist objectives.

At the end of 1936, therefore, Hungary stood at the crossroads and peered into an uncertain future.

Before 1937, Hungary's economic freedom of action was severely circumscribed by low global agricultural prices and depressed demands. Since overseas transportation to Western Europe was less costly than shipping goods from eastern Europe by rail, Hungary had few opportunities to sell its agricultural products in western Europe. Germany rescued Hungary's faltering economy in 1931, and thereafter helped absorb most of Hungary's excess agrarian production.

This situation changed in 1937. The agricultural depression eased, farm product prices rose, and Hungary was tempted to reap considerably higher profits derived from sales to countries other than Germany. By neglecting its contractual obligations to the Third Reich, Hungary established a poor reputation as being opportunistic and untrustworthy. Germany had just embarked on an ambitious Five-Year Plan that sought to establish regional autarchy in support of Germany's growing war machine. Instead of establishing itself as a reliable German trade partner, Hungary sent a clear message to Berlin that the National Socialist leaders interpreted as Hungarian unwillingness to abide by a bargain and to support a former wartime ally. This boded ill for Hungarian plans to recapture the territories lost in World War I. Without Germany's assistance, Hungary could not succeed in this quest.

The Germans turned increasingly to Romania and Yugoslavia to satisfy their needs for agricultural products. Germany refused to support Hungary's territorial claims in Romania and Yugoslavia, so that Hungary had to be content with the possible restoration of some of its lost territories in eastern Czechoslovakia. The prosperity of 1937 ended, and a depression struck with renewed force in 1938. More than ever before, Hungary was compelled to rely on the German market, having lost Italy and Austria as its most lucrative accounts. The desire for quick, temporary profit at the expense of Germany in 1937 cost Hungary dearly in the long-run in terms of economic loss and the forfeiture of Germany's trust and good will.

The year 1938 found Hungary in an economic conundrum. Having lost confidence in Hungary, Germany began making exceedingly heavy and unreasonable commercial demands. Defying Germany overtly would have been foolhardy. Hungary had no choice but to supply Germany's economic needs at low prices set by the Third Reich, and to accept unneeded manufactured items in return, including obsolete armaments. Germany also forced Hungary to pass anti-Jewish legislation, and intervened in Hungary's internal affairs by supporting Hungary's National Socialists and *völkisch* Swabians. By denying Hungary access to essential raw materials, Germany effectively curtailed Hungary's plan to launch an industrial revolution that might have relieved the misery and unemployment of the lower classes. Germany supported the Romanian and Yugoslav economies, and threatened to replace Hungary as its principal regional ally and supplier. Germany tried to frighten Hungary into signing a long-term trade agreement that would have turned Hungary into a German economic satellite. Although Germany had the upper hand, Hungary refused to succumb to pressure and barter away its independence. With Austria and most of Czechoslovakia in the German orbit by the end of 1938, Hungary found it increasingly more difficult to resist German economic demands. The German government realized that Hungary could not resist economic *Gleichschaltung* indefinitely, and at the end of 1938, assumed a wait-and-see attitude. Hungary's economic options had narrowed to few alternatives.

Although by 1939 Germany had made its political, military and economic supremacy abundantly clear in eastern Europe, Hungary continually defied the Third Reich on a wide range of vital economic issues. Hungary promised but refused to conclude long-range commercial agreements that would have tied Hungarian production and allocation of agricultural produce hand and foot to German requirements. Hungary reneged on a pledge to permit Germany to explore and exploit the natural resources of recently acquired Ruthenia. In particular, the Hungarians thwarted German efforts to exploit Hungarian fossil fuel deposits. Hungary would not ship food to Germany's satellite Slovakia at a time when the Slovaks were aiding the German war effort against Poland. The Hungarian authorities would not permit the country's railway system to be used to transport German or Slovak troops to the Polish front.

Hungary's most damaging and humiliating action against Germany when war began was to manipulate the Pengö to the detriment of Germany, and to make Hungarian goods more accessible and salesworthy in the Allied countries of western Europe. The sole concession to German demands, the passage of a law restricting Jewish economic activity, helped neither the Germans nor the Swabians. Perceived Hungarian duplicity convinced Berlin that Hungary disapproved of Germany's war against Poland, and that its leaders had no faith in an Axis victory. This message, Hungarian leaders hoped, would make a suitable impact not only in Berlin and Rome, but in London, Paris and Washington. As in the past, Hungary overestimated the ability and desire of the Western allies to intercede on behalf of Hungary. In fact, Hungary's destiny eventually would be decided by the outcome of the struggle between Nazi Germany and the Soviet Union.

In the years preceding World War II, Hungary's diplomacy excelled. Skillful diplomatic maneuverings comprised an important element in Hungary's short-run success to contain German advances in eastern Europe. These diplomatic contributions measured on a global scale might appear unimportant and hardly worth relating. It must be kept in mind, however, that even the great powers failed to stem the German tide short of war. The failure to curb Germany was not Hungary's fault, and thus should not detract from the considerable achievements, however temporary, of certain Hungarian statesmen. Their options were, after all, severely limited.[1] Negotiations seeking fullfledged rapprochement with the Little Entente, especially Czechoslovakia, would have invited German retaliations. Refusal to negotiate out of fear of Germany would have relegated Hungary to the level of a German satellite, and earned the West's disapproval. Limited negotiations with the Little Entente meant keeping Hungary's options open, Germany at bay, and gaining time.

Parleys with these three neighbors also proved to be the correct formula for possible reconciliation with them all, or with some of them. The Little Entente established the foundations for such a reconciliation in response to Hungarian encouragement at Şinaia in August 1937. This positive reaction considerably expanded Hungary's diplomatic options and improved the country's maneuverability. Foreign Minister Kánya's clever and adaptive diplomacy demonstrated that even a small, militarily and economically weak country such as Hungary could block the progress of a mighty imperialistic power, provided the former enjoyed the strategic advantage, had the courage to act, and possessed the wisdom to execute the appropriate policies.

The year 1938 brought mixed blessings to Hungary in the diplomatic arena. German-Italian parity, upon which Hungary depended for an equitable power distribution in eastern Europe, vanished, and German hegemony took its place. Revisionism became a trap for Hungary. Recapturing the lost territories could be achieved only with German help, but that assistance was fraught with peril. Far from emerging a regional powerbroker serving congenial German and Italian allies, Hungary faced the possibility of becoming an eventual victim of Nazi aggression. Romania and Yugoslavia appeared to compete successfully for German and Italian favor, and as the year progressed, Axis support for Hungary ebbed, whereas sympathy for Romania and Yugoslavia grew in Berlin and Rome. The fall of Austria and Czechoslovakia brought Nazi Germany closer to Hungary's frontiers. The Western powers had demonstrated their impotence at Munich, Italy was powerless to assist Hungary, and Poland, Hungary's sole remaining friend, was too insignificant to alter the balance in Hungary's favor. Worse still, the Soviet Union loomed as a threat exceeding, in Hungarian view, even that presented by Germany. Indeed, many Hungarians believed that they had no other choice than to rely on Germany as the lesser of two evils as a protector of Hungary from bolshevism.

Hungary's leaders responded to these multiple perils by continuing their *Realpolitik* with Germany and the Little Entente. They wanted to slow the Third Reich's eastward progress by various diplomatic expedients. One stratagem was to make the Germans believe that Hungary would actively participate in the projected military campaign against Czechoslovakia, but then to renege at the last moment. This forced Hitler to negotiate an unwanted compromise with the Western powers at Munich. This Hungarian action slowed Hitler's timetable in Czechoslovakia for half a year.

Another limited Hungarian diplomatic success in 1938 was the pacification of Romania and Yugoslavia. Hungary also wrecked the Little Entente by isolating Czechoslovakia from its allies. This plan succeeded, albeit only partially. Romania and Yugoslavia abandoned Czechoslovakia largely because its position proved hopeless in the face of German determination to destroy that country. Romania and Yugoslavia did, however, deny Hungary the freedom to acquire all of Slovakia by threatening to go to war to protect their battered ally from Hungarian aggression. They had no way of knowing, of course, that Hitler had no intentions to permit all of Slovakia to slip into Hungarian hands. Hungary's diplomacy to wreck the Little Entente by affecting to befriend Romania and Yugoslavia therefore bore only limited fruit, and earned Hitler's suspicion and anger at Hungary's apparent attempt to undermine Germany's diplomatic objectives in the Balkans. Furthermore, as a matter of principle, Hitler could not tolerate a small country such as Hungary to pursue an independent foreign policy, especially one that disrupted German blueprints and timetables. On the whole, therefore, although Hungary did succeed in temporarily checking the German advance, the cost was high. Germany, and to some extent Italy, ceased regarding Hungary as a reliable and valued ally. Their displeasure relegated Hungary to the status of being one among many expendable small states in eastern Europe.

In 1939, German-Hungarian diplomatic relations further deteriorated. Hungary incorporated Ruthenia with Germany's grudging permission. But the price for such a small gain was steep in terms of having to render economic and strategic accommodations to Germany, and in terms of having to offer the Swabians an extensive reform package. Hungarian concessions to Germany and the Swabians, however, turned out to be virtually worthless. Hungary broke its pledge regarding economic concessions to Germany, whereas the *völkisch* Swabians had their freedoms curtailed by a restrictive autonomous arrangement.

Hungary's alarm grew after the liquidation of Czecho-Slovakia in March 1939. Hungary's leaders did everything in their power to prevent, or at least delay, the German attack on Poland. Poland in German hands would terminate Hungary's advantageous strategic position in east-central Europe. Hungary would be in the same precarious position as Czechoslovakia had been a few months earlier. The beginning of the end for Hungarian sovereignty came on 23 August 1939. On that day, Germany and the Soviet Union settled their dispute and sealed Poland's doom. A few weeks later Poland was gone. Hungary was completely surrounded by Germany, Romania and Yugoslavia, and the USSR had moved much closer to Hungary's northeastern frontier.

Between 23 August and the day hostilities erupted between Germany and Poland, Hungary made a number of brave but futile defiant gestures to protest German aggression in Poland. Hungary rescued elements of the defeated Polish armed forces and helped to transplant them to western Europe. These actions, however, were damaging to Hungarian security. Hungary could no longer defy such German directives as participation in the growing war, economic *Gleichschaltung*, or introduction of laws that limited traditional Hungarian freedoms, such as the anti-Jewish legislation. With the occupation of Poland by German and Soviet forces, Hungarian sovereignty, which had survived six years of National Socialist assault, became fatally weakened.

Hungarian minority policy was also characterized by *Realpolitik*. At the end of 1936, the Hungarian government would have liked nothing better than to continue its current innocuous Swabian cultural policy indefinitely. In the struggle between the Hungarian government and the *völkisch* Swabians, education and language served as the chief battlegrounds. In practical terms, this meant the extension of limited cultural and educational concessions that seldom if ever filtered down to the Swabians effectively at the grass roots level. The government adopted a self-righteous attitude, but relied on local functionaries to ensure that modest concessions in increased German teacher training, over which the Ministry of Education had full control, would not be translated into a deluge of qualified German instructors in the Swabian minority village schools.

The government's refusal to provide German textbooks on financial grounds constituted another bottleneck to thwart effective German instruction. In a sense, the central government heeded the sentiments of most local officials, especially teachers. These individuals regarded German instruction as unnecessary, even unpatriotic. Many priests and ministers in Swabian areas concurred with their secular colleagues' views, as did numerous Swabian parents. While C-type schools were available, parents preferred those institutions to A-type schools because their children received a thorough Magyar education as well as daily German language instruction. Most parents deemed this limited formal tutoring, combined with home use of German, sufficient to carry their children through life. The B-type schools not only offered too much German, they confused the children by alternating Magyar and German subject matters in a confusing manner. After the introduction of the 1935 school law, many parents chose pure Magyar schools for their offspring. This had nothing to do with disloyalty to the German *Volk*. Parents merely wanted their children to learn the official language thoroughly and properly, and thus permit them to succeed socially and economically later in life.

A few hundred well-educated *völkisch* Swabians insisted on providing Swabian children with German instruction, but not on the basis of economic utility but of *Volkstum*. But for them, the Swabian issue in Hungary might have become slowly resolved through gradual assimilation. In view of the overwhelming power and propinquity of the deeply concerned Third Reich, however, the Swabians became radicalized along National Socialist lines. Many of them gradually turned into more or less willing tools in the hands of their German "protectors," to the detriment of their Hungarian homeland, their Hungarian compatriots, and their own long-term interests.

Under Prime Minister Darányi, Hungary had been attempting to pacify German-speaking citizens and to soothe Germany by offering minimal educational and cultural concessions to Swabians. By then, only Magyarized and semi-assimilated Swabians found these halfway measures satisfactory. Prime Minister Imrédy, however, tried to settle Swabian grievances and thus gain the confidence of the Third Reich, with which he sought closer cooperation.[2] The Prime Minister's pro-German posture offended not only Hungary's nationalistic Magyar and Magyarized public and officialdom, but dismayed the country's influential conservative political establishment as well. Its representatives feared that Imrédy's influence[3] and actions would open the floodgates to German penetration and would sooner or later destroy Hungarian independence. The public feared the growing aggressiveness of the Third Reich, and deplored its penchant for utilizing German minorities as Fifth Columns in countries that Hitler sought to subvert or destroy. Despite the protestations of *völkisch* Swabians that they would always remain *staatstreu, i.e.,* loyal to the Hungarian state, most Hungarians were convinced that, if offered the choice and the opportunity, those Swabians would support the Third Reich and the German *Volk*, and that therefore their professed fidelity to the Hungarian state was hypocritical. Conversely, most Swabians sensed that the price of their ungrudging acceptance into Hungarian society would have to be purchased at the cost of full assimilation into the Magyar lingual and cultural stream. A compromise between these two extreme ideological positions seemed out of the question as long as Nazi Germany threatened to use the *völkisch* Swabians as a Fifth Column in Hungary.

The fundamental parting of the ways between Hungary and *völkisch* Swabians became manifest in 1939. That year, the pressure on Hungary from Germany and the *völkisch* Swabians intensified. Both demanded incontrovertible proof that the government sincerely desired a rapprochement with the German minority. Hungary had no intentions of honoring any promise that would enable an autonomous *völkisch* Swabian society to exist side by side with the Magyar-dominated establishment. That is why the pro-German Imrédy was replaced as prime minister by the noted anti-Nazi and anti-Swabian Pál Teleki in the spring of 1939. Teleki introduced pro-Swabian pseudo-reforms by releasing the long-delayed autonomy statute for Swabians, and in the May elections, he permitted three Swabian *Volksbund* members to run on the MEP ticket. He also passed Hungary's first anti-Jewish legislation. These concessions proved illusory. The *Volksbund* won only meager cultural rights, while its rival, the *UDV*, not only continued operations, but had its government subsidies considerably increased. Minority education failed to improve. The anti-Jewish legislation did not benefit Swabians. Only two *Volksbund* members sat in Parliament on the government benches, and they exerted no influence on the government's internal or external policies. Since these concessions pleased Germany, the Swabians had no choice but to feign gratitude.

The question remains, why did the Hungarian government promise Swabian reform in November 1938, then renege on its pledge throughout the winter and early spring months of 1939, only to reemerge with concessions that appeared generous just when tensions with the Swabians had reached the breaking point? The Third Reich's growing influence on Hungarian domestic and foreign policy, and the Germans' oft-repeated concern for the welfare of the Swabians profoundly influenced and modified Hungarian strategy throughout these months. During the Munich Crisis, Imrédy had compared Hungary's past and future path to a "narrow mountain ridge with yawning abysses to the right and to the left of it."[4] Imrédy's allegory was still appropriate the following spring. Many of Hungary's political leaders admired certain features of National Socialism, even though their brutality repelled them. They were alarmed lest Germany's overwhelming predominance in Danubian Europe destroy Hungary's chances of remaining influential, let alone sovereign. Hungary feared that the National Socialist *Weltanschauung* would infect not only the Swabians, but ensnare Hungary's impoverished urban and rural proletarian masses as well.[5] They also recognized that the Third Reich demanded decent treatment for Germans in all those states that desired to transact profitable business with the National Socialist regime. Hence Hungarian leaders evolved the strategy of legislating Swabian pseudo-reforms to please Berlin.

To complicate Hungary's ethnic problems and physical isolation, Hungary's leaders realized after the Munich Crisis that the Western powers, especially Great Britain, were neither willing nor able to remedy the perceived injustices of Trianon.[6] Italy might have promoted Hungarian interests more vigorously had it not been eclipsed by the more dynamic and powerful Third Reich. Hopes of economic, political and territorial gains, as well as the desire for protection by Germany against the bolshevik menace, propelled Hungary into the Third Reich's orbit, despite the apprehensions of the country's leaders regarding Nazi Germany.[7]

Hungary's statesmen considered the *volksbewusst* Swabians no less perilous to national security than the power-hungry Third Reich, with its continual interference in Hungarian internal affairs and foreign diplomacy, and with its endless economic demands. The problem was how to balance Hungary's obligations to Germany and the risks involving perceived Swabian duplicity in formulating policies designed to please the Third Reich and the *Volksbund* without compromising Hungary's sovereignty? The Hungarian government wished to defer "the evil day" as long as possible. This explains why Hungary alternated between tendering promises to the German minority and not fulfilling these pledges.[8] The government's concessions to the *Volksbund* in April 1939 did not depart from this routine. The enabling decree was merely a gesture by the Hungarian government designed to propitiate the impatient Third Reich on an issue that was very close to its leaders' hearts. Hungary also wished to deny its restless *völkisch* Swabian citizens the excuse to agitate against Hungary in Germany during a trying period in German-Hungarian diplomatic and economic relations.

In the late 1930s, Germany and Hungary had emerged uneasy allies of convenience. They clashed on every conceivable issue, from military and diplomatic strategy and objectives to ideology and the treatment of the Swabians in Hungary. What had begun as merely "misunderstandings" [9] in the early 1930s grew into thinly disguised mutual animosity by the outbreak of World War II. [10] Ferenc Deak explained the underlying reasons for this schism: "The Horthy regime's Christian traditionalist ideology and liberal economic policy never really squared with Nazi Germany's un-Christian, radical ideology and centrally directed economy."[11] During the six-month interval before the war, Hungary enjoyed an unusual short-term strategic advantage over Germany. Romania proved unreliable for Germany's expansionary purposes, and this situation forced the Third Reich to defer to Hungary as its easternmost strategic outpost. Teleki skillfully exploited this opportunity. He delayed Germany's eastward expansion, gained new territory, strengthened Hungary's sovereignty,[12] albeit temporarily, parried German retaliations against Hungary, confined National Socialist subversion in Hungary within manageable bounds, and splintered the Swabian minority movement. He thus rendered the *völkisch* Swabians' potential collusion with the Third Reich temporarily less effective.

Teleki's short-term excursion into *Realpolitik* was therefore a modest success.[13] In the long-run, however, Hungary lacked both the might and the influence to sway events in which it became embroiled. Even with optimum diplomatic skills and the best of intentions, small countries surrounded by powerful adversaries can influence their environment only temporarily and to a limited degree. Considering Hungary's circumstances on the eve of World War II, the country's statesmen, especially Gömbös and Teleki, made the best possible use of their opportunities, and came close to achieving their limited domestic and foreign goals. In the long-run, however, the price Hungary had to pay for short-term gains was excessively steep. The country became a battleground between National Socialist and bolshevik forces. Germany could not save Hungary from a Soviet invasion. Ultimately, what Hungary's conservative leaders had feared most came to pass. Hungary exchanged German and domestic National Socialist despotism for Soviet bolshevik autocracy. Nazi Germany was in ruins. Its exploitation of the *völkisch* Swabians created a backlash. After the war, the Hungarian government expelled hundreds of thousands of collaborationist Swabians, and tried Franz Basch for high treason. He was found guilty and paid with his life for having chosen the losing side. Interference by powerful states in the affairs of ethnic brethren residing in neighboring countries aggravates prevailing problems and saddles the next generation with new difficulties.

NOTES

Chapter I
Hungary's Political, Economic and Ethnic Background
Prior to 1937

1. Georg von Lukács, "Die Tragödie Trianon-Ungarns," *Ungarischer Volkswirt*, VII, 10 (October, 1938), 4-7, summarizes the consequences of Trianon from the Hungarian perspective.

2. Magyar Királyi Belügyminisztérium, *Magyar statisztikai évkönyv és jelentés 1919-1922* (Budapest, 1925), *passim*. After the 1921 plebiscite in the western counties of Hungary that assigned 360,000 people, among them 232,000 Swabians and 65,000 Magyars to Austria, about 550,000 German-Hungarians remained in Trianon Hungary. Lukács, "Die Tragödie," 4. Although originally these Germans came from every part of southern Germany and Austria, they eventually acquired the appellation "Swabian" (Schwaben). Franz A. Basch, *Das Deutschtum in Ungarn* (Budapest, 1926), p. 7. N. G. Papp, "The German Minority in Hungary Between the Two World Wars: Loyal Subjects or Suppressed Citizens?" *East European Quarterly*, XXII, 4 (1989), 495-514.

3. C. A. Macartney, *National States and National Minorities* (London, 1934), p. 122.

4. Albert Apponyi, "Historic Mission of Hungary and the States Aggrandized to Her Detriment," *Justice for Hungary* (London, 1928), pp. 1-20.

5. *Évkönyv és jelentés* (1926-1929), *passim*.

6. Law 4800.923 M.E. *Budapesti Közlöny* (22 June 1923).

7. Law 7699/1924 M.E. II, 21 October 1924.

8. Law 11,000/1935.M.E., *Évkönyv és jelentés* (1936), pp. 94-95.

9. Robert F. Young, *In Command of France. French Foreign Policy and Military Planning, 1933-1940* (Cambridge and London, 1978), p. 119. For a coverage of events from 1919 to 1936, see Thomas Spira, *German-Hungarian Relations and the Swabian Problem from Károlyi to Gömbös 1919-1936* (Boulder and New York, 1977).

10. For a discussion of Gömbös's foreign policy, see Spira, *German-Hungarian Relations*, chapters VIII and IX.

Chapter II
The Diplomatic Picture - Europe in 1937

The author utilized the following works as his chief sources for reconstructing the European diplomatic situation in the year 1937.

Stephen Bethlen, "Hungary's Position after the Austrian Anschluss," *The Hungarian Quarterly*, VI (Old Series) (1938), 201-210.

John C. Dreifort, *Yvon Delbos at the Quai D'Orsay. French Foreign Policy during the Popular Front 1936–1938* (Lawrence, KS, 1973).

Nandor A. F. Dreisziger, *Hungary's Way to World War II* (Toronto, 1968).

Endre Bela Gasztony, "Revisionist Hungarian Foreign Policy and the Third Reich's Advance to the East, 1933–1939," unpublished doctoral dissertation, University of Oregon, 1970.

Gyula Juhász, *Hungarian Foreign Policy 1919–1945* (Budapest, 1979).

C. A. Macartney, *Hungary and Her Successors. The Treaty of Trianon and Its Consequences 1919–1937* (London, et al., 1937).

————. "Hungary and the Present Crisis," *International Affairs*, XVII, 11 (1938).

"Poland between Germany and the USSR, 1926–1939: The Theory of Two Enemies. The Pilsudski Institute Symposium," *The Polish Review*, XX, 1 (1975).

György Ránki, et al., *A Wilhelmstrasse és Magyarország. Német diplomáciai iratok Magyarországról 1933–1944* (Budapest, 1968).

Günter Reichert, *Das Scheitern der Kleinen Entente. Internationale Beziehungen im Donauraum von 1933 bis 1938* (Munich, 1971).

Thomas L. Sakmyster, *Hungary, the Great Powers, and the Danubian Crisis 1936–1939* (Athens, GA, 1980).

Gerhard L. Weinberg, *The Foreign Policy of Hitler's Germany. Starting World War II, 1937–1939* (Chicago, IL and London, 1980).

————. "Secret Hitler-Beneš Negotiations in 1936–37," *Journal of Central European Affairs*, XIX (1960), 366-374.

Chapter III
German-Hungarian Economic Relations - Late 1936–1937

1. Iván T. Berend and György Ránki, *Magyarország a fasiszta Németország "életterében" 1933–1939.* (Budapest, 1960), pp. 167*ff*.

2. David E. Kaiser, *Economic Diplomacy and the Origins of the Second World War. Germany, Britain, France, and Eastern Europe, 1930-1939* (Princeton, NJ, 1980), p. 130. Also see S. D. Zagoroff, Jenő Végh and Alexander D. Bilimovich, *The Agricultural Economy of the Danubian Countries 1935-1945* (Stanford, CA, 1955); Dietrich Orlow, *The Nazis in the Balkans. A Case Study of Totalitarian Politics* (Pittsburgh, PA, 1968); Rene Erbe, *Die nationalsozialistische Wirtschaftspolitik 1933-1939 im Lichte der modernen Theorie* (Zurich, 1958); Lajos Jócsik, *German Economic Influences in the Danube Valley* (Budapest, 1946); and Gerhard Schacher, *Germany Pushes South-East* (London, 1937).

3. Antonín Basch, *The Danube Basin and the German Economic Sphere* (New York, 1943), p. 171.

4. Cited in *Ungarisches Wirtschafts-Jahrbuch*, XIII (1937), 170.

5. Basch, *The Danube Basin*, pp. 174*ff.*, and Chapters 10 and 11. Also see Howard S. Ellis, *Exchange Control in Central Europe* (Cambridge, MA, 1941), pp. 80-81.

6. Basch, *The Danube Basin*, p. 184.

7. *Ibid.*, p. 178. Also see Schacher, *Germany*, espec. Ch. 13.

8. "German Bartering Failing in Balkans," *The New York Times* (31 December 1936).

9. Basch, *The Danube Basin*, p. 190.

10. Berend and Ránki, *Magyarország*, p. 159.

11. *Documents on German Foreign Policy 1918-1945 (DGFP)*. Series C (London, 1949), V, Item 490.

12. *Ibid.*, Item 589. Also see Kaiser, *Economic Diplomacy*, pp. 155-157.

13. *DGFP*, C, V, Item 612.

14. Berend and Ránki, *Magyarország*, p. 161, Note 224.

15. *Ibid.*, p. 134 (Table 9).

16. *Ibid*, pp. 160-161.

17. J. Feledy, "Hungaro-German Economic Relations," unpublished doctoral dissertation, McGill University, 1970, 289.

18. Berend and Ránki, *Magyarország*, p. 163, Note 227.

19. *Ibid.*, p. 164, Note 229.

20. Feledy, "Hungaro-German," 293.

21. Kaiser, *Economic Diplomacy*, p. 160. For example, imports of Yugoslav wheat cost Germany 151 Marks per ton in 1937, compared with 125 Marks per ton for Canadian wheat. Romanian corn cost 106.90 Marks per ton compared with 75 Marks per ton for the Argentinian variety.

22. *Ibid.*, p. 156. See letter of 18 December 1936, for example.

23. Feledy, "Hungaro-German," 292 and 293; and Berend and Ránki, *Magyarország*, pp. 162-163.

24. *Ibid.*

25. Feledy, "Hungaro-German," 295-296.

26. Kaiser, *Economic Diplomacy*, p. 156.

27. *Ibid.*, pp. 156-157.

28. Feledy, "Hungaro-German," 296.

29. H. Reischle, "Deutsch-ungarische Wirtschaftsprobleme," *Ungarischer Volkswirt*, VI, 7 (July, 1937), 8-10. For the Hungarian position, see Samuel Weiner, "Die Placierung der ungarischen Mehlüberschüsse auf den Auslandsmärkten," *ibid.*, 10ff.

30. I. Ferenczi, "Ungarische Handelspolitik," *Ungarisches Wirtschafts-Jahrbuch*, XII (1936), 159-168.

31. Jenő Végh, "Agriculture and Food in Hungary during World War II," in Zagoroff, *et al.*, *The Agricultural Economy*, pp. 157-162. Végh was Secretary General of the National Association of Manufacturers of Hungary before World War II.

32. I. Ferenczi, "Ungarns Handelspolitik," *Ungarisches Wirtschafts-Jahrbuch*, XIII (1937), 152-165.

33. Feledy, "Hungaro-German," 297-298.

34. Ferenczi, "Ungarns Handelspolitik."

35. Hungary to Germany, Export in 1936: 115.2 million Pengő — Hungary to Germany, Export in 1937: 141.6 million Pengő — Germany to Hungary, Export in 1936: 113.4 million Pengő — Germany to Hungary, Export in 1937: 124.8 million Pengő. Andreas Vitéz Mecsér, "Die Rückwirkungen des Anschlusses auf die wirtschaftlichen Beziehungen Ungarns zum Deutschen Reich," *Ungarisches Wirtschafts-Jahrbuch*, XIV (1938), 21.

36. Feledy, "Hungaro-German," 299.

37. Basch, *The Danube Basin*, pp. 200-201.

Chapter IV
Hungary's Abortive 1937 Rapprochement with
the Little Entente

1. For example, Jörg K. Hoensch, *Der ungarische Revisionismus und die Zerschlagung der Tschechoslowakei* (Tübingen, 1967), p. 46, claims that Hungarian Foreign Minister Kánya pursued a deceitful policy in negotiating with the Little Entente; he merely wished Italy and Germany to declare themselves in favor of Hungarian revisionism. György Ránki, "Adatok a magyar külpolitikához a csehszlovákia elleni agresszió idején 1937–1939," *Századok*, XCIII (1959), 117-159 and 356-372 (119), declares that Hungary rigidly rejected any kind of collaboration with Czechoslovakia, but he cites 1935–1936 sources to support this view. John A. Lukács, *The Great Powers and Eastern Europe* (New York, 1953), p. 89, only mentions Beneš's approaches to Hungary in late 1937, by which time reconciliation was "well-nigh too late." Magda Ádám, *et al.*, *Magyarország és a Második Világháború. Titkos diplomáciai okmányok a háború előzményeihez és történetéhez* (Budapest, 1966), p. 61, claim that, in 1937 Hungary might still have created a mutual defense pact with its neighbors to combat Nazi Germany, but that "Hungary's ruling classes" would not even hear of such an agreement. For precisely the same viewpoint, see Magda Ádám, *et al.*, *Allianz Hitler-Horthy-Mussolini. Dokumente zur ungarischen Aussenpolitik (1933–1944)* (Budapest, 1966), p. 23. In "Az ellenforradalmi rendszer revíziós külpolitikájához," in Erzsébet Andics, ed., *A magyar nacionalizmus kialakulása és története* (Budapest, 1964), p. 364, Ádám also claims that Hungary conducted sham negotiations with Czechoslovakia as a means of building bridges to the Western powers, but she offers no proof. Robert Machray, *The Struggle for the Danube and the Little Entente, 1929–1938* (London, 1938), p. 284, fails to mention the negotiations, but he does construct a plausible rationale for Hungary's willingness to negotiate at all. According to him, the Italian-Yugoslav treaty of March 1937 placed Hungary in an awkward economic and political position, and Darányi wished to redress the balance. C. A. Macartney's *October Fifteenth. A History of Modern Hungary, 1929–1945* (Edinburgh, 1956), I, 200, is ambiguous. Kánya felt obligated to accept negotiation offers, but only in

order "not to put himself in the wrong." But, "he had no intention of ever binding himself by a pact with Czechoslovakia (nor, one must think...with Rumania either)," only a settlement with Yugoslavia alone, and a provisional one with Rumania, leaving Czechoslovakia isolated. Yet, "if...the Little Entente States had offered Hungary really attractive terms, who shall say that he [Kánya] might not have accepted them?" In *Independent Eastern Europe* (London and Basingstoke, 1962), p. 361, co-authored with A. W. Palmer, Macartney reiterates the same views, with minor modifications. In *Das Scheitern*, pp. 72*ff*, Günter Reichert mentions some of the negotiations between Hungary and the Little Entente, but he fails to explain Hungarian policy or motives. Thomas Sakmyster, *Hungary*, pp. 74-77, alludes to the problem mainly from the vantage point of Hungary's relations with the great powers, but he does not discuss Hungary's negotiations with Austria and the Little Entente in early 1937 in detail. The most thorough survey is by Gyula Juhász, *Magyarország külpolitikája 1919-1945* (Budapest, 1969), pp. 166-171. Juhász's account is essentially accurate, although a few omissions tend to mislead. He minimizes Austria's role in Hungary's negotiations with the Little Entente; he ignores Hungary's fear of German expansion, omits Kánya's distrust of Yugoslavia, and he subtly insinuates that Hungarian diplomacy proceeded partly voluntarily, partly by accident, in conjunction with German aspirations.

2. Sakmyster, *Hungary*, p. 85.

3. *Ibid.*; and Ádám, "Az ellenforradalmi rendszer," pp. 364-365.

4. This emerged in a conversation involving Kánya, Darányi and Ciano. Galeazzo Ciano, *Ciano's Diplomatic Papers*, ed. by Malcolm Muggeridge (London, 1948), p. 117, citing discussions in Budapest, 19-22 May 1937. Horthy basically agreed with a strategy that would harmonize with British objectives. See Thomas L. Sakmyster, "Miklós Horthy, Hungary, and the Coming of the European Crisis, 1932-41," *East Central Europe*, III, 2 (1976), 220-232, especially 223-225; and Nikolaus von Horthy, *Ein Leben für Ungarn* (Bonn, 1953), pp. 179-180.

5. Ciano to Darányi and Kánya, Budapest, 21 May 1937. Ádám, *Allianz*, Item 17.

6. Franz von Papen, *Der Wahrheit eine Gasse* (Munich, 1952), p. 433. This represented von Papen's view on 12 January 1937.

7. This is allegedly what Hitler told George Bratianu, according to a Hungarian Foreign Ministry minute of January 1937. See Magda

Ádám, ed., *A müncheni egyezmény létrejötte és Magyarország külpolitikája 1936–1938* (Budapest, 1965), Item 53. This agrees with Ciano's understanding of Germany's position. See *Ciano's Diplomatic Papers*, Minutes of 24 October 1936, pp. 58-59.

8. Hitler to Guido Schmidt, Memorandum of 20 November 1936. *DGFP*, D, I, Item 181.

9. Ádám, "Az ellenforradalmi rendszer," p. 365.

10. Macartney, *October Fifteenth*, I, 193.

11. Wettstein to Kánya, Report of 4 April 1936, Ádám, *A müncheni egyezmény*, Item 8.

12. John L. Heineman, *Hitler's First Foreign Minister, Constantin Freiherr von Neurath, Diplomat and Statesman* (Berkeley, CA, 1979), p. 151; and Weinberg, "Secret Hitler-Beneš Negotiations," 366-374.

13. Machray, *The Struggle*, p. 255.

14. Lajos Kerekes, *Anschluss 1938. Ausztria és a nemzetközi diplomácia 1933–1938* (Budapest, 1968), pp. 244-245.

15. Sztójay to Kánya, Secret Report of 29 May 1937. *Országos Levéltár*. M. K. Külügyminisztérium, Pol. Oszt. 1780 - 6/4 - 1937.

16. Kerekes, *Anschluss 1938*, pp. 244-245. For a thorough coverage, see Thomas Spira, "Hungary and the Little Entente: The Failed Rapprochement of 1937," *Südost-Forschungen*, XL (1981), 144-163.

17. Ádám, *A müncheni egyezmény*, Item 54.

18. *Ibid.*, Items 56 and 57. Also see Reichert, *Das Scheitern*, pp. 147-148.

19. Ádám, *A müncheni egyezmény*, Item 56.

20. *Ibid.*

21. Kerekes, *Anschluss 1938*, pp. 246-247.

22. Alan Bullock, *Hitler. A Study in Tyranny* (New York, 1961), pp. 312-313.

23. William M. Shirer, *The Rise and Fall of the Third Reich. A History of Nazi Germany* (New York, 1960), p. 301.

24. Ádám, *A müncheni egyezmény*, Item 59.

25. *Ibid.*, Item 61.

26. *Ibid.*, Item 60.

27. *Ibid.*, Item 62.

28. *Ibid.*, Item 63.

29. *Ibid.*, Item 65.

30. Kerekes, *Anschluss 1938*, pp. 244-245.

31. For details, see J. B. Hoptner, *Yugoslavia in Crisis 1934-1941*(New York, 1962), pp. 62*ff.*

32. Johann Wuescht, *Jugoslawien und das Dritte Reich. Eine dokumentierte Geschichte der deutsch-jugoslawischen Beziehungen von 1933 bis 1945* (Stuttgart, 1969), *passim.*

33. Ciano, *Ciano's Diplomatic Papers*, pp. 117-120.

34. Machray, *The Struggle*, pp. 269*ff.*, and Reichert, *Das Scheitern*, pp. 103-104.

35. Eduard Beneš, *Memoirs of Dr. Eduard Beneš. From Munich to New War and New Victory* (London, 1954), pp. 30-33.

36. Sakmyster, *Hungary*, p. 76.

37. *The New York Times* (2 May 1937).

38. Kerekes, *Anschluss 1938*, pp. 246-247.

39. Ádám, *A müncheni egyezmény*, Item 74.

40. Macartney and Palmer, *Independent Eastern Europe*, pp. 358-359.

41. Secret Report of 30 April 1937. Ádám, *A müncheni egyezmény*, Item 75.

42. Ciano, *Ciano's Diplomatic Papers*, Minutes of 22-23 April 1937, pp. 108-115.

43. Kurt Schuschnigg, *Ein Requiem Rot-Weiss-Rot* (Zurich, 1948), pp. 184-185. Also see von Schuschnigg's conversation with Prince Starhemberg in November 1937, to the effect that the basis of Austria's foreign policy, even before Stresa, "was not broad enough," because it failed to consider the democratic sympathies of the Western powers. Ernst Rudiger Prince Starhemberg, *Between Hitler and Mussolini* (New York and London, 1942), p. 267.

44. *The New York Times* (4 May 1937).

45. *Ibid.*; and (6 May 1937). *Cf.*, G. E. R. Gedye, *Betrayal in Central Europe* (New York and London, 1939), pp. 202-203. Bethlen most ably explained why Hungary shied away from joining a Danubian scheme of this sort. See Bethlen, "Hungary's Position after the Austrian Anschluss," 203.

46. Ádám, *A müncheni egyezmény*, Item 77.

47. *Ibid.*

48. *The New York Times* (22 and 23 May 1937); and Ciano, *Ciano's Diplomatic Papers*, Minutes of 19-22 May 1937, pp. 117-120.

49. Machray, *The Struggle*, pp. 280-281.

50. Ádám, *A müncheni egyezmény*, Items 78 and 79.

51. *Ibid.*, Item 80.

52. Velics's Report of 27 May 1937. *Ibid.*, Item 78.

53. Kánya's notes on his conversation with Darányi and Ciano, 21 May 1937. Ádám, *Allianz*, Item 17.

54. Report of Neurath's conversation with Darányi and Kánya, 13 June 1937. *Ibid.*, Item 18.

55. *The New York Times* (6 June 1937).

56. O. L. M. K. Kül. pol. 1938 - 7/7 - 541 (1825).

57. Ádám, *A müncheni egyezmény*, Item 82.

58. Ádám, *Allianz*, Item 18. Also published in László Zsigmond, ed., *Diplomáciai iratok Magyarország külpolitikájához 1936–1945. Volume I 1936–1938* (Budapest, 1962), Item 264. Also see Hoensch, *Der ungarische Revisionismus*, pp. 45-47.

59. *The New York Times* (12 June 1937).

60. Joseph Rothschild, *East Central Europe between the Two World Wars* (Seattle, WA, and London, 1974), p. 177. On French policy, see Anthony A. Komjathy, *The Crises of France's East Central European Diplomacy 1933–1938* (New York, 1976), Chapter XI. On Great Britain's Eastern policy, see Arnold Wolfers, *Britain and France between Two Wars* (New York, 1966), Chapter XVII.

61. *The New York Times* (13 June 1937).

62. Sakmyster, *Hungary*, p. 25.

63. See Paul Einzig, *Bloodless Invasion. German Economic Penetration into the Danubian States and the Balkans* (London, 1938), pp. 67*ff.*

64. *The New York Times* (13 June 1937).

65. *Ibid.* (18 June 1937).

66. Macartney, *October Fifteenth*, I, 200.

67. Henry L. Roberts, *Eastern Europe. Politics, Revolution and Diplomacy* (New York, 1970), p. 62.

68. Flandin and François-Poncet did not share this optimistic view. See André François-Poncet, *The Fateful Years. Memoirs of a French Ambassador in Berlin 1931–1938* (New York, 1972), pp. 223-224.

69. Schacher, *Germany*, Chapter VIII. *Cf.*, Ivan Maisky, *Who Helped Hitler?* (London, 1964), p. 69.

70. Roberts, *Eastern Europe*, p. 206.

71. Edouard Calic, *Secret Conversations with Hitler* (New York, 1971), pp. 62-63.

72. Orlow, *The Nazis*, Chapter IV, especially pp. 110-111. Rauschning ably summarizes the outlines of such an imperium. See Hermann Rauschning, *Hitler's Aims in War and Peace* (London and Toronto, 1940), pp. 50-54.

73. László Zsigmond, *Adalékok a magyar ellenforradalmi rendszer külpolitikájához 1929–1945* (Budapest, 1953), pp. 35*ff.*

74. Adolf Hitler, *Mein Kampf* (Munich, 1943), p. 705; and Calic, *Secret Conversations*, second interview, throw light on these German plans.

75. France tried, in 1936 and 1937, to reassert its power in eastern Europe, but failed. See Dreifort, *Yvon Delbos*, Chapter VII.

Chapter V
German-Hungarian-Swabian Relations -
Late 1936–1937

1. Gustav Gratz, *Deutschungarische Probleme* (Budapest, 1938), p. 249. This chapter was originally prepared by Jakob Bleyer in 1930, but Gratz revised it and brought the vital statistics up-to-date.

2. Lutz Korodi, *Deutsche Bilanz in Südosteuropa* (Berlin, 1936), p. 100. *Nation und Staat*, X (1936–1937), 234-235, postulated the existence of a maximum of 58 elementary school teachers with German mother tongue in the Swabian minority school system.

3. *Grenzland* (July-August, 1937). Also see Kurt E. von Türcke, *Das Schulrecht der deutschen Volksgruppen in Ost- und Südosteuropa* (Berlin, 1938).

4. The communities involved in these struggles were Soroksár, Békásmegyér, Nagykovácsi, Decsés, Ceglédbercel, Kismányok, Almamellék, Kocsola, Gyorsóvenyháza, Kaposcsekcső, Gara, Albaliget, Katymár, Vertésboglár, Németker and Dunakömlőd. *Nation und Staat*, XI, 2 (1937–1938), 140-141.

5. *Ibid.*, 33.

6. *Ibid.*, X (1936–1937), 610.

7. *Ibid.*, 398.

8. Zenobius Păclisanu, *Der Ausrottungskampf Ungarns gegen seine nationalen Minderheiten* (Bucharest, 1941), pp. 140-141.

9. *Nation und Staat*, XI, 1 (1937–1938), 140.

10. *Ibid*, XI, 6 (1937–1938), 391-392.

11. G. C. Paikert, "Hungary's National Minority Policies 1920–1945," *The American Slavic and East European Review*, XII (April, 1953), 211.

12. *Évkönyv* (1935), p. 299.

13. *Nation und Staat*, X, 2-3 (1936–1937), 163.

14. See Note 28.

15. *Nation und Staat*, X, 8 (1936–1937), 610.

16. Gratz, *Deutschungarische Probleme*, pp. 247-251; Law X 18699-1937 V.K.M. See Évkönyv és jelentés (1938), p. 100.

17. *Nation und Staat*, X, 10-11 (1936–1937), 785-786.

18. "Wieder ein Jahr Deutscher Volksbote, deutsche Volkstumarbeit," *DV*, III (January, 1937), 1.

19. *Ibid.*, 2.

20. "Grundsätzliches zum Problem der konfessionellen Schulen des ungarländischen Deutschtums," *ibid.*, III (February, 1937), 1.

21. "Ministerpräsident Darányi über die Schulfrage," *ibid.*, III (June, 1937), 11-12.

22. "Unser Standpunkt zur Rede des Ministerpräsidenten. Die Lebengebiete des Volkstums," *ibid.*, III (June, 1937), 12-13.

23. Georg Goldschmidt, "Über die Durchführung der neuen Schulverordnung," *ibid.*, III (July, 1937), 1-3.

24. See *ibid.*, III (November, 1937), *passim.*

25. "Zur Erklärung des Innenministers v. Széll," *ibid.*, III (August, 1937), 8.

26. "Unser Standpunkt," *ibid.*, III (August, 1937), 9.

27. Georg Goldschmidt, "Ein ernstes Wort an die ungarische Gesellschaft," *ibid.*, III (October, 1937), 1.

28. Klemens Puhl, "Wie sehen wir die Schulfrage?" *ibid.*, III (October, 1937), 4.

29. *Nation und Staat*, X (1936-1937), 605-609.

30. *Ibid.*, 783-785.

31. Erdmannsdorff's report of Darányi's speech, see *BK*-Ministerium des Innern, R 18 33331. Also see *Berliner Börsenzeitung* (15 May 1937).

32. *Nation und Staat*, X (1936-1937), 783-785.

33. Mihály Szabados, "Kisebbségi kérdés—szentistváni gondolat," *Korunk Szava*, VII, 6 (16 March 1937), 172.

34. The secret ballot was introduced into urban areas in 1935.

35. Mihály Szabados, "A titkos választójog és a kisebbségi kérdés," *Korunk Szava*, VII, 18 (15 September 1937), 519-520.

36. *Magyar Statisztikai Szemle*, VIII (1930), 240.

37. *Ibid.*, 230.

38. Spectator (anon.) to Hans Steinacher, head of the *VDA*, *BK*, R 18 3330, fol. 1-215, Doc. VI, A 14140 7414.

39. Gratz, *Deutschungarische Probleme*, pp. 27-28.

40. *Ibid.*, pp. 211-213.

41. *Nation und Staat*, X (1936-1937), 161.

42. *Ibid.*; and 325-326.

43. *Ibid.*, 609.

44. Ránki, *A Wilhelmstrasse*, Item 72.

45. *Ibid.*, Item 73-1.

46. *Ibid.*, Item 74. These arguments and counterarguments dominated German-Hungarian conversations on the Swabian problem throughout 1937. See, for example, Item 101, Mackensen and Darányi, 22 November 1937.

47. *Ibid.*, Items 76, 76-1 and 76-2, 14-17 December 1937. Also see *BK*-Ministerium des Innern, R 18 3330.

48. *Ibid.*, letter of 23 December 1937.

49. Ránki, *A Wilhelmstrasse*, Item 80, Mackensen's telegram of 1 February 1937 to the Foreign Ministry.

50. *Ibid.*, Item 95, 12 June 1937.

51. *Nation und Staat*, X (1936–1937), 786-791; and *Völkischer Beobachter*, (16 July 1937). Also see the preliminary talks involving Hess, Kánya and Széll on 13 June 1937. Zsigmond, *Diplomáciai iratok*, I, 264.

52. *BK*-Minister des Innern, R 18 3331 (20 August - 17 September 1937).

53. Ránki, *A Wilhelmstrasse*, Item 102, 24 November 1937.

54. *Ibid.*, Item 105, 26 November 1937.

Chapter VI
The Diplomatic Picture - Europe in 1938

The author utilized the following works as his chief sources for reconstructing the European diplomatic situation in the year 1938.

Bethlen, "Hungary's Position after the Austrian Anschluss," 201-202.

Dreifort, *Yvon Delbos*.

Dreisziger, *Hungary's Way*.

Gasztony, "Revisionist Hungarian Foreign Policy."

Juhasz, *Hungarian Foreign Policy*.

Macartney, "Hungary and the Present Crisis."

Magyar Királyi Külügyminisztérium, *Külpolitikai adatok az 1938. évről* (Budapest, 1939).

Williamson Murray, *The Change in the European Balance of Power, 1938–1939. The Path to Ruin* (Princeton, NJ, 1984).

"Poland between Germany and the USSR, 1926–1939."

Ránki, *A Wilhelmstrasse.*

Reichert, *Das Scheitern der Kleinen Entente.*

Eric Roman, "Munich and Hungary: An Overview of Hungarian Diplomacy During the Sudeten Crisis," *East European Quarterly*, VIII, 1 (Munich, 1974), 71-97.

Thomas L. Sakmyster, "Hungary and the Munich Crisis: The Revisionist Dilemma," *Slavic Review*, XXXII, 4 (December, 1973), 725-740.

Ibid., Hungary.

Thomas L. Sakmyster, ed. and trans., "The Hungarian State Visit to Germany of August, 1938: Some New Evidence on Hungary in Hitler's Pre-Munich Policy," *Canadian Slavic Studies*, III, 4 (Winter, 1969), 677-691.

Telford Taylor, *Munich. The Price of Peace* (Garden City, NY, 1979).

Betty Jo Winchester, "Hungary and the 'Third Europe' in 1938," *Slavic Review*, XXXII, 4 (December, 1973), 741-756.

Weinberg, *The Foreign Policy of Hitler's Germany.*

Chapter VII
Hungary's Economic Problems in 1938

1. Ferenczi, "Ungarns Handelspolitik," 160.

2. Ellis, *Exchange Control*, p. 123.

3. Einzig, *Bloodless Invasion*, p. 67.

4. Macartney and Palmer, *Independent Eastern Europe*, p. 376.

5. *Ibid.*

6. The disproportion of large estates in Hungary was acute. In 1937, 840,000 smallholders shared half the arable land, 10,000 owners shared 10,000 middle-sized estates, and the rest had large landholders in possession. Worse still, state subventions depended upon the payment of consumption taxes, so that a major part of government

subsidies went to the large landed estates. See M. Körmendy-Ékes, "Big Estates in Hungary," *The Hungarian Quarterly*, V (Old Series) (Spring, 1937).

7. Ránki, *A Wilhelmstrasse*, Item 122.

8. Ferenczi, "Ungarns Handelspolitik," 160.

9. Basch, *The Danube Basin*, pp. 160-161.

10. *Ibid.*, p. 174, Note 7.

11. League of Nations Council, Economic, Financial and Transit Department, *The League of Nations Reconstruction Schemes in the Inter-War Period* (Geneva, 1945), p. 70.

12. *Ibid.*, p. 72.

13. For the evolution of this process, see *ibid.*, p. 149.

14. György Ránki, *Economy and Foreign Policy. The Struggle of the Great Powers for Hegemony in the Danube Valley, 1919-1939* (Boulder, CO and New York, 1983), p. 179.

15. Fritz von Bruck, "Neuer englisch-französischer Kapitalstrom zum Südosten?" *Ungarischer Volkswirt*, VII, 9 (September, 1938), 14-17.

16. See, for example, Ránki, *Economy and Foreign Policy*, Chapter 11; and Basch, *The Danube Basin*, pp. 201-202.

17. Basch, *The Danube Basin*, p. 203.

18. *The Economist* (14 May 1938), 356.

19. Basch, *The Danube Basin*, p. 205.

20. *Ibid.*

21. *Ibid.*, pp. 206-209.

22. Orlow, *The Nazis*, pp. 12-13.

23. *DGFP*, D, IV, Item 62.

24. *Cf.*, Berend and Ránki, *Magyarország*, pp. 182-185. Also see Sakmyster, *Hungary*, pp. 200, 207 and 218-219; and Ránki, *A Wilhelmstrasse*, Item 149.

25. *Ibid.*, Item 165; and *DGPF*, D, V, 252.

26. Ránki, *A Wilhelmstrasse*, Item 168; and *DGFP*, D, V, 256.

27. Ránki, *A Wilhelmstrasse*, Item 131.

Chapter VIII
Hungarian Foreign Policy in 1938 -
Germany, Italy and the Little Entente

1. See Ránki, "Adatok a magyar külpolitikához a csehszlovákia elleni agresszió idején 1937–1939,"117-159 and 356-372; Josef Hanč, *Tornado Across Eastern Europe. The Path of Nazi Destruction from Poland to Greece* (New York, 1942); Sakmyster, "Miklós Horthy;" Martin Broszat, "Deutschland-Ungarn-Rumänien. Entwicklung und Grundfaktoren nationalsozialistischer Hegemonial- und Bündnispolitik 1938–1941," *Historische Zeitschrift*, CCVI, 1 (February, 1968), 45-96; Lajos Kerekes, "Akten des ungarischen Ministeriums des Äusseren zur Vorgeschichte der Annexion Österreichs," *Acta Historica*, VII (1960); Erzsébet Andics, ed., *A Magyar nacionalizmus kialakulása*; Machray, *The Struggle*; Elizabeth Wiskemann, *The Rome-Berlin Axis. A Study of the Relations between Hitler and Mussolini* (London, 1966); Anthony Adamthwaite, *France and the Coming of the Second World War 1936-1939* (London, 1977); Václav Král, ed., *Das Abkommen von München 1938* (Prague, 1968); and Gasztony, "Revisionist Hungarian Foreign Policy."

2. Macartney, *October Fifteenth*, I, *passim*; and A. Mayor, *Ciano's Diary* , p. 60.

3. Ádám, *A müncheni egyezmény*, Item 101.

4. A. Mayor, trans., *Ciano's Diary 1937-1938* (London, 1951), p. 62.

5. *Ibid.*, p. 63

6. *Ibid.*, p. 58.

7. *Ibid.*, p. 60.

8. *Ibid.*, p. 88.

9. Kerekes, *Anschluss 1938*, pp. 289-290; and Mayor, *Ciano's Diary*, p. 52. See Macartney, *October Fifteenth*, I, 205, for an explanation why Ciano turned against Hungary.

10. In a 2 March 1938 letter, Kánya expressed a preference for Austria as a neighbor. See NA Budapest, Küm. res. pol., 1938. Pos. No. 17 and No. 138; cited in László Zsigmond, "Ungarn und das münchner Abkommen," *Acta Historica*, VI (1959), 262-264.

11. See Ádám, *A müncheni egyezmény*, Item 114; and Elek, *A németek*, Item 5.

12. Ádám, *A müncheni egyezmény*, Item 114.

13. *Ibid.*, Item 100, Note 86.

14. Mayor, *Ciano's Diary*, p. 86; Ádám, *Allianz*, Item 21; and Weinberg, *The Foreign Policy*, p. 323.

15. Ádám, *Allianz*, Item 22; and Dreisziger, *Hungary's Way*, pp. 70 and 72*ff.*

16. Ádám, *A müncheni egyezmény*, Item 120.

17. Komjathy, *The Crises, passim.*

18. Józef Lipski, *Papers and Memoirs of Józef Lipski, Ambassador of Poland, Diplomat in Berlin 1933-1939.* Ed. W. Jedrzejewicz (New York, 1968), p. 356; and Alfred D. Low, "Edvard Beneš, "The Anschluss Movement, 1918-38, and the Policy of Czechoslovakia," *East Central Europe*, X, Pts. 1-2 (1983), 83-91.

19. Ádám, *A müncheni egyezmény*, Item 111.

20. Zsigmond, "Ungarn," 255*ff.*

21. Ádám, *A müncheni egyezmény*, Items 113 and 116; and Weinberg, *The Foreign Policy*, pp. 226*ff.*

22. Ádám, *A müncheni egyezmény*, Item 111.

23. *Ibid.*, Items 122 and 123.

24. *DGFP*, D, II, Items 58-60, reveal Hungarian-Sudeten German negotiations on possible cooperation. These talks proved unproductive.

25. Ádám, *A müncheni egyezmény*, Items 116, 118 and 126.

26. *Ibid.*, Item 110.

27. *DGFP*, D, V, Item 173.

28. Ádám, *A müncheni egyezmény*, Note 112.

29. Horthy's 3 April 1938 radio speech, *The New York Times* (4 April 1938).

30. Elek Bolgár, *A németek Magyarországi politikája titkos német diplomáciai okmányokban (1937-1942)* (Budapest, 1947), Item 8.

31. *The New York Times* (16 March 1938).

32. *Ibid.* (13 March 1938).

33. Bolgár, *A németek,* Items 8-12, 14 and 16.

34. Ránki, "Adatok," 124-125.

35. Ádám, *A müncheni egyezmény,* Item 128.

36. *Ibid.,* Item 130.

37. *Ibid.,* Item 131.

38. *Ibid.,* Items 215 and 218.

39. *Ibid.,* Item 229.

40. Germany. Auswärtiges Amt, *DGFP,* Papen to Hitler, 17 April 1937, Item 220, pp. 413-415; and Ádám, *A müncheni egyezmény,* Item 229.

41. Ádám, *A müncheni egyezmény,* Item 220.

42. *DGFP,* D, II, Item 166.

43. In various conversations, the Germans kept dangling the possibility of a favorable settlement for Hungary in Czechoslovakia. See Ádám, *Allianz,* Items 24 and 27.

44. Ránki, "Adatok," 126-127.

45. András Hóry, *A kulisszák mögött. A Második Világháború előzményei ami és ahogy a valóságban történt* (Vienna, 1965), p. 30.

46. Macartney, *October Fifteenth,* I, 211.

47. Ádám, *A müncheni egyezmény,* Item 132.

48. *Ibid.,* Item 134.

49. *Ibid.,* Items 135, 137 and 149.

50. *Ibid.,* Item 136. Ciano conveyed these assurances periodically to Hungary. See Mayor, *Ciano's Diary,* pp. 93, 98-99, 117, 118 and 131.

51. Ádám, *A müncheni egyezmény,* Item 138.

52. *Ibid.,* Item 153.

53. Ádám, *Allianz,* Item 28.

54. Hoensch, *Der ungarische Revisionismus, passim.*

55. Ádám, *A müncheni egyezmény,* Item 154.

56. *Ibid.*, Item 156.

57. *Ibid.*, Items 159 and 165.

58. Ránki, *A Wilhelmstrasse*, Item 105.

59. *Ibid.*, Item 121.

60. *DGFP*, D, II, Items 198, 205 and 260.

61. Ádám, *A müncheni egyezmény*, Item 195.

62. *Ibid.*, Items 176, 178, 183 and 188.

63. *Ibid.*, Item 223.

64. *Ibid.*, Item 208.

65. *Ibid.*, Items 217 and 225.

66. *DGFP*, D, II, Item 275.

67. Ádám, *A müncheni egyezmény*, Item 236.

68. *Ibid.*, Item 242.

69. *Ibid.*, Items 248 and 253.

70. *Ibid.*, Item 251.

71. *Ibid.*, Item 256.

72. *Ibid.*, Item 264.

73. *Ibid.*, Item 266.

74. *DGFP*, D, II, Item 284.

75. *Ibid.*, Item 294.

76. Hoptner, *Yugoslavia*, p. 113.

77. Ádám, *Allianz*, Note 53, p. 394.

78. Mayor, *Ciano's Diary*, p. 138; and Hoensch, *Der ungarische Revisionismus*, pp. 53-54.

79. Mayor, *Ciano's Diary*, pp. 131 and 138.

80. Hoptner, *Yugoslavia*, p. 114.

81. *Ibid.*; and Mayor, *Ciano's Diary*, p. 139.

82. Macartney, *October Fifteenth*, I, 234-235; and Mayor, *Ciano's Diary*, p. 138.

83. Ádám, *A müncheni egyezmény*, Item 243.

84. *Ibid.*, Item 247.

85. *Ibid.*, Item 249.

86. *Ibid.*, Item 255.

87. Ránki, *A Wilhelmstrasse*, Item 128; and Ádám, *A müncheni egyezmény*, Item 259.

88. *Ibid.*, Item 261.

89. *Ibid.*, Items 263, 274 and 280; and Ránki, *A Wilhelmstrasse*, Items 129 and 132.

90. Ádám, *A müncheni egyezmény*, Item 298.

91. *Ibid.*

92. *Ibid.*, Items 293-296.

93. *Ibid.*, Item 298.

94. Mayor, *Ciano's Diary*, pp. 146 and 147.

95. *DGFP*, D, II, Item 306; and Ránki, *A Wilhelmstrasse*, Item 130.

96. Ádám, *A müncheni egyezmény*, Item 310.

97. Ránki, "Adatok," 127-131. Also see Pál Pritz, "A kieli találkozó," *Századok*, CVIII (1974), 646-679.

98. *DGFP*, D, II, Item 383.

99. Macartney, *October Fifteenth*, I, 241.

100. Ránki, *A Wilhelmstrasse*, Item 134.

101. *Ibid.*, Item 135.

102. *Ibid.*, Item 139; and *DGFP*, D, II, Item 390.

103. Ránki, *A Wilhelmstrasse*, Item 136; *DGFP*, D, II, Item 392; and Weinberg, *The Foreign Policy*, pp. 407*ff.*

104. *DGFP*, D, II, Items 395 and 402; Ránki, *A Wilhelmstrasse*, Items 137 and 138; Dreisziger, *Hungary's Way*, pp. 87-92; Sakmyster, *Hungary*, pp. 175*ff*; and Juhász, *Hungarian Foreign Policy*, pp. 136*ff.*

105. Macartney, *October Fifteenth*, I, 236-247; and *DGFP*, D, II, Item 395.

106. *DGFP*, D, II, Items 477 and 503; and Ádám, *A müncheni egyezmény*, Items 346, 351, 362, 363 and 365.

107. *DGFP*, D, II, Item 506; Ádám, *Allianz*, Item 34; and *idem*, *A müncheni egyezmény*, Item 361.

108. *DGFP*, D, II, Item 541. Also see Item 551; and Ádám, *A müncheni egyezmény*, Item 359, for Horthy's letter; and see Lipski, *Papers*, pp. 455-456.

109. *DGFP*, D, II, Item 554; and Ránki, *A Wilhelmstrasse*, Item 142.

110. Macartney, *October Fifteenth*, I, 207-208.

111. Mayor, *Ciano's Diary*, pp. 139 and 158-159.

112. *Ibid.*, p. 173.

113. *Ibid.*, p. 172.

114. Ádám, *A müncheni egyezmény*, Item 539.

115. Sakmyster, *Hungary*, pp. 185*ff.*; *idem*, "Hungary and the Munich Crisis," 725-740; and Roman, "Munich and Hungary," *passim*.

116. Mayor, *Ciano's Diary*, pp. 172-173.

117. Ádám, *A müncheni egyezmény*, Item 401.

118. *Ibid.*, Item 613.

119. Lipski, *Papers*, pp. 455-456.

120. Ádám, *A müncheni egyezmény*, Item 534, Note 123.

121. *Ibid.*, Item 560.

122. *Ibid.*, Item 535.

123. *Ibid.*, Items 615 and 560.

124. *Ibid.*, Item 541.

125. *Ibid.*, Item 544.

126. *Ibid.*, Item 551.

127. *Ibid.*, Item 557.

128. Hóry, *A kulisszák*, pp. 38-39.

129. Ádám, *A müncheni egyezmény*, Item 618.

130. *Ibid.*, Items 623-625.

Chapter IX
Swabian Cultural and Educational Controversies in 1938

1. Actually, by law, at intervals of at least five weeks.

2. The Third Reich recognized the *VK* as the sole and legitimate Swabian representative in Hungary. Officially, Germany denied interfering in Swabian affairs. Unofficially and quasi-officially, however, Reich funds and agents found their way to the *VK* through circuitous routes.

3. See, particularly, Fr. Christian Wirthoven, "Die deutsche Bevölkerungsfrage in Ungarn," *Neue Heimatblätter*, III, 1 (1938), 13-5; *ibid.*, 2, 1-57; and Franz Schittenhelm, "Das ungarländische Deutschtum in Zahlen," *Nation und Staat*, XI (1937-1938), 162-171. For example, the proportion of Swabians in various occupations in 1930 was as follows: armed forces, 1.8%, government officials, 0.9%; attorneys, 0.5%; physicians, 1.1%; veterinarians, 0.3%; elementary school teachers, 0.4%; and university professors, 1.7%. Another worrisome statistic for the Swabian nationalists concerned the relative age distribution of the Swabians versus the Magyars. At all age levels between birth and 19, the Magyar population exceeded the Swabian by an aggregate 8.9%. All statistics cited are based on official Hungarian statistics. Also see Alajos Kovács, "Népesedésünk fény- és árnyoldalai," *Magyar Szemle*, XVIII (January, 1933), 10-21; Herbert Sachse, "Die Verluste des ungarländischen Deutschtums im Spiegel der Statistik," *Schriften zur Volkswissenschaft* (1937); and András Rónai, "A németek számszerű csökkenése Csonka-Magyarországon," *Magyar Szemle*, XXXIV (1938), 74-78.

4. Schittenhelm, "Das ungarländische Deutschtum."

5. *Ibid.*, 170.

6. "Hat das ungarländische Deutschtum eine Zukunft?" *DV*, IV, 3 (May, 1938), 2-3.

7. See "Zur Frage der Bildungsschicht unseres Deutschtums," *DV*, IV, 4 (July, 1938), 2.

8. Georg Goldschmidt, "Gewissenlose Irreführung," *DV*, IV, 3 (May, 1938), 5.

9. Heinrich Mühl, "Noch immer die Schulfrage," *DV*, IV, 6-7 (October, 1938), 4.

10. Goldschmidt, "Gewissenlose Irreführung."

11. g.g. [Georg Goldschmidt], "Die Schulfrage und die jetzige Leitung des UDV," *DV*, IV, 1 (February, 1938), 3.

12. Georg Goldschmidt, "Gehen wir in der Schulfrage einer Lösung entgegen?" *DV*, IV, 2 (April, 1938), 9; and *idem*, "Schule und Volkscharakter," *ibid.*, 4 (July, 1938), 6-7.

13. Jakob Zumpft, "Die Schulnot in der Schomodei," *DV*, IV, 6-7 (October, 1938), 3.

14. Mühl, "Noch immer die Schulfrage."

15. Kaspar Hügel, *Abriss der Geschichte des Donauschwäbischen Schulwesens* (Munich, 1957), pp. 22-23; and all 1938–1939 issues of *Nation und Staat* (Vienna). For a dissenting view, see Paikert, "Hungary's Policies," 214-215.

16. Goldschmidt, "Klarheit."

17. Goldschmidt, "Die Schulfrage." Also see Walter Schneefuss, *Deutschtum in Süd-Ost-Europa* (Leipzig, 1939), p. 78.

18. For an exposition of this problem, see Paikert, "Hungary's Policies," 210-215.

19. 115.085/1937.IX.

20. Georg Goldschmidt, "Klarheit in die Durchführung der Schulverordnung," *DV*, IV, 1 (February, 1938), 2.

21. Mühl, "Noch immer die Schulfrage."

22. Goldschmidt, "Klarheit."

23. Goldschmidt, "Gewissenlose Irreführung."

24. Georg Goldschmidt, "Kultusminister Graf Teleki über die deutsche Frage," *DV*, IV, 4 (July, 1938), 6.

25. *Der Auslandsdeutsche*, XXI (1938), 783.

26. See Loránt Tilkovszky, "A Volksbund szerepe Magyarország másodk világháborús történetében," *Történelmi Szemle*, XI (1969), 296-297.

27. Mühl, "Noch immer die Schulfrage."

28. "Das Wesen unseres Volkstumpskampfes," *DV*, IV, 2 (April, 1938), 6.

29. Gustav Gratz, *Deutschungarische Probleme*, p. 8. Gratz spoke on 3 March 1938 to the Swabian student organization *Suevia*.

30. *Ibid.*, p. 9. Gratz spoke to *Suevia* in November 1937.

31. Emil Neugeboren, "'Nationalität' und 'Minderheit'," *Nation und Staat*, XI (1937–1938), 150-151.

32. Tilkovszky, "A német irredenta," 371.

33. "Staatsvolk, Volksgruppe, Muttervolk," *DV*, IV, 3 (May, 1938), 4.

34. "Volksgruppe und Mutterland," *DV*, IV, 1 (February, 1938), 2.

35. "Das Reich ist Hüter und Schirmheer aller Deutschen," *DV*, IV, 2 (April, 1938), 5.

36. "Adolf Hitler sprach," *DV*, IV, 1 (February, 1938), 1.

37. "Die Bedingungen der Versöhnung im U.D.V.," *Neues Sonntagsblatt* (20 March 1938); also see Gratz, *Deutschungarische Probleme*, pp. 240-241.

38. "Gustav Gratz ruft die magyarische Gesellschaft zum Kampf gegen die Volksdeutsche Bewegung auf," *DV*, IV, 2 (April, 1938), 10-11.

39. Georg Goldschmidt, "Verständigung," *DV*, IV, 2 (April, 1938), 8.

40. Franz Basch, "Der Entscheidung entgegen," *DV*, IV, 3 (May, 1938), 1-2; and "Wir stehen," *ibid.*, 6-7 (October, 1938), 1.

41. "Tatsachen, von denen wir ausgehen," *DV*, IV, 3 (May, 1938), 2.

42. "Wir schreiten der Entscheidung entgegen," *DV*, IV, 3 (May, 1938), 2.

43. Georg Goldschmidt, "Zurückgebliebene Gehirne," *DV*, IV, 4 (July, 1938), 4.

44. Georg Beer, "Der Sinn unseres Volkstumskampfes," *DV*, IV, 4 (July, 1938), 4. See also *Der Auslandsdeutsche*, XI (1938), 781-783.

45. Actually only seven points. See Franz Basch's seven-point program, reproduced in *Der Auslandsdeutsche*, XXI (1938), 782; and Franz Basch, "Deutscher Aufbruch in Ungarn," *Nation und Staat*, XII (1938–1939), 210-211.

46. Loránt Tilkovszky, "Die deutsche Minderheit in Ungarn in der Zeit des Faschismus vor dem zweiten Weltkrieg," *Jahrbuch für Geschichte der sozialistischen Länder Europas*, XV, 2 (1971), 74; and *idem, Ez volt a Volksbund. A német népcsoportpolitika és Magyarország 1938-1945* (Budapest, 1978), pp. 20-21.

47. Faulstich, "Volksgruppe," 2.

48. Georg Goldschmidt, "Gedanken am 900 jährigen Todestag Stefan des Heiligen," *DV*, IV, 5 (August, 1938), 1-3.

49. Georg Goldschmidt, "Unser Weg ist richtig," *DV*, IV, 6-7 (October, 1938), 1-2. See Paikert, "Hungary's Policies."

50. Although Gustav Gratz resigned in protest, the government continued and even increased its support of the *UDV* at the expense of the *VDU*. "Ungarn," *Der Auslandsdeutsche*, XXI (1938), 783.

51. Basch, "Deutscher Aufbruch," 204-211.

Chapter X
The Diplomatic Picture - Europe in 1939

The author utilized the following works as his chief sources for reconstituting the European diplomatic situation in the year 1939.

Dreisziger, *Hungary's Way.*

Gasztony, "Revisionist Hungarian Foreign Policy."

Juhasz, *Hungarian Foreign Policy.*

Murray, *The Change in the European Balance of Power.* "Poland between Germany and the USSR, 1926-1939."

Ránki, *A Wilhelmstrasse.*

Sakmyster, *Hungary.*

Weinberg, *The Foreign Policy of Hitler's Germany.*

Chapter XI
Hungary's Economic Dilemmas in 1939

1. Ránki, *Economy*, p. 190. Also see William Carr, *Arms, Autarky and Aggression. A Study in German Foreign Policy 1933–1939* (New York, 1973); Lothar Gruchmann, *Nationalsozialistische Grossraumordnung* (Stuttgart, 1962); Wilbert E. Moore, *Economic Demography of Eastern and Southern Europe* (Geneva, 1945); and Zagoroff, Végh and Bilimovich, *The Agricultural Economy.*

2. Orlow, *The Nazis*, pp. 8-9; and Ciano, *Ciano's Diaries 1939-1943*, p. 50.

3. Göring interview in *Le Temps* (20 September 1938).

4. Basch, *The Danube Basin*, p. 208.

5. *Ibid.*, pp. 219-220.

6. Ellis, *Exchange Control*, p. 191.

7. *Ibid.*, p. 124.

8. Ránki, *A Wilhelmstrasse*, Item 175b.

9. *Ibid.*, Item 176.

10. *Ibid.*

11. *Ibid.*, Item 177.

12. Ránki, *Economy*, p. 192; and Einzig, *Bloodless Invasion*, pp. 62-65.

13. Ránki, *A Wilhelmstrasse*, Item 188. Also see Loránt Tilkovszky, "Volksdeutsche Bewegung und ungarische Nationalitätenpolitik (1938-1941)," *Acta Historica*, XII, 1-4 (1966), 82.

14. Monica Curtis, ed., *Documents on International Affairs 1938* (London, *et al.*, 1943), II, 61.

15. Ránki, *A Wilhelmstrasse*, Items 188 and 207c.

16. *Ibid.*, Item 200.

17. *Ibid.*, Item 193.

18. *Ibid.*, Item 221.

19. *Ibid.*, Items 222, 224, 227 and 229, between 21 June and 26 July.

20. *Ibid.*

21. *Ibid.*, Item 236.

22. *Ibid.*, Item 250.

23. *Ibid.*, Item 251.

24. *Ibid.*, Item 254.

25. *Ibid.*, Item 255.

26. Zsigmond, *Diplomáciai iratok*, IV, 379.

27. Ránki, *A Wilhelmstrasse*, Item 261.

28. *Ibid.*, Item 262.

29. *Ibid.*, p. 440, Note 4.

30. *Ibid.*, Item 263.

31. *Ibid.*, Items 264 and 265.

32. *Ibid.*, Item 279.

33. *Ibid.*, Item 288.

Chapter XII
Swabian Cultural and Educational Difficulties
in 1939

1. See Matthias Annabring, *Volksgeschichte der Deutschen in Ungarn* (Stuttgart, 1954), I, 106.

2. A full report of the *Volksbund*'s establishment is in *Der Auslandsdeutsche*, XXI (1938), 781-782. Franz Basch's inaugural speech is in *Nation und Staat*, XII (1938–1939), 204-211.

3. Tilkovszky, "Volksdeutsche Bewegung," 81.

4. Tilkovszky, "Die deutsche Minderheit," 75.

5. "Volk und Volksgruppe," *DVW*, I (5 February 1939), 2.

6. See further, János Hajdú and Béla C. Tóth, *The "Volksbund" in Hungary* (Budapest, 1962), p. 14.

7. "Programmrede des Ministerpräsidenten. Ausführliche Erörterung der Innen- und Aussenpolitik der Regierung," *DVW*, I (1 January 1939), 1. Also see Imrédy's article in *Pester Lloyd* (Morgenblatt) (25 December 1938).

8. Tilkovszky, *Ez volt a Volksbund*, pp. 40-41.

9. "Unsere Staatstreue," *DVW*, I (8 January 1939), 1-2.

10. "Franz Basch spricht zur ungarischen Öffentlichkeit," *DVW*, I (8 January 1939), 2-3.

11. "Auch in Bataszék wurde die Schulfrage gelöst—aber wie!," *DVW*, I (5 February 1939), 4.

12. Tilkovszky, *Ez volt a Volksbund*, pp. 41-42; and G. C. Paikert, *The Danube Swabians. German Populations in Hungary, Rumania and Yugoslavia and Hitler's Impact on their Patterns.* (The Hague, 1967), pp. 167-168.

13. "Volksgruppe," *DVW*, I (15 January 1939), 3.

14. "Die neue nationale Front Bewegung des ungarischen Lebens. Grosse Rede des Ministerpräsidenten," *DVW*, I (15 January 1939), 3.

15. "Ist die Schulordnung durchgeführt?" and "Wie führt man die neue Schulordnung durch?," *DVW*, I (15 January 1939), 3. Also see subsequent *DVW* issues for village-by-village surveys on the school problem to document alleged pervasive violations of the school laws by the local authorities.

16. "Sturm im Parlament wegen des Volksbundes," *DVW*, I (22 January 1939), 2.

17. "Das Neueste. Die Schulfrage im Parlament," *DVW*, I (29 January 1939), 10.

18. "Kultusminister Graf Teleki zur Schulfrage. Eine Antwort auf die Interpellationen des Abg. Horvath und Baross," *DVW*, I (12 February 1939), 5-6.

19. "Unsere Stellungnahme zur Parlamentrede des Kultusministers," *DVW*, I (19 February 1939), 1.

20. Országos Levéltár, No. 53 cs.C.160/1939.

21. Loránt Tilkovszky, "A német irredenta és Magyarország. A magyarországi népinémet (volksdeutsch) mozgalom útja," *Történelmi Szemle*, XIII, 3 (1970); and *idem*, "Volksdeutsche Bewegung," 75-77.

22. Georg Goldschmidt, "Um ein neues Nationalitätengesetz," *DVW*, I (5 February 1939), 4.

23. The notion of separate Magyar-Swabian development, part of the *Volksbund*'s program, was soft-pedaled in the period under scrutiny.

24. "Asszimiláció és disszimiláció," *Budapesti Hírlap* (12 March 1939), based on Ravasz's 11 March 1939 lecture; and Georg Goldschmidt, "Eine kluge Politik, Antwort an den ref. Bischof Ladislaus Ravasz," *DVW*, I (19 March 1939), 1.

25. "Auf neuen Wegen?" *DVW*, I (2 April 1939), 1-2.

26. (18 March 1939).

27. *Virradat* (27 March 1939). Also see *Magyar Út* (18 March 1939), in a similar vein.

28. (8 March 1939).

29. *Az Est* (2 April 1939).

30. Georg Goldschmidt, "Einem neuen Ungarn entgegen," *DVW*, I (16 April 1939), 2.

31. "Ein sonderbarer Kameradschaftbefehl der Mohácser Obergruppe des Frontkämpfer Landesverbandes," *DVW*, I (26 March 1939), 5.

32. "Geht die Namenmagyarisierung weiter?" *DVW*, I (2 April 1939), 4.

33. "Gleiches Recht," *DVW*, I (9 April 1939), 1-2.

34. "Aus dem Osteraufsatz des Ministerpräsidenten Teleki," *DVW*, I (16 April 1939), 1.

35. Tilkovszky, *Ez volt a Volksbund*, pp. 47-48.

36. No. 104.213/1939-VII.a.

37. Michael Hillinger, "The German National Movement in Interwar Hungary," unpublished doctoral dissertation, Columbia University, 1973, 219. The *Volksbund* began functioning by virtue of Ministry of the Interior decree 104.213/1939 - VII a.

38. "Das neue Morgenrot," *DVW*, I (30 April 1939), 2.

39. "Das ungarländische Deutschtum im Wahlkampf," *DVW*, I (14 May 1939), 1.

40. See Tilkovszky, *Ez volt a Volksbund*, pp. 47-48, reporting on Franz Basch's early April Berlin trip.

41. Tilkovszky, "A német irredenta," 393. The consequences of these limitations were not realized at the time. See "Der Volksbund der Deutschen in Ungarn genehmigt," *Nation und Staat*, XII (1938–1939), 547-548.

42. Tilkovszky, "Volksdeutsche Bewegung," 85; and *idem*, "A Volksbund szerepe," 297.

43. "Der Volksbund genehmigt," *DVW*, I (23 April 1939), 1.

44. See Point 7 of the *Volksbund*'s seven-point program on the organization of a political party. See the text in *Der Auslandsdeutsche*, XXI (1938), 782; *Nation und Staat*, XII (1938–1939), 210-211; and Tilkovszky, *Ez volt a Volksbund*, p. 53.

45. *DVW*, I (14 May 1939), 7; and (28 May 1939), 2-3.

46. According to Hugh Seton-Watson, *Eastern Europe between the Wars 1918–1941* (Cambridge [England], 1946), p. 284, the *Volksbund* won two-thirds of the total Swabian vote.

47. *DVW*, I (18 June 1939), 5. On Hungary's right-radicals, see Nicholas M. Nagy-Talavera, *The Green Shirts and Others. A History of Fascism in Hungary and Rumania* (Stanford, CA, 1970); and Miklós Lackó, *Arrow-Cross Men, National Socialists 1935–1944* (Budapest, 1969). Translation of *idem*, *Nyilasok, Nemzetiszocialisták 1935–1944* (Budapest, 1966).

48. For details about the reasons for the moderate Swabians' meager election results see Tilkovszky, *Ez volt a Volksbund*, p. 55.

49. Heydrich to Lammers, report of 11 July 1939, Ránki, *A Wilhelmstrasse*, Item 230.

50. Csáky's 14 May 1939 Sopron speech, reported in "Graf Csaky über die Volksgruppenfrage," *DVW*, I (21 May 1939).

51. Speeches of 10 May 1939, reported in "Die Grafen Teleki und Csaky über die Volksgruppenfrage," *DVW*, I (21 May 1939), 5. Also see Teleki's speech in the newly convened Parliament in mid-June 1939, in a similar vein, *ibid.*, I (25 June 1939), 1.

52. *Szegedi Új Nemzedék* (7 May 1939), based on Szabó's 4 May 1939 Szeged speech. Also see R. M. Bigler, "Heil Hitler und Heil Horthy! The Nature of Hungarian Fascist Nationalism and Its Impact on German-Hungarian Relations," *East European Quarterly*, VIII, 3 (Fall, 1974), 262-263.

53. *Mohácsi Hírlap* (25 June 1939).

54. (2 July 1939).

55. *Mosonvármegye* (13 July 1939).

56. *Nemzet Szava* (23 July 1939).

57. (30 July 1939).

58. Hufnagel, "Nem kell nekünk a Volksbund," *Dunántúl* (August, 1939).

59. (30 July 1939).

60. *Egyetemi Híradó* (August, 1939).

61. *Előre* (13 August 1939).

62. *Magyar Nemzet* (27 August 1939).

63. "Verfassungsschutz? Antwort an Prof. Dr. Polner Ödön," *DVW*, I (1 September 1939), 1.

64. Before 1 January 1939, the *DV* appeared eleven times annually.

65. *DVW*, I (23 April 1939).

66. "Warum Volksgruppe?" *DVW*, I (13 April 1939), 8.

67. (6 April 1939).

68. "Namensmagyarisierung heute besonders notwendig?" *DVW*, I (16 April 1939), 5.

69. "Volkstumskampf," *DVW*, I (2 July 1939), 6.

70. "Magyarország és a németek" (27 June 1939).

71. "Kein Recht zu klagen," *DVW*, I (2 July 1939), 6.

72. Franz Basch, "Hetze und Aufwieglung um jeden Preis," *DVW*, I (30 July 1939), 1.

73. Johann Kuhn, "Schwabischer Patriotismus," *DVW*, I (16 July 1939), 5.

74. Heinrich Neun, "Die Provinzpresse, wie sie ist und wie sie sein sollte," *DVW*, I (23 July 1939), 5.

75. "Németajkú magyarok és magyarországi németek," *Pesti Napló* (25 July 1939).

76. "Antwort an den Hauptschriftleiter des jüdischen *Pesti Napló* Gustav Gratz," *DVW*, I (6 August 1939), 6.

77. "Die deutschfeindliche Front," *DVW*, I (27 August 1939), 4.

78. "Aufgeräumt!" *DVW*, 1 (26 November 1939), 1.

Chapter XIII
Hungary's Diplomatic Attempts to Resolve
the Swabian Problem in 1939

1. *Cf.*, Dreisziger, *Hungary's Way*, p. 106. In a sense, this action corroborates the view of several observers that ethnic chauvinism played only a minor role in interwar Hungarian society. See, *inter alia*, Rothschild, *East Central Europe*, p. 195; and Macartney, *Hungary and Her Successors*, pp. 451-452.

2. After his Berlin trip in early April, Basch threatened Teleki with German intervention, unless Hungary improved Swabian conditions immediately. See Tilkovszky, *Ez volt a Volksbund*, pp. 47-48.

3. András Hóry, Hungary's ambassador in Warsaw, to Csáky, letter of 12 May 1939. O. L. Küm: res. pol. 1939-73-17.

4. Endre B. Gastony, "Revisionist Hungarian Foreign Policy," pp. 184-185; also see Paikert, *The Danube Swabians*, pp. 154-155; Loránt Tilkovszky, *Revizió és nemzetiségpolitika Magyarországon (1938-1941)* (Budapest, 1967), pp. 11-12; and Sakmyster, *Hungary*, pp. 225-227. Aladár Kis, *Magyarország külpolitikája a második világháború előestején (1938 november-1939 szeptember)* (Budapest, 1963), assumes that Teleki continued in Imrédy's footsteps, and ignores the former's Machiavellianism. See especially chapter 4.

5. "Klarheit," *DVW*, I (5 February 1939), 1.

6. "Dr. Franz Basch: Die deutsche Volksgruppe in Ungarn. Grundsätze, die gelöst und Rechte, die gewährt werden müssen," *DVW*, I (5 March 1939), 1-2. Also see "Die Lage der deutschen Volksgruppe," *Nation und Staat*, XII (1938-1939), 446-448, in a similar vein.

7. "Reichsminister Frick über das ungarländische Deutschtum [aus "Magyar Nemzet" von 2. April 1939.]," *DVW*, I (9 April 1939).

8. Gábor Baross, *Hungary and Hitler* (Astor, FL, 1970), pp. 26 and 28; Anthony Komjathy, "The First Vienna Award (November 2, 1938)," *Austrian History Yearbook*, XV-XVI (1979-1980), 154; Juhász, *Hungarian Foreign Policy*, pp. 145 and 153; and Kis, *Magyarország külpolitikája*, pp. 178 *ff*.

9. Winchester, "Hungary and the 'Third Europe' in 1938," 741-756; and Weinberg, *The Foreign Policy*, pp. 496-497. Also see Zsigmond, *Diplomáciai iratok*, III, *passim*.

10. Teleki promised "to move forward, step by step, in the minority question." Teleki and Csáky at the German Foreign Ministry, 30 April 1939. Auswärtiges Amt, *Akten zur deutschen auswärtigen Politik 1918-1945. Serie D (1937-1945), Band VI. Die letzten Monate vor Kriegsausbruch. März bis August 1939* (Baden-Baden, 1956), Item 295 (hereinafter AA, *Akten*).

11. Macartney and Palmer, *Independent Eastern Europe*, p. 399; and Ránki, *A Wilhelmstrasse*, Weizsäcker's note concerning the conversation with Sztójay, 10 March 1939, Item 196.

12. Baross, *Hungary and Hitler*, pp. 27-28.

13. Juhász, *Hungarian Foreign Policy*, p. 153; Dreisziger, *Hungary's Way*, p. 110; and Erdmannsdorff's note concerning the conversation with Csáky, 11 March 1939, Ránki, *A Wilhelmstrasse*, Item 197.

14. Weizsäcker's note concerning the conversation with Sztójay, 16 March 1939. Ránki, *A Wilhelmstrasse*, Item 199. *Cf.*, Hillinger, "The German National Movement," pp. 223-224.

15. The government had raised the *UDV*'s annual stipend to 67,000 Pengő from 12,000 Pengő, and on 31 March 1939 Teleki secretly allocated an additional emergency fund of 435,000 Pengő. Tilkovszky, "Die deutsche Minderheit," 75; and *idem*, "A német irredenta," 393. Government aid failed to keep the *UDV* solvent. The organization gradually disintegrated, having "lost credibility by developing beyond loyalty to docility." Rothschild, *East Central Europe*, p. 393.

16. Macartney, *October Fifteenth*, I, 352; and Hillinger, "The German National Movement," pp. 225-226.

17. Weizsäcker to Ribbentrop, note of 25 March 1939, Ránki, *A Wilhelmstrasse*, Item 202.

18. Woermann's note concerning the conversation with Nemeshegyi, 12 April 1939, *ibid.*, Item 205.

19. See AA, *Akten*, especially Items 2, 6, 8, 13, 29, 30, 47, 91, 135, 153, 180 and 194, which deal with various Hungarian-Romanian territorial disputes.

20. Woermann's note concerning the conversation with Sztójay, 26 May 1939, Ránki, *A Wilhelmstrasse*, Item 215.

21. Weizsäcker's note concerning Sztójay's communication, 29 June 1939, *ibid.*, Item 223.

22. Tilkovszky, "Volksdeutsche Bewegung," 69 and 75.

23. Erdmannsdorff to Foreign Ministry, telegram of 20 February 1939, Ránki, *A Wilhelmstrasse*, Item 192; and Erdmannsdorff to Foreign Ministry, report of 22 February 1939, *ibid.*, Item 193.

24. Erdmannsdorff to Foreign Ministry, report of 28 February 1939, *ibid.*, Item 194.

25. Huber's note concerning the conversation with Van der Venne, 7 April 1939, *ibid.*, Item 204; and Erdmannsdorff's note concerning Ribbentrop's second discussion with Teleki and Csáky on 1 May 1939, *ibid.*, Item 210. Also see AA, *Akten*, Item 300.

26. See Anthony Komjathy and Rebecca Stockwell, *German Minorities and the Third Reich. Ethnic Germans of East Central Europe between the Wars* (New York and London, 1980), pp. 147-148, on the role of the *Volksdeutsche Mittelstelle* (*VoMi*) in these illicit contacts. Also see MacAllister Brown, "The Third Reich's Mobilization of the German Fifth Column in Eastern Europe," *Journal of Central European Affairs*, XIX (July, 1959), 128-148. Also see AA, *Akten*, Item 436.

27. Erdmannsdorff to Foreign Ministry, telegram of 25 May 1939, Ránki, *A Wilhelmstrasse*, Item 213; and Erdmannsdorff to Foreign Ministry, report of 25 May 1939, *ibid.*, Item 214.

28. *Ibid.*, p. 399.

29. Weizsäcker's note concerning the conversation with Sztójay, 19 July 1939, *ibid.*, Item 233. Also see Kis, *Magyarország külpolitikája*, pp. 165 *ff.*

30. Erdmannsdorff to Foreign Ministry, telegram of 22 July 1939, Ránki, *A Wilhelmstrasse*, Item 235. See also AA, *Akten*, Item 712.

31. Erdmannsdorff's note concerning the Hitler-Csáky discussion of 8 August 1939, Ránki, *A Wilhelmstrasse*, Item 241. On 10 August, Hungary officially "withdrew" the two letters under German pressure, but Teleki's opposition to Germany's projected Polish campaign continued. Kis, *Magyarország külpolitikája*, pp. 211-213. Also see AA, *Akten*, Item 919.

32. Weizsäcker to Mackensen, telegram of 19 August 1939, Ránki, *A Wilhelmstrasse*, Item 242.

33. Horthy, *Ein Leben für Ungarn*, p. 219, claims that on 9 September 1939, Ribbentrop demanded use of the railway line from Kassa (Košice) to invade Poland from the south.

34. Woermann to Sztójay, note of 31 August 1939, Ránki, *A Wilhelmstrasse*, Item 250.

35. Erdmannsdorff to Foreign Ministry, report of 21 August 1939, *ibid.*, Item 245.

36. *Ibid.*, Item 250.

37. Ribbentrop to Erdmannsdorff, telegram of 1 September 1939, *ibid.*, Item 251.

38. Erdmannsdorff to Foreign Ministry, telegram of 1 September 1939, *ibid.*, Item 252.

39. Erdmannsdorff to Foreign Ministry, telegram of 27 October 1939, *ibid.*, Item 284.

Chapter XIV
Conclusion

1. On this, see C. A. Macartney, *Hungary. A Short History* (Chicago, 1962), pp. 226-227; and *idem, October Fifteenth*, I, 153. *Cf.*, Juhász, *Magyarország külpolitikája*, p. 171.

2. Sakmyster, *Hungary*, pp. 208*ff*.

3. *Ibid.*, pp. 219-221.

4. Speech of 1 October 1938, cited in Sakmyster, *Hungary*, p. 209; also see *idem*, "Hungary and the Munich Crisis," 740.

5. Tilkovszky believes that greed for territorial gain overruled the Hungarian leaders' judgment which submerged fears of National Socialism. See his *Revizió*, pp. 11-12.

6. Sakmyster, *Hungary*, pp. 234-235.

7. Roman, "Munich and Hungary," 84.

8. See Hillinger, "The German National Movement," 217-219.

9. On German-Hungarian antipathy, see, *inter alia*, Stephen Kertesz, *Diplomacy in a Whirlpool* (Notre Dame, IN, 1953), p. 38; and Horthy, *Ein Leben*, p. 214.

10. See C. A. Macartney, "Foreword," Nicholas Kallay, *Hungarian Premier* (Westport, CT, 1970 [1954]), p. xxiv; and Mayor, *Ciano's Diary*, p. 207; Ciano noticed deteriorating German-Hungarian relations at the end of 1938; and Weinberg, *The Foreign Policy*, p. 497, who considered German-Hungarian differences as minor frictions.

11. "Collaborationism in Europe, 1940–1945: The Case of Hungary," *Austrian History Yearbook*, XV-XVI (1979–1980), 160. Also see Sakmyster, *Hungary*, pp. 235-237.

12. Deak, "Collaborationism," 160; and Kertesz, *Diplomacy*, p. 38.

13. Juhász, *Hungarian Foreign Policy*, p. 155.

BIBLIOGRAPHY

I. UNPUBLISHED DOCUMENTS

Auswärtiges Amt. Politische Abteilung. Bonn.

Bundesarchiv. Koblenz.

Deutsches Zentralarchiv. Potsdam.

Magyar Királyi Belügyminisztérium. Országos Levéltár. Budapest.

Österreichisches Staatsarchiv. Neue Politische Abteilung. Vienna.

II. PUBLICATIONS OF DOCUMENTS, SPEECHES, MEMOIRS AND AUTOBIOGRAPHIES

Ádám, Magda, ed. *A müncheni egyezmény létrejötte és Magyarország külpolitikája 1936-1938.* Budapest, 1965.

——, et al. *Dokumente zur ungarischen Aussenpolitik (1933-1944). Allianz Hitler-Horthy-Mussolini.* Budapest, 1966.

———. *Magyarország és a Második Világháború. Titkos diplomáciai okmányok a háború előzményeihez és történetéhez.* Budapest, 1966.

Auswärtiges Amt. *Akten zur deutschen auswärtigen Politik 1918–1945. Serie D (1937-1945). Band VI. Die letzten Monate vor Kriegsausbruch. März bis August 1939.* Baden-Baden, 1956.

Beneš, Eduard. *Memoirs of Dr. Eduard Beneš. From Munich to New War and New Victory.* London, 1954.

Bolgár, Elek, ed. *A németek Magyarországi politikája titkos német diplomáciai okmányokban* (1937-1942). Budapest, 1947.

Ciano, Galeazzo, ed. by Malcolm Muggeridge. *Ciano's Diplomatic Papers.* London, 1948.

Curtis, Monica, ed. *Documents on International Affairs 1938.* London, *et al.*, 1943, vol. 2.

Documents and Materials Relating to the Eve of the Second World War. Volume I November 1937–1938. Salisbury, NC, 1978.

Documents and Materials Relating to the Eve of the Second World War. Volume II Dirksen Papers (1938–1939). Salisbury, NC, 1978.

Françoit-Poncet, André. *The Fateful Years. Memoirs of a French Ambassador in Berlin 1931-1938.* New York, 1972.

Germany. Auswärtiges Amt. *Documents on German Foreign Policy 1918–1945.* Series C. London, 1949.

Hitler, Adolf. *Mein Kampf.* Munich, 1943.

Horthy, Nikolaus von. *Ein Leben für Ungarn.* Bonn, 1953.

Kerekes, Lajos. "Akten des ungarischen Ministeriums des Äussern zur Vorgeschichte der Annexion Österreichs." *Acta Historica,* VII (1960), 355–390.

———. *Anschluss 1938. Ausztria és a nemzetközi diplomácia 1933–1938.* Budapest, 1968.

League of Nations Council. Economic, Financial and Transit Department. *The League of Nations Reconstruction Schemes in the Inter-War Period.* Geneva, 1945.

Lipski, Józef. *Papers and Memoirs of Józef Lipski, Ambassador of Poland, Diplomat in Berlin 1933–1939.* Ed. W. Jedrzejewicz. New York, 1968.

Magyar Királyi Belügyminisztérium. *Magyar statisztikai évkönyv és jelentés 1919—.* Budapest, 1925—.

Magyar Királyi Külügyminisztérium. *Külpolitikai adatok az 1936. évről.* Budapest, 1937.

———. *Külpolitikai adatok az 1937. évről.* Budapest, 1938.

———. *Külpolitikai adatok az 1938. évről.* Budapest, 1939.

———. *Külpolitikai adatok az 1939. évről.* Budapest, 1940.

Magyarországi Rendeletek Gyüjteménye, 1919–1939. *Vallás- és közoktatásügyi miniszteri rendeletek.* Budapest, 1942.

Maisky, Ivan. *Who Helped Hitler?* London, 1964.

Mayor, A., trans. *Ciano's Diary 1937–1938.* London, 1952.

Ránki, György, et al. *A Wilhelmstrasse és Magyarország. Német diplomáciai iratok Magyarországról 1933–1944.* Budapest, 1968.

Schuschnigg, Kurt. *Ein Requiem Rot-Weiss-Rot.* Zurich, 1948.

Starhemberg, Ernst Rudiger Prince. *Between Hitler and Mussolini.* New York and London, 1942.

Von Papen, Franz. *Der Wahrheit eine Gasse.* Munich, 1952.

Zsigmond, László. *Adalékok a magyar ellenforradalmi rendszer külpolitikájához 1929–1945.* Budapest, 1953.

———, ed. *Diplomáciai iratok Magyarország külpolitikájához 1936–1945. Volume I 1936–1938.* Budapest, 1962.

III. SECONDARY WORKS
BOOKS

Adamthwaite, Anthony. *France and the Coming of the Second World War 1936-1939.* London, 1977.

Andics, Erzsébet, ed. *A magyar nacionalizmus kialakulása és története.* Budapest, 1964.

Annabring, Matthias. *Volksgeschichte der Deutschen in Ungarn.* Stuttgart, 1954, vol. I.

Baross, Gábor. *Hungary and Hitler.* Astor, FL, 1970.

Basch, Antonín. *The Danube Basin and the German Economic Sphere.* New York, 1943.

Basch, Franz A. *Das Deutschtum in Ungarn.* Budapest, 1926.

Berend, Iván T. and Ránki, György. *Magyarország a fasiszta Németország "életterében" 1933-1939.* Budapest, 1960.

Bullock, Alan. *Hitler. A Study in Tyranny.* New York, 1961.

Calic, Edouard. *Secret Conversations with Hitler.* New York, 1971.

Carr, William. *Arms, Autarky and Aggression. A Study in German Foreign Policy 1933-1939.* New York, 1973.

Dreifort, John E. *Yvon Delbos at the Quai d'Orsay. French Foreign Policy during the Popular Front 1936-1938.* Lawrence, KS, 1973.

Dreisziger, Nandor A. F. *Hungary's Way to World War II.* Toronto, 1968.

Einzig, Paul. *Bloodless Invasion. German Economic Penetration into the Danubian States and the Balkans.* London, 1938.

Ellis, Howard S. *Exchange Control in Central Europe.* Cambridge, MA, 1946.

Erbe, Rene. *Die nationalsozialistische Wirtschaftspolitik 1933-1939 im Lichte der modernen Theorie.* Zurich, 1958.

Gedye, G. E. R. *Betrayal in Central Europe.* New York and London, 1939.

Gratz, Gustav. *Deutschungarisehe Probleme.* Budapest, 1938.

Gruchmann, Lothar. *Nationalsozialistische Grossraumordnung.* Stuttgart, 1962.

Hajdú, János and Tóth, Béla C. *The "Volksbund" in Hungary.* Budapest, 1962.

Hanč, Josef. *Tornado Across Eastern Europe. The Path of Nazi Destruction from Poland to Greece.* New York, 1942.

Heineman, John L. *Hitler's First Foreign Minister, Constantin Freiherr von Neurath, Diplomat and Statesman.* Berkeley, CA, 1979.

Hoensch, Jörg K. *Der ungarische Revisionismus und die Zerschlagung der Tschechoslovakei.* Tübingen, 1967.

Hoptner, J. B. *Yugoslavia in Crisis 1934–1941.* New York, 1962.

Hóry, András. *A kulisszák mögött. A Második Világháború előzményei ami és ahogy a valóságban történt.* Vienna, 1965.

Hügel, Kaspar. *Abriss der Geschichte des Donauschwäbischen Schulwesens.* Munich, 1957.

Jócsik, Lajos. *German Economic Influences in the Danube Valley.* Budapest, 1946.

Juhász, Gyula. *Hungarian Foreign Policy 1919–1945.* Budapest, 1979.

―――. *Magyarország külpolitikája 1919–1945.* Budapest, 1969.

Kaiser, David E. *Economic Diplomacy and the Origins of the Second World War. Germany, Britain, France, and Eastern Europe, 1930–1939.* Princeton, NJ, 1980.

Kállay, Nicholas. *Hungarian Premier.* Westport, CT, 1970 [1954].

Kertesz, Stephen. *Diplomacy in a Whirlpool.* Notre Dame, IN, 1953.

Kis, Aladár. *Magyarország külpolitikája a második világháború előestején (1938 november–1939 szeptember).* Budapest, 1963.

Komjathy, Anthony. *The Crises of France's East Central European Diplomacy 1933–1938.* New York, 1976.

Komjathy, Anthony and Stockwell, Rebecca. *German Minorities and the Third Reich. Ethnic Germans of East Central Europe between the Wars.* New York and London, 1980.

Korodi, Lutz. *Deutsche Bilanz in Südosteuropa.* Berlin, 1936.

Král, Václav, ed. *Das Abkommen von München 1938.* Prague, 1968.

Lackó, Miklós. *Arrow-Cross Men, National Socialists 1935–1944.* Budapest, 1969. (Transl. of *Nyilasok, Nemzetiszocialisták 1935–1944* [Budapest, 1966]).

Lukács, John A. *The Great Powers and Eastern Europe.* New York, 1953.

Macartney, C. A. *Hungary and Her Successors. The Treaty of Trianon and Its Consequences 1919–1937.* London, et al., 1937.

———. *Hungary. A Short History.* Chicago, 1962.

———. *National States and National Minorities.* London, 1934.

———. *October Fifteenth. A History of Modern Hungary, 1929–1945.* Edinburgh, 1956, 2 vols.

Macartney, C. A. and Palmer, A. W. *Independent Eastern Europe.* London and Basingstoke, 1962.

Machray, Robert. *The Struggle for the Danube and the Little Entente, 1929–1938.* London, 1938.

Moore, Wilbert E. *Economic Demography of Eastern and Southern Europe.* Geneva, 1945.

Murray, Williamson. *The Change in the European Balance of Power, 1938–1939. The Path to Ruin.* Princeton, NJ, 1984.

Nagy-Talavera, Nicholas M. *The Green Shirts and Others. A History of Fascism in Hungary and Rumania.* Stanford, CA, 1970.

Orlow, Dietrich. *The Nazis in the Balkans. A Case Study of Totalitarian Politics.* Pittsburgh, PA, 1968.

Păclisanu, Zenobius. *Der Ausrottungskampf Ungarns gegen seine nationalen Minderheiten.* Bucharest, 1941.

Paikert, G. C. *The Danube Swabians. German Populations in Hungary, Rumania and Yugoslavia and Hitler's Impact on Their Patterns.* The Hague, 1967.

Ránki, György. *Economy and Foreign Policy. The Struggle of the Great Powers for Hegemony in the Danube Valley, 1919–1939.* Boulder, CO and New York, 1983.

Rauschning, Hermann. *Hitler's Aims in War and Peace.* London and Toronto, 1940.

Reichert, Günter. *Das Scheitern der Kleinen Entente. Internationale Beziehungen im Donauraum von 1933 bis 1938.* Munich, 1971.

Roberts, Henry L. *Eastern Europe. Politics, Revolution and Diplomacy.* New York, 1970.

Rothschild, Joseph. *East Central Europe between the Two World Wars*. Seattle, WA and London, 1974.

Sakmyster, Thomas L. *Hungary, the Great Powers, and the Danubian Crisis 1936–1939*. Athens, GA, 1980.

Schacher, Gerhard. *Germany Pushes South-East*. London, 1937.

Schneefuss, Walter. *Deutschtum in Süd-Ost-Europa*. Leipzig, 1939.

Seton-Watson, Hugh. *Eastern Europe between the Wars 1918–1941*. Cambridge [England], 1946.

Shirer, William M. *The Rise and Fall of the Third Reich. A History of Nazi Germany*. New York, 1960.

Spira, Thomas. *German-Hungarian Relations and the Swabian Problem from Károlyi to Gömbös 1919–1936*. Boulder, CO and New York, 1977.

Taylor, Telford. *Munich. The Price of Peace*. Garden City, NY, 1979.

Tilkovszky, Loránt. *Ez volt a Volksbund. A német népcsoportpolitika és Magyarország 1938–1945*. Budapest, 1978.

———. *Revizió és nemzetiségpolitika Magyarországon (1938–1941)*. Budapest, 1967.

Von Türcke, Kurt E. *Das Schulrecht der deutschen Volksgruppen in Ost- und Südosteuropa*. Berlin, 1938.

Weinberg, Gerhard L. *The Foreign Policy of Hitler's Germany. Starting World War II, 1937–1939*. Chicago, IL and London, 1980.

Wiskemann, Elizabeth. *The Rome-Berlin Axis. A Study of the Relations between Hitler and Mussolini*. London, 1966.

Wolfers, Arnold. *Britain and France between Two Wars*. New York, 1966.

Wuescht, Johann. *Jugoslawien und das Dritte Reich. Eine dokumentierte Geschichte der deutschjugoslawischen Beziehungen von 1933 bis 1945*. Stuttgart, 1969.

Young, Robert F. *In Command of France. French Foreign Policy and Military Planning, 1933–1940*. Cambridge and London, 1978.

Zagoroff, S. D., Végh, Jenö and Bilimovich, Alexander D. *The Agricultural Economy of the Danubian Countries 1935–1945*. Stanford, CA, 1955.

IV. SECONDARY WORKS
Articles and Dissertations

Ádám, Magda. "Az ellenforradalmi rendszer reviziós külpolitikájához." In Andics, ed., *A magyar nacionalizmus kialakulása.*

Apponyi, Albert. "Historic Mission of Hungary and the States Aggrandized to Her Detriment." In *Justice for Hungary.* London, 1928.

Basch, Franz. "Antwort an den Hauptschriftsteller des jüdischen *Pesti Napló* Gustav Gratz." *Deutscher Volksbote, Wochenblatt für Kultur, Politik und Wirtschaft (DVW),* I (6 August 1939), 6.

———. "Deutscher Aufbruch in Ungarn." *Nation und Staat,* XII (1938–1939), 204-211.

———. "Franz Basch spricht zur ungarischen Öffentlichkeit." *DVW,* I (8 January 1939), 2-3.

———. "Hetze und Aufwieglung um jeden Preis." *DVW,* I (30 July 1939), 1.

Beer, Georg. "Der Sinn unseres Volkstumskampfes." *Deutscher Volksbote (DV),* IV, 4 (July, 1938), 4.

Bethlen, Stephen. "Hungary's Position after the Austrian Anschluss." *The Hungarian Quarterly,* VI (Old Series) (1938), 201-210.

Bigler, R. M. "Heil Hitler and Heil Horthy! The Nature of Hungarian Fascist Nationalism and Its Impact on German-Hungarian Relations." *East European Quarterly,* VIII, 3 (Fall, 1974), 251-272.

Broszat, Martin. "Deutschland-Ungarn-Rumänien. Entwicklung und Grundfaktoren nationalsozialistischer Hegemonial- und Bündnispolitik 1938–1941." *Historische Zeitschrift,* CCVI, 1 (February, 1968), 45-96.

Brown, MacAllister. "The Third Reich's Mobilization of the German Fifth Column in Eastern Europe." *Journal of Central European Affairs,* XIX (July, 1959), 128-148.

Deak, Ferenc. "Collaborationism in Europe, 1940–1945: The Case of Hungary." *Austrian History Yearbook,* XV-XVI (1979–1980), 157-164.

Faulstich, Ägidius. "Das neue Morgenrot." *DVW,* I (30 April 1939), 2.

———. "Volksgruppe und Mutterland." *DV,* IV, 1 (February, 1938), 2.

———. "Volk und Volksgruppe." *DVW,* I (5 February 1939), 2.

Feledy, J. "Hungaro-German Economic Relations." Unpublished doctoral dissertation, McGill University, 1970.

Ferenczi, I. "Ungarische Handelspolitik." *Ungarisches Wirtschafts-Jahrbuch,* XII (1936)¡ 159-168.

———. "Ungarns Handelspolitik." *Ibid.,* XIII (1937), 152-165.

Gasztony, Endre Bela. "Revisionist Hungarian Foreign Policy and the Third Reich's Advance to the East, 1933–1939." Unpublished doctoral dissertation, University of Oregon, 1970.

Goldschmidt, Georg. "Auf neuen Wegen." *DVW,* I (2 April 1939), 1-2.

———. "Das ungarländische Deutschtum im Wahlkampf." *DVW,* I (14 May 1939), 1.

———. "Die Schulfrage und die jetzige Leitung des UDV." *DV,* IV, 1 (February, 1938), 3.

———. " 'Eine kluge Politik', Antwort an den ref. Bischof Ladislaus Ravasz." *DVW,* I, (19 March 1939), 1.

———. "Einem neuen Ungarn entgegen." *DVW,* I (16 April 1939), 2.

———. "Ein ernstes Wort an die ungarische Gesellschaft." *DV,* III (October, 1937), 1.

———. "Gedanken am 900 jährigen Todestag Stefan des Heiligen." *DV,* IV, 5 (August, 1938), 1-3.

———. "Gehen wir in der Schulfrage einer Lösung entgegen?" *DV,* IV, 2 (April, 1938), 9.

———. "Gewissenlose Irreführung." *DV,* IV, 3 (May, 1938), 5.

———. "Gleiches Recht." *DVW,* I (9 April 1939), 1-2.

———. "Grundsätzliches zum Problem der konfessionellen Schulen des ungarländischen Deutschtums." *DV,* III (February, 1937), 1.

———. "Klarheit in die Durchführung der Schulverordnung." *DV,* IV, 1 (February, 1938), 2.

——. "Kultusminister Graf Teleki über die deutsche Frage." *DV*, IV, 4 (July, 1938), 6.

——. "Schule und Volkscharakter." *DV*, IV, 4 (July, 1938), 6-7.

——. "Über die Durchführung der neuen Schulverordnung." *DV*, III (July, 1937), 1-3.

——. "Um ein neues Nationalitätengesetz." *DVW*, I (5 February 1939), 4.

——. "Unser Weg ist richtig." *DV*, IV, 6-7 (October, 1938), 1-2.

——. "Verständigung." *DV*, IV, 2 (April, 1938), 8.

——. "Zurückgebliebene Gehirne." *DV*, IV, 4 (July, 1938), 4.

Gratz, Gustav. "Die Bedingungen der Versöhnung im U.D.V." *Neues Sonntagsblatt* (20 March 1938).

——. "Németajkú magyarok és magyarországi németek." *Pesti Napló* (25 July 1939).

Gündisch, Guido. "Unsere Staatstreue." *DVW*, I (8 January 1939), 1-2.

Hillinger, Michael. "The German National Movement in Interwar Hungary." Unpublished doctoral dissertation, Columbia University, 1973.

Huss, Richard. "Wieder ein Jahr Deutscher Volksbote, deutsche Volkstumarbeit." *DV*, III (January, 1937), 1.

Komjathy, Anthony. "The First Vienna Award (November 2, 1938)." *Austrian History Yearbook*, XV-XVI (1979–1980), 131-156.

Körmendy-Ékes, M. "Big Estates in Hungary." *The Hungarian Quarterly*, V (Old Series) (Spring, 1937).

Kovács, Alajos. "Népesedésünk fény- és árnyoldalai." *Magyar Szemle*, XVIII (January, 1933), 10-21.

Kuhn, Johann. "Schwabischer Patriotismus." *DVW*, I (16 July 1939), 5.

Low, Alfred D. "Edvard Beneš, the Anschluss Movement, 1918–38, and the Policy of Czechoslovakia." *East Central Europe*, X, Pts. 1-2 (1983), 46-91.

Lukács, Georg von. "Die Tragödie Trianon-Ungarns." *Ungarischer Volkswirt*, VII, 10 (October, 1938), 4-7.

Macartney, C. A. "Hungary and the Present Crisis." *International Affairs*, XVII, 11 (1938), 749-768.

Mecsér, Andreas Vitéz. "Die Rückwirkungen des Anschlusses auf die wirtschaftlichen Beziehungen Ungarns zum Deutschen Reich." *Ungarisches Wirtschafts-Jahrbuch,* XIV (1938), 21.

Mühl, Heinrich. "Noch immer die Schulfrage." *DV,* IV, 6-7 (October, 1938), 4.

———. "Staatsvolk, Volksgruppe, Mutterwolk." *DV,* IV, 3 (May, 1938), 4.

Neugeboren, Emil. " 'Nationalität' und 'Minderheit'." *Nation und Staat,* XI (1937–1938), 150-151.

Neun, Heinrich. "Die Provinzpresse, wie sie ist und wie sie sein sollte." *DVW,* I (23 July 1939), 5.

Paikert, G. C. "Hungary's National Minority Policies 1920–1945." *The American Slavic and East European Review,* XII (April, 1953), 201-218.

Papp, N.G. "The German Minority in Hungary between the Two World Wars: Loyal Subjects or Suppressed Citizens?" *East European Quarterly,* XXII, 4 (1989), 495-514.

"Poland between Germany and the USSR, 1926–1939: The Theory of Two Enemies. The Pilsudski Institute Symposium." *The Polish Review,* XX, 1 (1975).

Pritz, Pál. "A kieli találkozó." *Századok,* CVIII (1974), 646-679.

Puhl, Klemens. "Wie sehen wir die Schulfrage?" *DV,* III (October, 1937), 4.

Ránki, György. "Adatok a magyar külpolitikához a Csehszlovákia elleni agresszió idején 1937–1939." *Századok,* XCIII (1959), 117-159 and 356-372.

Reischle, H. "Deutsch-ungarische Wirtschaftsprobleme." *Ungarischer Volkswirt,* VI, 7 (July, 1937), 8-10.

Roman, Eric. "Munich and Hungary: An Overview of Hungarian Diplomacy During the Sudeten Crisis." *East European Quarterly,* VIII, 1 (March, 1974), 71-97.

Rónai, András. "A németek számszerű csökkenése Csonka-Magyarországon." *Magyar Szemle,* XXXIV (1938), 74-78.

Sachse, Herbert. "Die Verluste des ungarländischen Deutschtums im Spiegel der Statistik." *Schriften zur Volkswissenschaft.* Berlin, 1937.

Sakmyster, Thomas L. "Hungary and the Munich Crisis: The Revisionist Dilemma." *Slavic Review*, XXXII, 4 (December, 1973), 725-740.

———. "Miklós Horthy, Hungary, and the Coming of the European Crisis, 1932–41." *East Central Europe*, III, 3 (1976), 220-232.

———. ed. and trans. "The Hungarian State Visit to Germany of August, 1938: Some New Evidence on Hungary in Hitler's Pre-Munich Policy." *Canadian Slavic Studies*, III, 4 (Winter, 1969), 677-691.

Schittenhelm, Franz. "Das ungarländische Deutschtum in Zahlen." *Nation und Staat*, XI (1937–1938), 162-171.

Spira, Thomas. "The German-Hungarian-Swabian Triangle and the Teleki Regime on the Eve of World War II." *Prace Polonijne*, XI (1986), 188-197.

———. "Hungary and the Little Entente: The Failed Rapprochement of 1937." *Südost-Forschungen*, XL (1981), 144-163.

———. "Nation and State: The Swabian *Volksbund* and Hungarian Public Opionion in Early 1939." *Ungarn-Jahrbuch*, XVIII (1986), 188-197.

———. "The Radicalization of Hungary's Swabian Minority After 1935." *Hungarian Studies Review*. XI, 1 (Spring, 1985), 9-22.

———. "The *Volksdeutsche Kameradschaft* and the Swabian Demands on the Eve of World War II." *East Central Europe*, XII, Pt. 2 (1985), 146-163.

Szabados, Mihály. "A titkos választójog és a kisebbségi kérdés." *Korunk Szava*, VII, 18 (15 September 1937), 519-520.

———. "Kisebbségi kérdés—szentistváni gondolat." *Korunk Szava*, VII, 6 (16 March 1937), 172.

Tilkovszky, Loránt. "A német irredenta és Magyarország. A magyarországi népinémet (volksdeutsch) mozgalom útja." *Történelmi Szemle*, XIII, 3 (1970), 369-395.

——. "A Volksbund szerepe Magyarország második világháborús történetében." *Történelmi Szemle*, XI (1969), 294-312.

———. "Die deutsche Minderheit in Ungarn in der Zeit des Faschismus vor dem zweiten Weltkrieg." *Jahrbuch für Geschichte der sozialistischen Länder Europas*, XV, 2 (1971), 57-81.

————. "Volksdeutsche Bewegung und ungarische Nationalitätenpolitik (1938–1941)." *Acta Historica,* XII, 1-4 (1966), 59-112 and 319-346.

Végh, Jenő. "Agriculture and Food in Hungary during World War II." In Zagoroff, *et al., The Agricultural Economy,* pp. 157-162.

Von Bruck, Fritz. "Neuer english-französischer Kapitalstrom zum Südosten?" *Ungarischer Volkswirt,* VII, 9 (September, 1938), 14-17.

Weinberg, Gerhard L. "Secret Hitler-Beneš Negotiations in 1936–37." *Journal of Central European Affairs,* XIX (1960), 366-374.

Weiner, Samuel. "Die Placierung der ungarischen Mehlüberschüsse auf den Auslandsmärkten." *Ungarischer Volkswirt,* VI, 7 (July, 1937), 10*ff.*

Winchester, Betty Jo. "Hungary and the 'Third Europe' in 1938." *Slavic Review,* XXXII, 4 (December, 1973), 741-756.

Wirthoven, Fr. Christian. "Die deutsche Bevölkerungsfrage in Ungarn." *Neue Heimatblätter,* III, 1 (1938), 13-55; 2, 1-57.

Zimmermann, Wilhelm. "Die Schulverordnung 1935 und das Jahr 1936–37." *DV,* III (January, 1937), 3.

Zsigmond, László. "Ungarn und des Münchner Abkommen." *Acta Historica,* VI (1959), 251-286.

Zumpft, Jakob. "Die Schulnot in der Schomodei." *DV,* IV, 6-7 (October, 1938), 3.

V. ADDITIONAL LITERATURE

Ádám, Magda, ed. *Magyarország külpolitikája 1938–1939.* Budapest, 1970.

Bahr, Richard. *Deutsches Schicksal im Südosten.* Hamburg, 1936.

Barsy, Julius. "Zur Methodenfrage der Muttersprache mit Rückblick auf das Deutschtum im Rumpfungarn." *Journal de la Societé Hongroise de Statistique,* No. 3 (1937), 306-332.

Berber, Fritz. *Europäische Politik 1933–1938 im Spiegel der Prager Akten.* Essen, 1941.

Beyer, Hans Joachim. "Der Südosten im Spiegel der Wilhelmstrasse 1919–1939." *Südostdeutsche Heimatblätter*, III (1954), 150-170.

Bodensieck, Heinrich. "Der Plan eines 'Freundschaftsvertrages' zwischen dem Reich und der Tschechoslowakei im Jahre 1938." *Zeitschrift für Ostforschung*, X (1961), 462-476.

Bohmann, A. *Menschen und Grenzen, Bevölkerung und Nationalitäten in Südosteuropa.* Cologne, 1969, 2 vols.

Bratianu, Gheorge I. *Rumänien und Ungarn. Demographische und wirtschaftliche Betrachtungen.* Bucharest, 1940.

Brausch, Gerd. "Deutschland-Ungarn. Die diplomatische Beziehungen vom Herbst 1937 bis Frühjahr 1939." Doctoral dissertation, University of Göttingen, 1956.

Broszat, Martin. "Faschismus und Kollaboration in Ostmitteleuropa zwischen den Weltkriegen." *Vierteljahrshefte für Zeitgeschichte*, XIV (July, 1966), 225-251.

Bullock, Alan. "Hitler and the Origins of the Second World War." *Proceedings of the British Academy*, LIII (1967), 259-287.

Churchill, Winston S. *The Gathering Storm. The Second World War.* Boston, 1948.

Ciano, Galeazzo. *Ciano's Hidden Diary 1937–1938.* New York, 1953.

De Battaglia, Otto Forst. *Zwischeneuropa von der Ostsee bis zur Adria.* Frankfurt am Main, 1954.

Funk, Walther. "Deutschlands Wirtschaftsbeziehungen zum Südosten." *Völkischer Beobachter* (16 October 1938), 19.

Gasztony, Endre B. "Hungarian Foreign Minister Kálmán Kánya's Grand Design, 1933–1936." *East European Quarterly*, XIX (Summer, 1985), 175-189.

Gehl, Jürgen. *Austria, Germany, and the Anschluss, 1931–1938.* London, 1963.

Gilbert, Martin and Gott, Richard. *The Appeasers.* London, 1963.

Göllner, Hans Otto. *Die Katastrophie des Südostdeutschtums. Das Schicksal der südostdeutschen Volksgruppen im Zweiten Weltkrieg.* Graz, 1957.

Grátz, Gustav. "A magyarországi németség ügye." *Magyar Szemle*, XXXII, 4 (128) (1938), 357-367.

Hagen, Walter. *Die Geheime Front.* Stuttgart, 1952.

Heimler, Heinrich and Spiegel-Schmidt, Friedrich. *Deutsches Luthertum in Ungarn.* Düsseldorf, 1955.

Henderson, Nevile. *Failure of a Mission. Berlin 1937–1939.* Toronto, 1940.

Hennyey, Gustav. *Ungarns Schicksal zwischen Ost und West.* Mainz, 1975.

Hertz, Frederick. *The Economic Problem of the Danubian States. A Study in Economic Nationalism.* London, 1947.

Hildebrand, Klaus. *The Foreign Policy of the Third Reich.* Berkeley, 1973 [1970].

Hillgruber, Andreas. *Deutschlands Rolle in der Vorgeschichte der beiden Weltkriege.* Göttingen, 1967.

Hoeft, K-D. "Die Agrarpolitik des deutschen Faschismus als Mittel zur Vorbereitung des zweiten Weltkrieges." *Zeitschrift für Geschichtswissenschaft,* VII, 6 (1959), 1205-1230.

Hoffmann, Walter. *Donauraum Völkerschicksal,* Leipzig, 1939.

Jacobsen, H-A. *Nationalsozialistische Aussenpolitik 1933–1938.* Frankfurt am Main, 1968.

Juhász, Gyula. *Magyarország külpolitikája a II. világháború kitörésének időszakában 1939–1940.* Budapest, 1962.

Kerekes, Lajos, ed. *Allianz Hitler-Horthy-Mussolini.* Budapest, 1966.

———. *Anschluss 1938 Ausztria és a nemzetközi diplomácia 1933–1938.* Budapest, 1968.

Kis, Aladár. *Magyarország külpolitikája a Második Világháború előestéjén (1938 November—1939 Szeptember).* Budapest, 1963.

Klein, Burton H. *Germany's Economic Preparations for War.* Cambridge, 1959.

Krugmann, Robert Werner. *Südosteuropa und Grossdeutschland. Entwicklung und Zukunftsmöglichkeiten der Wirtschaftsbeziehungen.* Breslau, 1939.

Kühl, J. "Das ungarländische Deutschtum zwischen Horthy und Hitler." *Südostdeutsche Heimatblätter,* IV (1955), 117-147.

Kuhn, Axel. *Hitlers aussenpolitisches Programm. Entstehung und Entwicklung 1919–1939.* Stuttgart, 1970.

League of Nations Council, Economic, Financial and Transit Department. *The League of Nations Reconstruction Schemes in the Inter-War Period.* Geneva, 1945.

Lemberg, Eugen. "Zur Geschichte der deutschen Volksgruppen in Ost-Mitteleuropa." *Zeitschrift für Ostforschung,* I (1952), 321-345.

Low, Aldred D. "The Soviet Union, the Austrian Communist Party, and the Anschluss Question, 1918-1938." *Slavic Review,* XXXIX (March, 1980), 1-26.

Macartney, C. A. "Hungary and Czechoslovakia." *Contemporary Review* (December, 1938), 677-683.

———. *Hungary and Her Successors. The Treaty of Trianon and Its Consequences 1919-1937.* London, *et al.,* 1937.

McKale, Donald M. *The Swastika Outside Germany.* Kent, OH, 1977.

Némedi, Ludwig. *Das Gesamtdeutschtum im ungarischen Blickfeld.* Budapest, 1938.

Noguères, Henri. *Munich 'Peace for Our Time'.* New York, 1965.

Ottlik, G. "Hungary's Foreign Relations." *Hungarian Quarterly,* VI (1938), 18-32.

Ormos, Mária. "A Rajna-vidék német megszállásának közép-európai hatása." *Századok,* CIII (1969), 664-689.

———. *Franciaország és a keleti biztonság 1931-1936.* Budapest, 1969.

Pethö, T. "Contradictory Trends in Policies of the Horthy Era." *New Hungarian Quarterly,* IV, 12 (1963).

Poole, DeWitt C. "Light on Nazi Foreign Policy." *Foreign Affairs* (October, 1946), 130-154.

Rauschning, Hermann. *The Voice of Destruction.* New York, 1946.

Renouvin, Pierre. *World War II and Its Origins, International Relations, 1929-1945.* New York, 1958.

Rich, Norman. *Hitler's War Aims. Ideology, the Nazi State, and the Course of Expansion.* New York, 1973.

Riedl, Franz H. *Das Südostdeutschtum in den Jahren 1918-1945.* Munich, 1962.

Ripka, Hubert. *Munich. Before and After.* New York, 1969.

Robertson, E. M. *Hitler's Pre-War Policy and Military Plans 1933–1939.* New York, 1967.

Rosenberg, Alfred. "Unterdrückte Völker und Revisionen." *Völkischer Beobachter* (15 November 1936).

Schneefuss, Walter. *Das Reiches neue Nachbarn. Unter Mitarbeit namhafter Wissenschaftler.* Salzburg and Leipzig, 1939.

———. *Ungarn.* Leipzig, 1939.

Schuman, Frederick L. *Europe on the Eve. The Crises of Diplomacy 1933–1939.* New York, 1939.

Seide, Gernot. "Die Deutschen in Ungarn zwischen den beiden Weltkriegen." *Ungarn-Jahrbuch,* VI (1974–1975), 148-161.

Spiegel-Schmidt, Frederich. *Franz Anton Basch 1901–1946.* Ulm, 1957.

Spira, Thomas. "Connections Between Trianon Hungary and National Socialist Germany and the Swabian Minority School Problem." *Internationales Jahrbuch für Geschichts- und Geographie-Unterricht,* XV (1974), 240-258.

———. "Worlds Apart: The Swabian Expulsion from Hungary after World War II." *Nationalities Papers,* XIII, 2 (Fall, 1985), 188-197.

Sziklay, János, ed. *A Magyar revizió 1920–1941.* Budapest, 1942.

Taylor, A. J. P. *The Origins of the Second World War.* London, 1969.

Thamer, Hans-Ulrich and Wippermann, Wolfgang. *Faschistische und neo-faschistische Bewegungen.* Darmstadt, 1977.

Tilkovszky, Loránt. "A magyarországi németség a Darányi-kormány idején." *Századok,* CXV, 5-6 (1981), 883-1135.

Ullmann, Hermann. *Pioniere Europas. Die Volkdeutsche Bewegung und ihre Lehren.* Munich, 1956.

Vambery, Rustem. *The Hungarian Problem.* Oberlin, OH, 1942.

Villari, Luigi. *Italian Foreign Policy under Mussolini.* New York, 1956.

Volgyes, Ivan. "The German Question in Hungary." *East European Quarterly,* XXIII (June, 1989), 145-157.

Von Auer, P. "Das neue Mitteleuropa." *New Commonwealth Quarterly* (December, 1938), 267-275.

Von Ribbentrop, Joachim. *Zwischen London und Moskau.* Leoni, 1953.

Weinberg, Gerhard L. *The Foreign Policy of Hitler's Germany. Diplomatic Revolution in Europe, 1933-36.* Chicago and London, 1970.

————. "German Foreign Policy and Poland, 1937-38." *Polish Review,* XX (1975), 5-23.

————. "The May Crisis, 1938." *Journal of Modern History,* XXIX, 3 (1957), 213-225.

Wheeler-Bennett, John W. *Munich. Prologue to Tragedy.* London, 1963.

Woodward, E. L. and Butler, R. eds. *Documents on British Foreign Policy 1919–1939.* Second Series. London, 1946–.

Zernatto, Guido. *Die Wahrheit über Österreich.* New York and Toronto, 1939.

INDEX